Shopping
for Identity

Also by Marilyn Halter

Between Race and Ethnicity
New Migrants in the Marketplace

Shopping for Identity

The Marketing of Ethnicity

Marilyn Halter

Schocken Books New York

Two charts on pages 52 and 54: "Agreement with Statements" and
"Type of Sneaker" (*MSR & C Ethnic Market Report*, pp. 321, 346).
Reprinted courtesy of The Market Segment Group.

Library of Congress Cataloging-in-Publication Data

Halter, Marilyn.
Shopping for identity: the marketing of ethnicity / Marilyn Halter.
p.   cm.
Includes bibliographical references and index.
ISBN 0-8052-1093-8
1. United States—Ethnic relations.   2. United States—Race
relations.   3. Ethnicity—Economic aspects—United States.
4. Assimilation (Sociology)—Economic aspects—United States.
5. Popular culture—Economic aspects—United States.
6. Marketing—Social aspects—United States.   7. Consumption
(Economics)—Social aspects—United States.   I. Title.

E184.A1 H214 2000   305.8'00973—dc21   00-022505

www.schocken.com

Book design by Johanna Roebas

Printed in the United States of America
First Paperback Edition
2 4 6 8 9 7 5 3

To the Memory of Toby Medoff Besner (1916–1966)
and Mary DePina Timm (1923–1999),
two aunts who made a difference

Contents

Acknowledgments

For his vision and implementation of a convivial interdisciplinary academic setting where ideas truly are freely exchanged, for his unfailing ability to amuse, and for his personal and staunch support of my work over the last decade, I am deeply indebted to Peter L. Berger, director of the Institute for the Study of Economic Culture at Boston University.

Funding to support this project was generously provided by the Lynde and Harry Bradley Foundation and by a grant from the Irish American Cultural Institute's O'Shaughnessy Irish Research Endowment. I have benefited from the excellent research assistance of Gini Laffey, Julie Plaut, Michael Goodman, and Irene Maksymjuk. At Schocken, I have had the good fortune of two outstanding editors. Cecelia Cancellaro has been an absolute treasure; most especially, her keen insights and clever eye are what helped to give this unwieldy subject matter its shape. Susan Ralston, editorial director, shepherded the volume to completion with meticulous care. Thanks also to Dassi Zeidel, editorial assistant. A phone conversation held several years ago with my American Studies mentor, Lawrence Fuchs, sparked the idea for this study in the first place. Once again, his influence has made all the difference in my career.

I am grateful for the spectacular friendship and collegiality of Doris Friedensohn. Over the last decade we have been engaged in an ongoing "seminar" on ethnicity and identity, writing and shopping that has informed this book considerably. From start to finish, Donna Gabaccia has also been especially supportive of this project. For leads, feedback, personal and professional advice, I wish to thank Boris Maksimov, Hasia Diner, Mary Waters, Steve Cornell, Clara Rodriguez, Larry Glickman, Viviana Zelizer, Shuli Berger, Ellen Garvey, Ruth Gallagher, John Carroll, Joan Nathan, Sivagami Sub-baraman, Lois Rudnick, Diane Hotten-Somers, Kathy Newman, my cousin Zelda Porte, and my parents, Marcella and Cyril Halter. Finally, I want to thank my own multiracial and always in style immediate family—Jonathan, Conor, Marcy, and Portia, all of whom navigate the marketplace effortlessly and, as far as I'm concerned, exhibit absolutely exquisite taste in doing so.

Shopping for Identity

One

Longings and Belongings:
An Introduction

My first real faculty position after returning to graduate school to finish my Ph.D. in the mid-1980s was a year-long stint in the history department at Boston College, where I filled in for two professors on leave, teaching various Americanist courses, including the hugely popular HI 101, "America in the 1960s." Three-hundred-plus students thronged the lecture hall; many more who had not preregistered for the class had to be turned away, including, rumor had it, the late Robert Kennedy's youngest offspring. As most other course offerings focused on the turbulent '60s, my class covered the social movements of the decade thoroughly, not just the grass-roots activity but the pivotal legislative acts, notably, of course, Civil Rights in 1964 and Voting Rights in 1965, which marked the government's endorsement of initiatives that would reshape the nation's social polity and civic culture for years to come. Yet what I had overlooked completely in my teaching of the explosive events of the period, indeed, what was absent from both the scholarly and popular texts at the time, was any mention whatsoever of what could arguably be called the most transformative measure of all in that decade of upheaval—the quiet passage of the Immigration Reform bill in 1965 ending preferential quotas for Europeans. Here was legislation that, in the years since its approval, has led to kaleidoscopic demographic change and to so complete a shake-up of the country's racial and ethnic composition that by 2050, when today's preschoolers will have reached middle age, there will be no white majority; every American will belong to a minority group.

The other significant legacies of the 1960s related to the contours of American ethnic identities today (and that did make it into my syllabus) were the movements by traditionally oppressed groups for recognition and self-determination within the wider culture, spearheaded by black nationalism and quickly followed by the American Indian Movement and the stirrings of a new Chicano militancy. These largely political initiatives were embellished by momentous cultural transformations that included unearthing buried roots and occluded histories as well as celebrating distinctive heritages. Moreover, the worldview of the '60s counterculture and of its New Left politics legitimized cultural hybridity, since much of it was based on rebellion against the previous decade's penchant for humdrum conformity. The colorless "organization man" gave way to the colorful nonconformist whose individuality could readily be expressed in ethnic terms. Indeed, '60s radical Tom Hayden, founding member of Students for a Democratic Society and an author of the organization's Port Huron Statement, a visionary document articulating the connections between the personal life of individuals and the politics of nations, went on to become not only a California state senator but also a proponent of Irish pride, who today lectures widely on the history and psychology of the culture that is his heritage.

By the mid-1970s, initially driven by a backlash against minority group movements for racial power, white descendants of immigrants who had arrived primarily from southern and eastern Europe during the sweeping second wave in the late nineteenth and early twentieth centuries, and who had also faced discrimination from the native population at the time, began to assert their own brand of ethnic pride. At first construed largely as a defense against the perceived threats of black power and the encroachment of African Americans into white ethnic neighborhoods, the ethnic resurgence ultimately went beyond such narrow aims to encompass a cultural alternative to assimilation and a political alternative to individualism for both black and white ethnics.

Thus, these early, often reactive impulses to reclaim roots had evolved by the century's end into a full-blown and multifaceted ethnic revival across a broad spectrum of the population that carries a much more benign rhetoric of rainbows and salad bowls to explain the dynamics of what historian David Hollinger has labeled America's communities of descent.[1] After decades in which assimilation was the leading model for the incorporation of diverse populations, cultural pluralism emerged to take its place as the reigning paradigm. When Congress passed the Ethnic Heritage Act in 1974 to support the funding of initiatives that promote the distinctive cultures and histories of the nation's ethnic populations, it was clear that this philosophy had taken hold at even the highest levels of government. The so-called roots phenomenon accounts for such developments as the growth of ethnic celebrations, a zeal for genealogy, increased travel to ancestral homelands, and greater interest in ethnic artifacts, cuisine, music, literature, and, of course, language.

One of the strongest influences on this vibrant cultural fluorescence has been the evolution of modern consumer capitalism. By the early 1970s, change was permeating the cultural front and the parameters of the American marketplace were shifting quite dramatically. After reaching its peak as the decade began, mass marketing was on the wane in many sectors of the economy. Parity in the production and technology of consumer goods had, for the most part, been achieved, so that customers could no longer differentiate between the quality of value and services rendered by Westinghouse versus Kenmore washing machines, Tide versus Cheer detergent, or even between the Coke or Pepsi that might spill on the clothes that ended up in the laundry basket. Companies needed to find new ways to hook consumers on their particular brands and to make customers loyal in an increasingly competitive and saturated marketplace.

Corporate industry leaders began taking a different tack, turning away from mass advertising campaigns to concentrate on segmented marketing approaches. One of the most successful of the segmenting strategies has been to target specific ethnic constituencies. Yuri

Radzievsky, founder of YAR Communications, a multicultural brand management firm that develops print and broadcast advertising for markets both in the United States and abroad, explained it this way:

> There aren't any more products so revolutionary that just by reciting a spec sheet, you win the marketplace. The sell today is an emotional sell. The products are coming closer and closer to each other. When you pick up this phone and you hear a dial tone, can you say whether it's AT&T, MCI, Sprint or anybody else? So how do you sell that service where there is so little differentiation in quality and product benefits? In order to reach the marketplace's pockets, you have to reach their minds and hearts first. How do you do it with one advertising fits all? You need to get on the home turf of that person. What's home turf? It's culture. We position our agency specializing in multicultural brand management.[2]

The demassification of American cultural identity during the last three decades has been reflected, even paralleled, in the ways that the business world has reshaped its own marketing tactics. The salience of ideas about diversity and differentiation pertains whether applied to people or to products. In the introduction to one of the new textbooks for business school students on the subject of ethnic marketing, the author points to this very confluence of academic concern with multiculturalism and the interests of the business sector when she writes, "Looking at advertising from the standpoint of ethnic audiences offers a chance to teach simultaneously segmentation, racial sensitivity, good copywriting technique, research, strategy, management, psychology, and consumer behavior.[3]

This fascinating and changing relationship between ethnic identity formation and consumer culture as it evolved across the American landscape during the second half of the twentieth century will be explored in the following pages. Whereas at one time the relationship between human beings and material objects resulted in identities that were acquired with the possessions one inherited, in modern times, people most often construct their own identities and define others through the commodities they purchase. With the rise of individualism and the evolution of mass consumerism objects become an extension of the self, and this has come to include one's ethnic identification as well, a new brand of cultural baggage. Through the consumption of ethnic goods and services, immigrants and their descendants modify and signal ethnic identities in social settings no longer sharply organized around ethnic group boundaries and the migration experience.

Earlier generations of ethnic Americans typically wanted to assimilate into the mainstream as rapidly as possible, but they found themselves defining themselves and being defined by the larger society according to their compatriot community affiliations and the constraints of ghetto life. They were surrounded by definitive and distinguishing ethnic group markers, most notably language, but also the still vibrant cuisines, music, literature, and religious practices of their native lands. They felt tied to neighborhoods, parishes, local politics, and an active network of voluntary organizations. Since the mid-twentieth century, however, the institutional structures of America's traditional ethnic enclaves have experienced significant erosion. Thus, today, the flux inherent in such an individualistic society—still holding within it large numbers of diverse religious, racial, and nationality groups—has led people to reflect and create the ethnic components of their identity through the process of acquisition instead. Ethnicity is increasingly manifest through self-conscious consumption of goods and services and, at the same time, these commodities assist in negotiating and enforcing identity differences. As the authors of a study exploring the favorite possessions of Asian Indians concluded, "While an Indian home is considered rich if it is filled with people, an American home is considered rich if it is filled with things, and especially things regarded as expressing individual identity."[4] Without consumer goods, certain acts of self-definition in this culture would be impossible. Shopping for an ethnic identity has become big business for contemporary consumer society.

Novelty is, perhaps, the most significant characteristic of modern consumer capitalism. As Daniel Boorstin has written, "We expect new heroes every season, a literary masterpiece every month, a dramatic spectacular every week, a rare sensation every night."[5] Back in the 1820s, in the budding years of St. Valentine's Day celebrations in the United States, printers promoted "valentine writers," chapbooks of model verse that could then be copied onto handmade cards, by calling the books "new" and "original," even when the volumes themselves were cribbed word for word from British versions. By the late nineteenth century, reverence for the new and the improved, for being in vogue and in season, had become so intrinsic to the development of mass commercial culture that fashion, style, and innovation became the central features of the evolving American marketplace. Even though corporate culture is in the business of perpetually manufacturing desires for the new and fashionable, consumers still resist giving themselves over completely to ceaseless innovation. They seek continuity and familiarity as well. Thus, they will buy the very latest in products, services, and technologies to re-create an old-fashioned and bygone world, and marketers respond by designing goods that might satisfy this craving for novelty without risk.[6] Indeed, most consumers today see absolutely no discrepancy in wanting what is both classic and fresh, timeless and ephemeral. They seek and expect to find what is essentially contradictory—the original recipe that is somehow "new and improved."

One of the latest innovations to galvanize consumers and hold out the promise of that magical potion that mixes the security of the old with the excitement of the new is a broad-based appeal to our romantic search for an ethnic identity. Advertising trends demonstrate that ethnicity is highly combustible, fueling free enterprise and molding our consumer patterns. The days when mainstream America meant Norman Rockwell, Ozzie and Harriet, and meat-and-potatoes are gone. There's a new, evolving, and complicated ethnic mainstream for which salsa has become a staple (indeed, since 1991 salsa has outsold ketchup as the top-ranking condiment of choice in the United States), Szechwan beef has replaced the standard hamburger, and movie actresses with "classic" Anglo-Saxon features are routinely having plastic surgery to embellish and fill out their now too-thin lips.

Much has changed in the almost thirty years since Margaret Mead pronounced that "Being American is a matter of abstention from foreign ways, foreign food, foreign ideas, foreign accents."[7] Although cultivating a foreign accent may not yet be a sign of true Americanness, relearning one's ancestral tongue, eating ethnic cuisine, displaying ethnic artifacts, fostering a hyphenated identity, and even reverse name-changes (back to the old-country original) have become the American way. What some viewed as a passing fad of the 1970s has only intensified. This renaissance is a form of voluntary ethnicity that has made any conflict between identifying oneself as American and affirming one's foreign heritage disappear. Indeed, as sociologist Robert Wood has pointed out, "In an age that celebrates diversity and multiculturalism, it has become almost a civic duty to have an ethnicity as well as to appreciate that of others."[8]

In a society in which individualism is so highly valued, this type of "convenience" or "portable" ethnicity works very well. Third- and fourth-generation upwardly mobile ethnics are now secure enough to proclaim their distinctiveness without risk of it becoming a hindrance to achieving middle-class respectability. In fact, it can be a plus in the workplace as a way not only of establishing connections among co-ethnics but also of relating to those of cultural backgrounds different from one's own.[9] Such flexibility of identification is also eminently suitable in a society with increasing rates of intermarriage.

New studies of the children, grandchildren, and the great-grandchildren of immigrants question the extent to which ethnicity is a factor in their identity formation after three or four generations in this country.[10] To the surprise of many, the results have shattered the assumption that over time and with greater structural integration, ethnicity would simply disappear. Ethnic identification persists and the research demonstrates that higher socioeconomic status and increased educational levels have strengthened rather than weakened it.[11] These findings run directly counter to the earlier assertions that movement up the social ladder is an assimilating force.

Ethnicity has typically been associated with the lifestyle of the lower classes.[12] However, increasingly, explicit ethnic identification has become an indicator of economic success and integration. In her study of Puerto Ricans in the United States, Clara Rodríguez found that those who had achieved a modicum of success tended to maintain a strong Puerto Rican or Hispanic identification. Similarly, in her survey of Americans of Armenian descent in metropolitan New York and New Jersey, Anny Bakalian concluded that the upwardly mobile respondents were just as likely to demonstrate public pride in their heritage as others in the population and that there was absolutely no stigma attached to doing so.[13] What used to be a liability has now become an asset, a luxury of assimilation. The requirement of optional or part-time ethnicity is a prior sense of belonging *enough* to be able to freely distinguish oneself from mass society on the basis of cultural difference. Getting ahead financially and getting back to one's cultural roots are perfectly compatible personal aspirations in America today.

This formula provided the rationale for the coffee-table magazine *Attenzione*, first published in 1979, in the flush of the revival of white ethnicity. The publishers hoped "to make hundreds of thousands of Italian-Americans prouder than ever of their heritage." Their strategy was to present articles reflective of upper middle-class tastes, including upscale renditions of the food that is so central to Italian ethnicity overall as well as the latest in fashion and home furnishings from Italian designers and glossy photo-essays depicting Italian Renaissance art. *Attenzione* also profiled successful Italian-Americans who had not lost their strong sense of ethnic identity. The magazine carried advertisements for classic high-status items—sports cars, luxury cruises, ski vacations—catering to an increasingly numerous, upwardly mobile but still ethnically oriented readership.[14]

Indeed, the 1990 U.S. Census indicated that among whites, a complete reversal has occurred in the relationship of ethnic identification to social class. Those of European descent who answered the question about ancestry on the census forms with "American" rather than a specific ethnic heritage had higher rates of poverty and lower levels of education than those who listed their ethnic designation. For example, of those who wrote "American," only 10 percent had college degrees, compared to 25 percent of those who reported a specific ancestry. Similar differentials were found with poverty rates. Lawrence Fuchs, formerly the vice-chairman of the U.S. Commission on Immigration Reform, explained the dynamic in this way: "Americans who cannot remember whether their ancestry was Scotch or Scotch-Irish or Irish or English . . . tend to live in areas of rural poverty. They are sure about their American identity and uncertain about their particular ancestral origins. Compared to the descendants of more recent immigrants—Italian Americans, Polish Americans, etc.—they tend to be poor."[15] Given this trend, it is not surprising that corporate America would employ ethnicity as a marketing tool directed at a sector of society with definitive buying power—middle-class, ethnic-identified consumers.

Warren Belasco's research on the development of ethnic fast food confirms this pattern, demonstrating that the revivalists tend to be affluent and well educated. Moreover, marketing experts have predicted a growing desire among the prosperous middle class for products that could suggest more permanence or stability in their lives. Belasco cites both oak furniture and ethnic foods as examples of consumer goods that convey a sense of continuity and rootedness. He points out that oftentimes ethnic eating revolves around ritual and ceremony, activities that further the semblance of community among those overwhelmed by the displacement and transitory nature of modernity.[16]

It could simply be stated that cultural commodification is inherent in the capitalist system, an inevitable outcome of the workings of the marketplace. However, the relationship of ethnic identity to commercial endeavors turns out to be much more complicated and, thus, far more interesting to dissect. Certainly for many, the ethnic revival represents the search for recognizable or familiar points of reference in a cold, impersonal, and fragmented world. Furthermore, these people see direct links between the modern life of material abundance and a perception of spiritual impoverishment. In this way, ethnic identities are continually being reinvented to fulfill our longing to feel anchored to a secure, harmonious, and localized past, although we are living amid the vast and chaotic landscapes of consumption that characterize the present.

Despite the voluminous attention paid to the permutations of American identity in the twentieth century, commentators have shied away from exploring the underlying economic issues involved. The sensibilities surrounding the romance of ethnicity—the nostalgia—do not readily invite an analysis that might be equated with what are often viewed as the crasser elements of such behavior. Most cultural critics paint a worst-case scenario of vulgar market forces co-opting all individual creative expression. Moreover, many still hold to a bias in favor of production, whereby an individual's occupation is the defining element of social identity, leaving no room for consumer behavior as a significant factor in identity formation. Thus, the story of the rise of a mass consumer society from the late nineteenth century to the end of the twentieth becomes a tale of continuous declension from the virtues of a producer-oriented society, in which individuals had some measure of control over their own lives, to one in which multinational corporations dictate its contours.

The Victorian values of saving over spending, frugality over acquisitiveness, and prudence over indulgence meant that engagement in the marketplace signified degenerative impulses.[17] The barely disguised moralistic critique of modern consumerist practice as necessarily self-indulgent, superficial, and excessive, along with the focus on individuals as workers only, has hampered sound research about an immensely important sphere of human behavior. A schism exists between the business people who view consumerism as constructive to American character and society and the academics who see it as detrimental. Either way consumerism has become so completely woven into American life that it is not necessary to judge its effects to give the phenomenon thoughtful attention.

Initially, if the ethnic revival was assessed at all in terms of its relationship to the business world, it was thought of as representing a strike against corporate culture. This was largely a grass-roots movement discontented with the rapid pace and high turnover of mass consumption, seeking instead more constant and meaningful connections to people and things. Representing some of the same sensibilities of the 1970s counterculture, those who turned back to their roots were not that different from their communal living, environmentalist back-to-nature counterparts. New ethnics, in their search for authentic homeland foods and the sense of community associated with it, would seek out local immigrant businesses involved in small-scale food production and retailing rather than consuming the products of corporate giants.

However, it has become clear that commercial goods produced at both the corporate and small-scale levels are increasingly being consumed by Americans as a form of ethnic expression. Similarly, ethnic festivals, commemorative events, museum and popular culture offerings, retreats, and courses of study have provided a temporary sense of community that, in an intensive and optional way, gratifies such longings for meaningful interpersonal contact. More and more, these consumer products and services are replacing traditional neighborhood and community affiliations as the connective tissue of postmodern life.

My research suggests that although the impetus to reclaim roots often stems from disdain for commercial interests, paradoxically, consumers look to the marketplace to revive and reidentify with ethnic values. Though a crucial component of the rationale for the creation of ethnic pride groups and related culture-specific practices may be to protest against the ills of consumer society, the new ethnics demonstrate that they are nonetheless deeply tied to consumerist practices. In effect, the market serves to foster greater awareness of ethnic identity, offers immediate possibilities for cultural participation, and can even act as an agent of change in that process. Thus, consumerism simultaneously disrupts and promotes ethnic community and can be both subversive and hegemonic. Commercialism may indeed dissipate tradition, community, and meaning, but it can also enhance and reinforce such identifications.

Consider the case of Cajun identity, the heritage of those French-speaking descendants of Acadians who had settled along the chilly Bay of Fundy in the early seventeenth century and who, by the late eighteenth century, had been exiled south to the semitropical Louisiana bayou country. After more than two centuries of adaptation to American society, the contemporary Louisiana Cajun community had lost many of its distinctive cultural features. But in the mid-1970s a steady stream of tourists began to arrive in the area looking for an "authentic" Cajun experience. They came especially from Francophone regions such as Quebec, France, and Belgium, inspiring the largely assimilated local population to probe its own cultural uniqueness. Indeed, many of the Francophone tourists evinced a stronger interest in Cajun culture than natives did. Thanks to these tourists, Cajun identity was reawakened in Louisiana. A full-fledged cultural revival has occurred, and visitors can now find restaurants serving traditional and reinvented Cajun fare, ethnic festivals featuring Cajun music, exhibits that carefully trace the history of migration and settlement, and a renewed attention to distinctive language use. Given how sweeping the ethnic renaissance has been nationally over the last two decades, Louisiana Cajuns might eventually have moved in this direction on their own initiative, but, in fact, tourism definitely played a significant part in accelerating the renewal of ethnic consciousness.[18]

The usual assumption is that the sheer scale of mass consumption means that the products themselves will necessarily be uniform and undifferentiated. Yet both segmented marketing strategies on the corporate level and more localized ethnic ventures that may even stem from grass-roots movements have generated a much more diverse and varied array of choices for the consumer than is typically acknowledged.[19] Even as the marketplace itself becomes increasingly globalized and the more superficial aspects of commercialism converge, actual consumer practice remains embedded in local codes of behavior that are culturally defined within particular social contexts. In Hawaii, an evolving sense of both native culture and local identity has made goods that convey a distinctive regional stamp extremely popular. Apparel with slogans proclaiming ethnic pride and artifacts with designs that vividly represent the particular ethnic mix of the local population were initially adopted primarily by the residents, but it wasn't long before vacationers from the mainland and from all over the world were purchasing this merchandise as well.[20] In this way, consumers can become part of a global culture and a local community in tandem.

Another example of consumer culture contributing to the reinvention of ethnicity is the way certain national holidays become far more important in the American context than in their native lands, largely because of corporate sponsorship. Cinco de Mayo, the commemoration of the May 5, 1862, Mexican victory over an occupying French army is hardly celebrated in Mexico, but it has become a widely recognized holiday in the United States in recent years. The U.S. Postal Service even issued a Cinco de Mayo stamp in 1998. During the month of April that year a full-page advertisement for Pace brand salsa and picante con queso served with Coca-Cola appeared with one line of text: "Create a Cinco de Mayo Party." Significantly, the ad ran in a national circular for a general audience with no further commentary—the creators assumed that consumers everywhere would know what a Cinco de Mayo party was.

St. Patrick's Day has become so popular in certain parts of the country that it is being extended far beyond March 17, much the way the Christmas season has become longer and longer. Early in

March, the Home Shopping network holds a 24-hour all-Irish merchandise event. A waitress at a New York pub, recently arrived from Ireland herself, griped about the long hours and exaggerated Irish pride required of her in the days leading up to March 17, "The boss was packing the place all week with the Tender Loving Care dinners. Old people from all over Long Island were bused in, everyone wearing green. We did the serving and had to mouth along to all the Irish songs. The boss made a packet out of it." St. Patrick's celebrations now start in February and carry right through March. In February 1997 the *Boston Irish Reporter* announced a gala Irish Heritage Day event scheduled for March 9 explaining, "With about 40 million Americans claiming some form of Irish heritage, it's understandable that St. Patrick's Day celebrations have extended to an entire month in many places. And Boston is no exception."[21]

Since the end of World War II, Chanukah, a relatively minor festival in the Jewish ritual calendar, commemorating the upset victory in 165 B.C. of a small band of Jews over the Greek army, and the rededication of the Temple in Jerusalem, has steadily become more and more commercialized in the United States. Indeed, one commentator, as early as 1950, was already chiding that the December holiday falling so close to Christmas had become a "major competitive winter sport." Also known as the Festival of Lights, Chanukah is celebrated for eight days and candles are lit each evening in a candelabra called a menorah. By 1998, amid all the excess of Chanukah-themed gifts and decorations, the Disney company was offering no fewer than five different Mickey Mouse menorah designs and three Winnie the Poohs, while shoppers could find Chanukah travel mugs at Starbucks shops around the country.[22]

The African-American festival of Kwanzaa, celebrated for a week from the day after Christmas to New Year's Day, is an invention of the 1960s Black Pride movement that illustrates well the complex and problematical relationship of ethnic celebration to consumerism. Inspired initially by the desire to bring distinctive season's greetings to African Americans during the European-based

December holidays, it was also conceived as an alternative to the excessive and overwhelming commercial spree that increasingly marks this time of year. Over the years, however, commemoration of Kwanzaa has also succumbed to marketplace influences, to the dismay of some of its founding figures, but to the simultaneous delight of those artists and entrepreneurs who benefit from the sale of specially designed gift items, crafts, toys, greeting cards, clothing, and music with putative African motifs. At a recent Kwanzaa Expo held in New York City, more than three hundred exhibitors showed their wares to an eager crowd of holiday shoppers, a scene that is replicated on a smaller scale at local festivals throughout the country.[23]

Exalting a particular culture and making money while doing it are not necessarily antithetical. Naturally, the bottom line is increasing sales, and in these times one of the primary strategies to accomplish this goal is to broaden the consumer base by finding new audiences. Yet the way this dynamic plays out is not simply that commercial forces end up necessarily controlling the cultural realm, nor can they be said to automatically erode authentic expression. Rather the relationship is a much more dialectical give-and-take between culture and commerce. People interested in showcasing their own culture can draw on corporate funding to make that happen and, in many cases, are able to have definitive input into the process as well. There is a broad gray area between the two extremes: on one side, authentic cultural purity and, on the other, cultural expression that has been so commercialized that it has been robbed of any distinctive meaning.

The search for authenticity is very much related to nostalgia for an idealized and fixed point in time when folk culture was supposedly untouched by the corruption that is automatically associated with commercial development. Hence, the more artificiality, anonymity, and uncertainty apparent in a postmodern world, the more driven are the quests for authentic experiences and the more people long to feel connected to localized traditions seeking out the timeless and true. Studies of contemporary tourism report a similar search for "the real thing." Increasingly, tourists want their travel agents to find sites to visit that offer fine weather *and* an authentic cultural encounter.

In the tourist-dependent economy of Hawaii, hotel and Visitors Bureau personnel now routinely receive cultural training in "Hawaiian" values. The demand to experience the local "aloha spirit," along with some fun in the sun, is so great that the state government has indulged the grass-roots Hawaiian movement for self-determination, despite its militant political challenges to the status quo; officials realize that they need to foster such expressions of authenticity to sustain touristic appeal. Funding has been provided for Hawaiian Studies programs, local craft initiatives, and training workshops in indigenous arts. The transformation of the competitive hula dance into a specialized art form in recent years is an example of how such initiatives can simultaneously symbolize Hawaiian pride and sovereignty and satisfy tourist desires to capture on film an authentic experience in paradise. Such an approach has conferred legitimacy on certain pro-Hawaiian demands, as can be seen in the strident concern for native burial grounds, which forced the government to prohibit hotel developers from building over them.[24]

Whether as tourists or as long-term excavators of their ethnic roots, people are pursuing experiences that ring true, feel untainted, and taste authentic. As Jennifer Gates has demonstrated in her study of ethnic tourism in Manhattan, the quest for authenticity can extend even to evaluating entire neighborhoods on this basis.[25] Although commercialism stands as the archenemy of cultural purity, corporate interests have nonetheless begun vying with one another to claim their particular output as the most authentic in the marketplace. Not surprisingly, when market forces are at play, authenticity itself becomes a hot commodity. Companies are already under pressure to become culturally sensitive to remain competitive, and when they can combine pitches to wider multicultural markets with successful cultivation of the authentic, they are likely to see good outcomes.

As a result, concern with authenticity figures prominently in the ethnic marketing literature. Typical is this guidance offered in the trade journal *Progressive Grocer:* "Latinos are looking for products that are authentic and they have a more rigorous standard for product quality. The non-Latino group is looking for 'new tastes,' but is still not as knowledgeable about product use, preparation and taste." Or when the director of the International Food Distributors Association admonishes supermarket planners to keep up with the trend: "If these people can't get what they want from the supermarket, they'll buy it at a restaurant. Supermarkets have been beaten to the punch. The real shift is to a more authentic cuisine. More people are demanding it, and I don't think grocery stores are ready for that at all." One Los Angeles restaurant with a panethnic menu simply calls itself The Authentic Café. New record labels that specialize in popular and world music reflect the desires of their audiences for authentically primal listening experiences, with names such as Roots Records, Real World, City of Tribes, Original Music, and Redwood Cultural Work. The YAR Communications agency underlines the critical value of cultural authenticity by casting the approach in military terms, calling it a "weapon" and "among the most potent forces in today's marketing arsenal."[26]

When individuals purchase something considered representative of a culture, whether buying a piece of their own heritage or branching out to expose themselves to another's, they expect a certain level of legitimacy. Yet determinations of authenticity are extremely arbitrary, and which items are and are not considered genuine expressions of ethnic identity is based on highly subjective criteria. In his 1975 essay "Travels in Hyperreality," Umberto Eco exposes such contradictions when he goes in search "of instances where the American imagination demands the real thing and, to attain it, must fabricate the absolute fake."[27] The tourists who visit Hawaii and bring home the requisite "aloha" shirt or maybe even a colorful muumuu as souvenirs of their true experience of local culture are unlikely to realize that these "authentic" items were probably made in Taiwan or mainland China.

Furthermore, notions of authenticity are closely intertwined with ideas about social class. There is a tendency to romanticize working-class communal sensibilities, especially the dynamics of lower-class racial and ethnic groups.[28] The simple assumption is that those who are working-class are more genuinely ethnic. Hence when middle-class people proclaim ethnic pride, their legitimacy often comes into question. They are not the true representatives of their culture but rather synthetic copies of their lower-class counterparts who are the *real* ethnics of their group. Are the third-generation Irish-American banker and his attorney wife living in a Boston suburb, who are active members of the Irish Cultural Centre, who make regular excursions to Ireland, and whose two daughters take step-dancing classes any less bona fide than their third-generation Irish-American counterparts residing in Southie not far from where they grew up, where he's a factory worker who likes to spend his free hours at Sully's Bar, she's a nurse active in her parish, and all six of their children attended Catholic schools?

What, then, makes for an authentic ethnic identification? Is it the intent, the function, the history, the purity of representation? Some cases are clear-cut. Cultural initiatives consciously designed to resist commercial intrusions are the most likely to be vigilant about upholding standards of purity. The National Indigenous Festival in Puerto Rico is a good example. The event celebrates the legacy of Taino contributions to Puerto Rican culture and has as its center-piece an elaborate pageant with the crowning of an Indigenous Queen. The winner is chosen largely on the basis of the purity of her costume, which, according to strictly imposed guidelines, can be made only from natural materials gathered locally: bark, feathers, seeds, or corn. The use of anything synthetic, such as glue or plastic, immediately disqualifies the candidate. Although the festival and pageant are supported jointly by government and business—mostly local, though at one point in its history, Winston cigarettes was a sponsor—commercial backers are not allowed to advertise or in any way to detract from the goal of delivering a supposedly unadulterated cultural experience. As a by-product, the usually sagging local economy does get an annual tourist boost, but the celebration itself maintains its aura of authenticity and purity of expression. Ironically, of course, even holding an event like this, reminiscent of a competitive beauty pageant, is already a marker of assimilation into a modern consumer ethic.[29]

By contrast, another Puerto Rican festival, the Bacardi Folk Arts Fair, offers a fascinating example of a cultural activity that also adheres to rigorous standards of authenticity, perhaps even more stringent than its nonprofit counterparts, but which has its origins solely in the corporate sector. The event was initially part of a campaign to reshape the image of Bacardi rum from a Cuban to a Puerto Rican product. Bacardi's corporate publicity team worked closely with the Institute of Puerto Rican Culture (ICP), the official government agency charged with regulating the parameters of what constitutes Puerto Ricanness. Thus, the Bacardi Fair accepted only those artisans who were registered with the ICP, and all the exhibits had to pass its criteria of cultural purity. The festival soon became known as a high-quality event, one that was *not* tainted by commercialism.

The overall promotion was so successful that Bacardi expanded its market share on the island fifteenfold, from 3 percent in the 1970s to 45 percent by the 1990s. At the same time, the merchandise itself has become so closely associated with a local legacy of production by traditional Puerto Rican artisans that the underlying economic motives for creating the Folk Arts Fair in the first place have been completely overshadowed by the event's reputation as being a purely cultural celebration that preserves exacting standards of authenticity. Furthermore, the festivities have proved so lucrative for the artists and artisans themselves that unofficial cultural vendors who are not subject to Bacardi or ICP qualifications began setting up shop outside the actual fairgrounds to pick up the spillover. Hence, the irony that specifications of authenticity are rigorously imposed by the corporate entity, Bacardi, while its grass-roots counterparts just outside the official festival walls are free to present their own individualized renditions of the meaning of Puerto Ricanness.[30]

Controversy about the efficacy of ethnic identities that are voluntary or optional also informs this discussion. Even those who recognize that ethnicity still matters are likely to assert that it has been steadily eroding into a purely symbolic form that lacks substance and real meaning. Nonetheless, evidence abounds to indicate that despite commercialization, much of this behavior can still uphold authentic, if ambiguous, ethnic identities. Events such as festivals with rows of vendors, organized tours to visit the homeland, fund-raising projects to sponsor ethnic programs in universities, and museums dedicated to the preservation and interpretation of ethnic history and culture all benefit from a highly evolved consumer society, even though, oftentimes, the motivation to re-create such ties is in reaction to an overly consumer-oriented culture. The values, interests, and activities of the new consumption classes in relation to this more situational and transitory ethnicity simultaneously gratify both spiritual and instrumental aims. As the president of the National Foundation for Jewish Campus Life (Hillel) explained, "If there is any culture that this generation is familiar with, it's the consumer culture. . . . They know how to shop. Their cultural place is not the town square, it's the mall—with all of both the superficiality and the abundance that that creates and it is here that they are looking to be consumers of a life that makes sense."[31]

Last March, one of my research assistants, Gini Laffey, was walking a dog on an Oregon beach when a man in his fifties approached, also with a dog, and as the two pets sniffed each other, he and Gini began a conversation. He was unremarkable in appearance, of medium build, dressed in casual L.L. Bean–type attire, and with a pleasant enough face, except that he had a fairly good-sized tattoo in an abstract design etched into the skin on one of his cheeks. Perhaps because of the contrast between the bold placement of body art and the man's otherwise understated style, Gini couldn't help wondering about it as they chatted. She found herself getting more and more curious until finally, she just came right out and asked him about his facial stamp. He responded eagerly, even thanking her for posing the question, because it gave him the chance to speak about the subject that he said most animated him in life.

He went on to explain excitedly that he was a sixth-generation Irish-American and that he and two of his brothers had decided they wanted to find a way to signal and celebrate their Celtic heritage. He created the actual design, a symbol that, according to Gini, who is also Irish-American, did not appear to have particularly Irish characteristics. The three siblings had agreed to get the same tattoo, but he was the only one to choose to have it burned into his face. When Gini asked, "You mean, like a coat of arms?" He agreed that, yes, that was how he thought of it. At first she had speculated that perhaps he was a Maori, coming from a culture that has a tradition of facial tattoos, or an American Indian, but she never expected that this literal in-your-face statement of cultural identity would turn out to be representative of a (much removed) Irishness and that the man sporting it was actually a member of Gini's own tribe.

Perhaps nothing better illustrates the extent to which the ethnic revival has permeated our culture than hearing the renowned baby and child care expert Dr. T. Berry Brazelton proclaim: "Every baby should get to know their heritage." In the fundamentals of end-of-the-century American child-rearing, roots training comes even before potty training. Not surprisingly, the mainstream Gerber corporation has followed with a new line of baby foods called Gerber Tropicals designed for Hispanic families. In their advertising, however, it is clear that the company has broader aims. Not content to corner the Latino market, it is touting the sixteen different varieties, such as mangoes, papayas, and beans and rice, for their tasty and nutritional appeal to babies of all ethnic backgrounds.

At times, the commodification of culture goes to such extremes that the result can be ludicrous, as in the case of a California-based company that sells a dog biscuit shaped like a dreidel, the four-sided top spun in the game traditionally played as part of the Jewish celebration of Chanukah. Whether shopping for a brand-name trinket or a brand-new identity (or even literally branding oneself with that identity), the creative quest for ethnic particularity is a driving passion in today's America that the nation's market economy embraces with an equally supple ardor.

Two

From Community to Commodity: The Color of Money

In order to preempt potential criticism of an article in a 1905 edition of New York's Yiddish daily *Forverts* on the latest fashion in hats, a story that in focusing on a manifestation of consumer capitalism could offend his large socialist readership, Abraham Cahan, the editor of what became the most popular foreign-language newspaper in the United States, wrote that, "Perhaps it can be said that women's hats is not such an important topic to be worthwhile to write about in a newspaper. Not at all! It absolutely is an important topic. If it does not touch the heart, it does touch the pocket, and how far is the distance nowadays from the pocket to the heart?"[1] If the distance between the heart and the pocket was already shrinking at the start of this century, it all but disappeared by century's end. Pulling at the heartstrings and pocketbooks of many Americans are the well-designed advertising campaigns developed by major corporations to tap into the lucrative market for products that reflect ethnic sensibilities.

In the aftermath of reports from the 1990 U.S. Census demonstrating that minorities represented the majority of population growth in the 1980s, one toy company executive declared: "How can you ignore these ethnic streams of revenue? You can't. The color of money is green, and you get it from whatever skin tone has got it." Or, putting it slightly differently, another commentator writes, "Black is beautiful—especially if you're black and have some green.

Or if you're Korean, Latino or part of a few other ethnic groups."[2] Whatever the clever turn of phrase, enormous amounts of money are being allocated for research and marketing development across ethnic and racial lines. U.S. companies now spend close to $2 billion a year on ads designed to win or keep the loyalty of minority customers with buying power estimated at over $1 trillion annually, of which over $700 billion will be spent on consumer goods each year. This target group, comprised of thirty-five million blacks, thirty million Hispanics, and ten million Asians, a total of seventy-five million people, represents one-quarter of the nation's current population and is projected to constitute one-third of the total by the year 2010. They have particularly transformed the demographic makeup of California, Florida, Texas, and New York, but the trend is nationwide. Less publicized but perhaps as significant were the data from the 1990 Census that revealed not only that the non-Anglo population was increasing in size but that it was also growing in affluence. These "New Americans," as they are sometimes referred to by marketers, were largely marginalized in the past, but given that they now hold such a significant aggregate share of the nation's buying power, they can no longer be discounted in the current scramble for corporate profit.[3]

Overlapping with this large target population are those who are truly new to America, the just-arrived immigrants who continue to stream into the country in such significant numbers. This is a population with enormous buying potential, especially when it comes to durable goods, such as appliances, home furnishings, and cars, which are the necessities immigrants seek to make a fresh start and, in some instances, may be once-in-a-lifetime purchases. As brand loyalty is typically established with the initial acquisition of essential household items, even when these newcomers trade these products in for pricier models as they move up the social ladder, they will return to the same companies that catered to them when they were still unaccustomed to this country. Catering to the needs of new immigrants makes even more good business sense if the most recent population totals are taken into account. Figures released in 1999 show that the number of immigrants living in the United States has tripled since 1970, rising from 9.6 million to 26.3 million today and far outpacing the growth of the native-born population, which means that immigrants account for nearly one in ten residents, the highest proportion in seven decades.

Two related approaches to marketing ethnicity escalated in the 1990s. One taps the lucrative niche markets, targeting emergent ethnic communities in the United States, often with separate messages for each language or racial group. This usually translates into appeals to the three main population categories of Hispanics, Asian Americans, and African Americans and includes the newest consumers, recent immigrants. The other approach is more broad-based and includes descendants of European immigrants, capitalizing on the "roots" phenomenon. It may even encompass pitches to multiethnic identities. Yet the two strategies rely on similar rationales. Whether they are recently arrived immigrants seeking a nostalgic taste of their homeland or third-generation ethnics attempting to reconnect with their heritage, the impetus to want to identify with a common cultural ancestry is nearly universal in America today.

Fueled by the demographic changes, corporations of all kinds are taking minority marketing seriously despite the risks of crossing the fine line between appealing to minority tastes and creating racial or ethnic stereotypes. Cosmetics and toy manufacturers have often led the way, but efforts to appeal to ethnic and minority customers have a wide product range. Even the U.S. Postal Service, the ultimate symbol of bureaucratic mass marketing with some 730,000 employees and over a hundred different products, has followed the trend and hired ethnic marketing specialists to reach African Americans, Hispanics, and even eastern Europeans. This has resulted in such initiatives as a new print ad campaign developed for the Express Mail International Service that includes a Santa Claus with Asian features urging potential customers—in Japanese—to remember relatives back home during the holidays. The Postal Service also gets involved at the grass-roots level, sponsoring community cultural events in relation to their ethnic-theme stamps. For example, in conjunction with the debut of the Lunar New Year stamp, ceremonies were held in the Chinatown neighborhoods of Los Angeles, San Francisco, and New York, while the release of the 1998 Cinco de Mayo stamp was accompanied by a parade in Los Angeles with a float trumpeting services available from the post office.

Major advertising campaigns for big corporations such as AT&T, United Airlines, Hallmark, and Pepsi have been designed to appeal to ethnic diversity and the interest in ancestral ties. AT&T committed a sizable slice of its marketing budget to hire a separate communications firm to focus solely on consumers who call relatives and friends outside the United States. The highly successful national campaign created print, broadcast, direct mail, and community-event-based advertising in nearly twenty languages. When a public radio reporter who was doing a story on the Asian-Indian community in upstate New York visited a Hindu temple in Schenectady and began to ask a few questions, one of the congregants immediately produced the *Handbook for Asian Indians*, put out by none other than AT&T. She offered the pamphlet enthusiastically, declaring it the best way for the reporter to learn about her culture. In this instance, AT&T's handbook was presented as the authoritative voice, not just for the inquiring outsider but as a document that was illuminating to the Asian-Indian community itself. Inside the front cover of the booklet, which contains information on both the nation of India and on Asian Indian-Americans, AT&T's advertisement, in both English and Hindi, boasts of its staff of Hindi-speaking operators with the headline—"On one hand, we greet you with a 'hello.' On the other, we greet you '*Namaste.*' "—and ends with the telephone number to dial for this service. For the back cover of this 1997 "heritage" edition, the telecommunications company capitalized on the fiftieth anniversary of India's independence with a commemoration design featuring photos and quotes from such figures as Gandhi and Nehru. The AT&T name and logo are simply placed underneath this tribute with the single phrase: "It's all within your reach."

A United Airlines television commercial uses vintage footage of immigrants arriving at Ellis Island and bustling about New York's Lower East Side to sell their "Flights to Europe" options. The narration accompanying these images entreats the viewer to "go back," to "return," by vacationing in your European homeland. Northwest Airlines utilizes a similar pitch.

In 1994 when Hallmark executives were first promoting their Common Threads collection, greeting cards that target consumers who recognize and celebrate cultural diversity, the sales staff was told that this product concept could best be understood by looking at the phrase on a dollar bill "*E Pluribus Unum*"—out of the many, one. The founding fathers could never have envisioned that the motto of the new republic would someday be employed to help the sale of greeting cards. In the context of promotion and sales training, the only significance of this essential maxim of American life was its placement on the almighty dollar.

Such attention to winning the loyalties of ethnic-identified customers has certainly not always been the American way of business, however. Historical studies of the development of advertising in America reveal the almost complete absence of representations of ethnic or racial minorities as consumers. Notions of modernity simply did not include such variations in identity. Despite the huge influx of southern and eastern European immigrants in the early part of the century, none appear in the imagery of the newly evolving advertising industry. Except for the occasional black trademark figure, such as Aunt Jemima, the only representations of African Americans were either servile depictions of porters, washerwomen, janitors, and the like or grotesque and exaggerated images reminiscent of stereotypes of minstrelsy that were meant to be humorous and entertaining and, thus, a viable strategy for selling to the white population. Often such caricatures were used in advertising designs for products associated with blackness—such as black shoe polish, coal stoves, certain soaps, or black thread. Occasional Chinese figures can also be found in these early ads, but, once again, their images are distorted and they are depicted in servile roles, usually

ROOTS
Trace them to Ireland on Northwest Orient.

Experience the land of your grandparents' past. A land that continues to change, all while it remains rich in ancestral heritage. Northwest Orient makes it easy, with service to Shannon and Dublin from cities all across the U.S.A. Enjoy 747 wide cabin service across the Atlantic. And we've simplified overseas travel so you won't have to change airlines or make connections in unfamiliar foreign airports.

If you like, you can fly in the luxury of our Executive Suite. Or opt for low individual or package tour fares, which include accommodations, rental cars and escorted tours.

Your travel agent can give you more information and make reservations. Or call us directly at (800) 447-4747.

Let Northwest Orient help you say hello to an old friend. Your homeland.

People who know...go
NORTHWEST ORIENT

associated with laundry products. Whether Chinese, African Americans, or European immigrants, these populations were never shown purchasing or using the products themselves.

However, the evidence suggests that early in the development of the advertising industry a national marketing strategy was addressed that would have included African Americans as part of the consumer base before this sector was completely discounted as viable customers. An 1895 article on "The Negro in Advertising" in the widely read weekly advertising journal *Printer's Ink* (precursor to *Advertising Age*) discussed whether ads should be placed in local southern newspapers when the black population of this region had such a high rate of illiteracy, but then the article concluded that, despite this liability,

> In thousands of negro homes the paper is not only read by that member of the family who is able to read it but he also reads it to others who are unfortunate in the matter of education. Considering these facts, it becomes evident that advertisements distributed judiciously among the local papers will reach a large percentage of negroes as well as white people.

In 1917, at least one ambitious and far-sighted individual saw the potential of targeting blacks when he took out a classified ad in *Printer's Ink* in which he touted the myriad opportunities that an "undeveloped" sector of "ten million Negro-Americans" presented for the advertising industry. But the young man's precocious ideas went completely unnoticed at the time. Moreover, it would take several more decades for corporate America in general to begin to recognize the buying power of African Americans and nearly to the end of the twentieth century for business to invest wholeheartedly in ethnic marketing strategies.[4]

The exceptions were certain manufacturers of beauty and skin care products, as well as recording companies. Beginning in the 1920s, labels such as Paramount and Columbia pitched their records to urban black consumers primarily through the vehicle of the African-American press. Similarly, in the 1920s and 1930s, purveyors of skin lighteners and hair straighteners began marketing their preparations through black newspapers, as did promoters of patent medicines.[5] Although this certainly stands as an early form of market segmentation, the sell, particularly in the case of cosmetics and beauty care merchandise, was the reverse of today's marketing rationale. The products were hailed for their promise to give African Americans a more Euro-American look—to lighten, straighten, and whiten—whereas contemporary beauty and skin care companies are trying to court African Americans by creating products that are specifically designed to enhance a wider variety of skin tones and textures of hair rather than molding all customers into a uniform Anglo model.

Thus, although ad campaigns did not historically feature ethnic or racial models, that does not mean that there was no attention paid to galvanizing the immigrant and ethnic consumer prior to the 1970s revival. However, unlike contemporary ethnic marketing, which promotes cultural difference as consumable, these ad campaigns were attempts to make standard "American" products appealing to ethnic outsiders. As early as the 1920s, the idea was promulgated that widely distributed branded merchandise was one of the more likely means by which a homogeneous people could be made out of a nation of immigrants.

In *Becoming Mexican American*, George Sanchez's prize-winning study of the Mexican immigrant community of Los Angeles during the first half of the twentieth century, the author discusses how retailers in the late 1920s, long before the advent of the segmented marketing approach, discovered the potential profits to be made by targeting local Mexican consumers. Manufacturers of such items as coffee, cigarettes, medicines, and records, some with a national distribution, began advertising in the Spanish-language press and sponsoring Spanish programming on the radio. At the local level some department stores in the downtown area started to compete for Mexican-American customers, many of whom resided in the nearby Plaza neighborhood, by offering special sales, extended credit lines, and even promotional merchandise geared toward increasing their Mexican clientele. One large retailer gave away free Cinco de Mayo pennants to any Mexican-American shopper who made a purchase there, while the Hidalgo pharmacy placed an Aztec eagle stamp on some of its merchandise as a mark of authenticity.

Along with pitches to particular ethnic groups came the familiar quest for authenticity. Sanchez tells us, "Advertisements usually stressed that their particular establishment was the most 'genuinely Mexican' of the group." We also learn that the big companies focused especially on the youthful consumer. In keeping with proto-typical generational modes of adaptation, adolescents in California's Mexican-American immigrant community during the 1920s were most likely to be the first in the family to break away from tra-ditional customs, clothing styles, foods, or entertainment and to Americanize by participating in mass-consumer society, by buying makeup or going to the movies. Thus, businesses designed their pro-motions to appeal particularly to young people.[6] This pattern has persisted right down to the present. Consulting firms that specialize in Hispanic marketing always stress the importance of teenage buy-ers within this consumer base; almost 40 percent of the current pop-ulation is between the ages of sixteen and thirty-four. More than any other age cohort within the Latino community, the young peo-ple live in two worlds—Spanish- and English-speaking. Today, how-ever, they are most likely to identify themselves first as Mexican or Puerto Rican or Cuban, second as Hispanic, and only third as American.[7]

Within the Jewish sector and largely because of the need for kosher products, brand-name advertising has also had historical precedents: in 1913 Procter & Gamble proclaimed that "The Hebrew Race Has Been Waiting 4,000 Years" for their recently invented all-vegetable Crisco shortening. The company published a cookbook, *Crisco Recipes for the Jewish Housewife*, in Yiddish and En-glish. This campaign was a very early example of what we now call segmented marketing. Moreover, in the process of developing and perfecting the shortening, the company even convened "Crisco teas" for urban clubwomen at which recipes that used the new product were sampled, gatherings that can be viewed as precursors to the specialized focus groups that are now standard features of corporate product testing. But, unlike today's segmented marketing efforts designed to capitalize on the merchandising of difference, Crisco's innovative kosher shortening was peddled as a way for foreigners to be able at last to make the American-style, lard-based dishes that had been prohibited in the past. Thus, Crisco served as a vehicle for greater Americanization and uniformity rather than for heightening distinctive ethnic tastes.[8]

Another early example of segmented marketing was seen in the mid-1930s, when the head of Maxwell House Coffee determined that coffee beans were classified as berries and thus could be declared kosher for Passover. He went on to popularize the brand by widely distributing Maxwell House Passover Haggadoth (booklets recounting the story of Passover) free to Jewish customers. Many Jewish families today still remember the Maxwell House Haggadah; and the company has started using them again, this time as a bonus with the purchase of a can of coffee in advertisements that read, "Maxwell House—Great Passover Traditions Last a Lifetime." Such early experimentation within the kosher sector led to the development of foods that more resembled the "nouvelle" specialty items of today, such as "Jewish bacon," a kosher meat product that purportedly tasted like the forbidden pig, which became available to consumers in the 1930s.

The confluence of interest in levels of dietary purity shared by Jews and non-Jews alike today actually dates back to the turn of the century and the early years of kosher marketing in this country, according to Andrew Heinze in his study of Jewish identity and consumer culture, *Adapting to Abundance*. Just when the influx of observant eastern European Jews was heightening the demand for kosher products, the native-born were expressing concern about unsanitary conditions and diminished food quality within rapidly urbanizing areas, and progressive reformers were targeting especially the abuses of the meat-packing industry. In 1910 in response to such pressures, the Borden Condensed Milk Company, one of the firms that regularly ran ads in Yiddish newspapers, came up with a clever new slogan, "Pure Means Kosher—Kosher Means Pure."[9]

The earlier acceptance and greater prevalence of advertising copy in the Yiddish press not just from Borden's but from such other major brands as Gold Medal Flour, Coca-Cola, Palmolive Soap, Kellogg's Corn Flakes, Chevrolet, Lucky Strike cigarettes and Pabst's Blue Ribbon Beer indicate that Jewish immigrants were more receptive than Italians or Germans to national advertising and participation in American consumer culture. Since the *Forverts* had the largest circulation among the Yiddish newspapers, some companies advertised only there. The majority, however, ran ads in all of them.

Even before these national firms began buying up space in the Yiddish media, their pioneering predecessors in the patent medicine business realized that the Jewish community was a promising target for their ad campaigns. Promoters of these magical elixirs had successfully used print ads in American newspapers throughout the second half of the nineteenth century. When they decided to cross over to the Yiddish press, they found a ready audience who proved to be enthusiastic consumers of Anglo brand-name potions such as Warner's Safe Cure, Allen's Lung Balsam, Beecham's Pills, and Mrs. Winslow's Soothing Syrup.

The Irish quickly followed suit. By the 1880s, advertisements for these same home remedies appeared in newspapers regularly. Although most of the early ads in the Irish press pitched merchandise associated with making it into American mainstream culture such as gold watches, pianos, and chandeliers, turn-of-the-century readers could also find ways to maintain their ethnic identity via ads for goods from Ireland, such as woolens, bank bonds, and books, especially novels by Irish and Irish-American authors.[10]

Market segment research may be a recent phenomenon, but it is not an entirely new business strategy. In her study of the workers' culture of Chicago during the interwar period, *Making a New Deal*, Lizabeth Cohen found evidence of initiatives by manufacturers of brand-name products, such as Colgate, to reach working-class ethnic consumers as early as the 1920s. They may have been influenced by an even earlier pamphlet called *Winning a Great Market on Facts*

(1916), which included advice on how to attract Chicago's immigrant customers. Advertising companies were hired to figure out the shopping preferences of targeted foreign-born populations in selected cities—Czechs in Chicago, Poles in Buffalo, Jews in New York, Germans in Philadelphia—and to attempt to change their consumer patterns so that they would frequent the newly developed chain stores rather than neighborhood shops.

Cohen's research also documented the impact that the availability of the mass-produced Victor Victrola had on Chicago's immigrant communities, especially Italian-Americans. She has evidence of the extent to which having the technology to listen to Italian operas, recordings of Sicilian comedians, or the popular Italian folk songs of the day reinforced ethnic solidarity. But it wasn't only the Italians in Chicago who equipped themselves with a Victrola and bought ethnic music. Immigrants of many nationalities, including even smaller clusters like Chicago's Mexican enclave, were so eager to buy foreign-language recordings that by the 1920s the city had become a hub for a burgeoning foreign-record industry.[11]

Big business quickly realized the potential of an appeal to nostalgic sensibilities and the desire for cultural familiarity among immigrant consumers. Naturally the marketing of ethnic music went hand in hand with creating the consumer need for a phonograph to play it on. Indeed, early commercial phonograph records may actually have been the first nationally marketed merchandise of any sort to be ethnically categorized. Sears and Roebuck might organize the goods in their catalog by age and gender, but turn-of-the-century national record brands such as Victor, Columbia, and Edison advertised instead on the basis of cultural and ethnic categories—not only Italian and Mexican music and lyrics but Hungarian, Bohemian, Hawaiian, and Jewish offerings, and even Chinese songs recorded in Mandarin. The records were marketed by categories, since the primary consumer base within a particular foreign-language genre was made up of compatriot buyers, but the merchandise was actually disseminated to a much more culturally mixed population. Italians were not the only ones who wanted to be able to listen to the great Caruso.[12]

Some of the earliest evidence of attention to ethnicity in music-making—and of a fascination with multiethnic identities and an optimistic belief in the possibilities of the melting-pot ideal—can be found in sheet music. The intersection of Irish and Jewish populations was a particularly favored subject as songs with titles like, "If It Wasn't for the Irish and the Jews" (1912) and the 1916 release "Moysha Machree (They're proud of their Irisher, Yiddisher Boy)," demonstrate. The lyrics in the former pay tribute to the contributions both groups have made to the American success story, highlighting politics, entertainment, transportation, and medicine. In this stanza the focus is on occupational niches:

> *What would this great Yankee nation really, really ever do?*
> *If it wasn't for a Levy, a Monahan or Donahue.*
> *Where would we get our policemen?*
> *Why Uncle Sam would get the blues.*
> *Without the Pats and Isadores*
> *You'd have no big department stores*
> *If it wasn't for the Irish and the Jews.*

"Moysha Machree" goes even further by telling the light-hearted story of harmonious ethnic and religious intermixing in a marriage between an Irish girl and the Jewish boy next door. They have a child and the upbeat lyrics continue:

> *Sure they were married and mother Machree said*
> *Please name the first girl after me.*
> *The first though was a blue-eyed boy.*
> *And he brought both luck and joy;*
> *Her son-in-law was wise so he said we'll compromise*
> *The idea was nifty, and to make it fifty-fifty*
> *He named him Patrick Moysha Machree Levee*

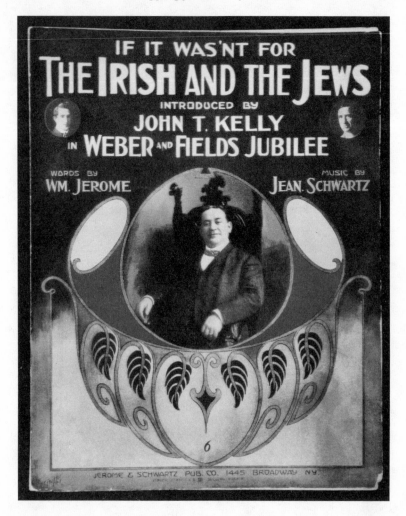

As the boy grew up they discovered that he had a voice that was rich
 with melody.
Someone said he'd surely rage,
If he changed his name and went upon the stage; and he did.
He dropped the Patrick and he dropped the Levee,
And he called himself just plain Moysha Machree.

Now he packs the theaters wherever he plays,
And for him the critics have nothing but praise.

The chorus goes on to relay the effortless melding of the two traditions:

Tis on Sunday he sings the rosary,
And on Friday night to make things right
He sings Jerusalem, Jerusalem, for his dear old Father . . .
He also owns two automobiles,
A Jew-ick (Buick) and a Cad-ollac (Catholic)
That bring him great joy
And they're proud of their Irisher-Yiddisher boy.

Perhaps the most unusual representative of this genre is the 1905 sheet music titled, "Cleopatra Finnegan: An Afro-Celtic Intermezzo." There are no lyrics, but the green-and-gold cover design shows a dark-haired but light-skinned beauty surrounded by a circle of shamrocks with one clover-leaf as a clasp at her breast.

Although my analysis throughout this investigation supports the notion of ethnic identities as fluid rather than fixed, at times it might be in the strategic interest of a particular group to insist that they are indeed primordially determined. Such was the case for the Navaho silversmiths of the southwest. Between 1900 and 1936 white consumers played a significant role in defining what constituted a putatively authentic Navaho identity. Silver jewelry was beginning to be made in factories at this time, but when serious collectors and eventually tourists became aware of this, they insisted that the jewelry be hand-made. It was of value only if it reflected premodern craftsmanship using primitive tools. Navaho ethnic identity came to be fused to their production of the silver jewelry, an identification that was influenced by market demands. It was the consumer, then, who turned Navaho silversmith production into an expression of traditional culture and the worker into a primitive artisan. Thus, Navaho identity became associated with a relatively new practice while paradoxically that identity melded with a sense of Navahoness that was premodern and unchanged by time. Economic survival turned on the creation of a cultural franchise supported by people who romanticized and idealized the craftspeople but who certainly cared nothing about their actual working or living conditions.[13]

Today ethnic jewelry is still very much in vogue, and marketing strategies continue to emphasize individualized craftsmanship and the romance of authentic ancestral cultures. In 1992 *Self* reported:

In today's relentlessly mass-market world, a growing number of aficionados have come to relish ethnic jewelry . . . prized not just for its intrinsic value, but also for its uniqueness, rich symbolism and culture heritage. An ethnic piece gives you the feeling of being transported to a faraway place. It evokes a mystique because it wasn't commercially conceived on a grand scale, but lovingly rendered in an extremely limited quantity . . . People who love ethnic jewelry are individualists.[14]

As the economy boomed after World War II, participation in mass consumer society had a homogenizing effect. The drive of the second generation to assimilate as rapidly as possible coincided with the availability and affordability of goods and an accompanying mass marketing approach. This was an era when socioeconomic advancement often meant denial of one's immigrant past and ethnic heritage, a betrayal that could readily translate into self-hate or anomie. The sustenance of face-to-face, co-ethnic communities was replaced by the palliative of mass-produced material goods that rapidly filled suburban households but often left the inhabitants inside with a profound sense of spiritual dislocation and emptiness.

The 1990 Census certainly was a wake-up call to marketers, but even before the findings were widely released, corporate America had begun to realize just how critical this demographic transition had become, and that it was causing a gradual shift from the notion of a single homogeneous marketplace to a segmented approach. This demassification had become necessary for several reasons. The first had to do with advances in technology. Whereas in the era of mass marketing brands were distinguished by quality and cost value, in today's marketplace most products have equality in value and proven benefits. With an increasing number of competitive offerings cluttering the media and battling for limited shelf space, mass marketers are finding it more difficult to dominate the product categories and score large-scale victories. No longer can they win customers simply by offering a better product; nor can an advertising strategy be directed solely at the consumer's income level. Rather than assuming that certain purchasing patterns are based on income alone, marketers must also be concerned with attitudes and lifestyle issues. Thus, the sell is an emotional one and this means an appeal to the home turf or the cultural background of the consumer. The Chisholm-Mingo group, a New York-based multicultural marketing firm, boasts of itself: "To Reach the Head, We Touch the Heart—For advertising that gets to the heart of the consumer without missing a beat." Ethnicity, of course, is an emotional pitch that automatically segments the marketplace.

Efforts to cultivate the African-American consumer predate the more broad-based ethnic marketing approach and challenge the view that all marketers of the postwar era simply assumed a standardized white middle-class consumer base. As early as the 1940s, Pepsi-Cola and Esso (Standard Oil) systematically began to court black customers. In this same period, radio stations featuring programming created for African-American audiences emerged for the first time and quickly became immensely popular vehicles for advertising to what was then called "The Negro Market." In 1954 and again in 1957 *Time* magazine ran feature stories on the buying power of blacks, noting that "the Negro market is crucial to the national market." But the real pioneers in corporate America were the African-American specialists who formed their own professional organization, the National Association of Market Developers (NAMD), in the early 1950s to press for recognition of the efficacy of promotions tailored to reach black consumers.[15] The NAMD was a trailblazer in market segmentation strategy, and recent trends have only reinforced their earlier initiatives. In every year since 1990 the purchasing power of black consumers has grown faster than the national average. Blacks consistently spend more than their white counterparts on luxury items such as cars, clothing, and home furnishings. Although total black buying power has been highest in New York, gains have been made in all fifty states. In a related trend, the black population is increasing at a faster rate than that of the United States overall. During the 1990s, the black population grew by 14 percent as compared with 9 percent for the nation as a whole.[16] Such figures underline the efficacy of targeting African-American shoppers.

In 1992 J. C. Penney, a mass marketing pioneer, jumped on the bandwagon with a highly successful line of imports from West Africa. In twenty stores Penney's set up "Authentic African" boutiques to display specialized clothing and home furnishings. The strategy worked so well that Penney's quickly launched similar promotions in hundreds of other locations. The gift departments carry African artifacts and artwork, for example, a mask bearing a tag that tells what the mask was traditionally used for and gives the country or tribe of origin. Mail-order customers can also purchase these items, billed as designed with "Afrocentric flair," from Penney's catalog. Some of the descriptions epitomize the excesses of cultural commodification; e.g., woven cotton throws and matching needle-point pillows are offered in four different patterns: Kwanzaa, Kente, Martin Luther King, and Malcolm X. Could Malcolm X, whose name was associated with the *overthrow* of the system a mere thirty-five years ago, ever have imagined that his image would be invoked as the code for the perfect *throw* in a system of home decor?

Initially, Penney's strategy was aimed only at a black clientele. Like the Afrocentric boutiques, its Iman line of oil-free cosmetics formulated for women of color also proved lucrative, accounting for 20 percent of the chain's cosmetics sales. This outcome surely influenced Penney's decision in 1996 to become the exclusive retail outlet for another line of cosmetics, the Zhen collection. According to the Zhen company's founder, Minneapolis entrepreneur Susan Yee, "Zhen was created by my sisters and me after years of frustration in trying to find the right colors for our Asian skintones. The Zhen color palette is especially chosen to work with yellow to pink undertones and was developed . . . to fill the void in the cosmetic world." To launch the Zhen line, Penney's brought the Yee sisters to key store locations in California, Hawaii, New York, and Washington State for personal appearances, which included complimentary makeovers for their customers. The overwhelming success of campaigns such as these has led J. C. Penney to further explore segmented marketing techniques. In 1998 the company hired Inter-Trend, a California-based ethnic marketing firm, to create a blitz of print ads, free-standing inserts, and radio spots in communities with significant numbers of Asian-American residents.

Major toy companies such as Mattel, Hasbro, and Disney have introduced multicultural figures from black Barbies and G.I. Joes to Pocahontas and Aladdin dolls. But it also took the expertise of ethnic marketing specialists to make these new items a financial success. Although Mattel was already manufacturing a line of black, Asian, and Latina Barbies in the 1980s, their ads depicted only the white models. It was not until 1990, when the company launched a "go ethnic" marketing plan, that sales began to pick up. There were targeted print ads in publications like *Essence* magazine and television spots in Latino media outlets, as well as the development of a new group of black Barbie-like dolls—Shani, Asha, and Nichelle—and their male counterpart, Jamal. Unlike the first black Barbies, which were simply made from "white" molds and dyed a darker shade, the new dolls purportedly had distinctive African-American features.

The results of the ethnic marketing campaign were impressive. Within a year sales of black Barbies and Barbie versions had doubled. Returns such as these make more high-minded rationales about the educational or self-esteem value of such merchandising persuasive to corporations that are still wavering about whether they should take the multicultural marketing plunge.[17] The notion that culture can be transposed onto molded plastic is what prompted the manufacturers of the popular and expensive series of American Girl dolls—which represent different periods of American history and come with accompanying storybooks, historically accurate clothing, and a myriad of other pricey accoutrements—to add to their catalog a choice of twenty permutations of skin, hair, and eye color, each with its own wardrobe of contemporary fashions so she can "look just like you."

Because of such compelling fiscal results, affluent minorities have become the latest targets of major investment firms, brokerages, and individual financial advisers. At a gathering held in early 1998,

Federal Reserve Chairman Alan Greenspan admonished Wall Street to broaden its base, saying that "Discrimination is patently immoral but it is now increasingly being seen as unprofitable." Current promotion and advocacy emphasizes the bottom line, not political correctness as motivation. As Kevin Boston, a financial adviser, author, and television personality, told the audience at a minority marketing conference, firms and brokerages that are courting nonwhite consumers are "not doing any goodwill stuff. It's about money."

With estimates that put the combined spending power of blacks, Asians, and Latinos as high as $1 trillion, financial services has become one of the most important sectors of the economy to turn to multicultural marketing. American Express, Merrill Lynch, and Prudential Securities have all hired in-house ethnic marketing specialists or sent corporate representatives to financial service seminars for training in multicultural strategizing. Some of the leading financial houses are pursuing both avenues to expedite their outreach to potential investors.[18]

For example, when California Federal Bank wanted to tap the Latino market, they hired Muse Cordero Chen & Partners (MCC&P), a multicultural advertising agency, to develop a print campaign and a series of collaterals to encourage investments in the form of CDs, real estate, and home mortgages. With the assistance of MCC&P, the bank developed a home-lending kit to walk Latino customers through the procedures of securing a home loan. Because this can often be a confusing process, a maze was used as a visual metaphor, and the instructions and worksheets in the kit were written in concise Spanish, all designed to guide the prospective borrower through each step. Although financial services are in general undermarketed to the Hispanic population, advisers at MCC&P are sensitive to the diversity within the Latino segment.

In another advertising campaign for Pueblo Financial Corporation, which included TV, radio, and print media, MCC&P devised a strategy to encompass a wide audience of assimilated, bilingual, and predominantly Spanish-speaking consumers by executing the slogan "I can do it" in English and Spanish, depending on the targeted constituency. Rather than lumping all Hispanics or Asians together, MCC&P specializes in customized campaigns to particular sub-groups, such as its branding effort for Home Savings of America to reach Chinese markets in Los Angeles, San Franciso, New York, and Houston. It works with the theme "As solid as Mount Tai"—which is China's tallest peak.

Common to all these endeavors is the recognition of a major para-digm shift in the popular perception of America as a melting pot. Despite all the limitations of this model and the voluminous schol-arly and public debates concerning its validity, the melting pot mythos held strong throughout the middle decades of the century. Furthermore, for years the basic premise underlying mass marketing itself has been assimilation. Immigrant groups supposedly wanted to blend into the American way of life and become part of the mass consumer mainstream. Concurrent with this widespread cultural assumption was the development of mass marketing as the corner-stone of an amalgamated consumer society. The melting pot was a metaphor perfectly suited to an age of uniformity.

Since the 1970s, however, both the notion of a homogeneous melting pot and the success of mass consumption have been called into question. The soup in the melting pot was far too bland for the post-'60s palate, its ingredients too difficult to distinguish. As one ethnic marketing specialist put it, "Assimilation is a real myth. Peo-ple have not assimilated. They are not going to assimilate. It's like putting people in a blender and pushing the button. And nobody wants to be mush."[19] Many have come to realize that the images of the cultural mosaic or tossed salad more accurately describe not only the newest arrivals to this country but many of its long-standing members who seek to retain hyphenated identities. The appeal of blending together while still maintaining separate identi-ties has permeated our economic culture.

Three

The New Ethnic
Marketing Experts

The fluctuating demographic trends in the United States over the last three decades have inspired the initiation of entirely new kinds of businesses and services created to reach a culturally diverse consumer base. The increasingly fragmented market not only calls for advertising campaigns tailored to specific groups but also requires a determination of which media are most effective in such initiatives. More and more, consumers themselves are expressing culturally distinctive desires, needs, and wants in their shopping habits, and these demands as well as patterns of product loyalty prompted consulting, research, and communications firms to begin specializing in multiethnic niche marketing. Some cater to specific ethnic groups such as the California-based Hispanic Market Connections (HMC) or the even more narrowly focused Talkline Communications Network, an agency in the business of reaching Jewish consumers with the amusing motto "It takes more than gefilte fish to reel in the Jewish market." Others have a broader scope and provide expert population and zip code breakdowns nationwide. When such agencies do specialize, they usually focus on one of the primary "New American" umbrella groups: Hispanics, Asians, or African Americans. Still another approach is that of Muse Cordero Chen & Partners (MCC&P), which seeks to design promotions that find a "zone of commonality" that centers on similarities rather than differences.

Instead of the traditional monoethnic message, MCC&P develops crossover advertising in a process they call transcreation.

Ethnic marketing has become an industry in its own right, bringing together experts with the latest technological training and advanced research methods to investigate attitudes, culture, heroes, trusted organizations, and lifestyles. Some of the most recent training programs include workshops on marketing on-line, touting multicultural e-commerce as the next frontier. In the 1999–2000 edition of *The Source Book of Multicultural Experts*, a reference guide published by Multicultural Marketing Resources, Inc., no fewer than two hundred companies and individuals in the business were listed. Since 1996 the organization has also produced the bimonthly newsletter *Multicultural Marketing News*. At a 1998 roundtable on niche marketing, sponsored by the magazine *Advertising Age*, Gilbert Davila, director of multicultural marketing for Sears, Roebuck & Co., observed: "Ten years ago, I never got a résumé from anybody coming out of a business school saying, 'I want to pursue a career in multicultural or ethnic marketing.' And we get them today. And that to me is fascinating."[1]

Ferreting out information such as the brand of soft drink favored by California Mexicans or the percentage of African-American households that own microwaves, the reason Hispanics are less likely to use credit cards, or the preference of Korean immigrants for commercials that show viewers how to use merchandise have all become essential to successful product promotion. Even academics are conducting segmentation surveys. A study comparing Korean-immigrant and American-born product selections showed differences in consumption of automobiles, stereo systems, laundry detergent, and coffee. The most significant discriminating variable was that the least acculturated Koreans put family wants above individual consumer choices.[2] In their search for messages and strategies that would be the most emotionally compelling and motivating, HMC found patterns among Latinos that resembled those of the Korean sector. The agency developed a rewards programs for Hispanics. Female customers could choose jewelry, a day at a spa, a new kitchen, or a family vacation. A similar list was offered to a general market group. What HMC discovered was consistent with their expectations: Latina women repeatedly opted for those rewards that were directed toward the family, such as having the kitchen remodeled or the vacation package, but most of the women in the general market category, particularly those of working age, preferred a day at a spa—alone. The rewards were more for themselves, to gratify individual desires.

Traditionally, ethnic enterprises capitalize on catering to a co-ethnic clientele, the culture with which they are most familiar. Sometimes they conduct their businesses in their native language, utilizing the ethnic press, taking advantage of advertising possibilities within the compatriot community's calendar of special events, specializing in indigenous merchandise and culturally specific services, and making a point of getting to know their customers' distinctive consumer preferences well. Corporate target marketing specialists are simply attempting to master the approach that local ethnic entrepreneurs have always based their business ventures on, but the big companies have to try to adapt these techniques to work on a much broader scale.

However, the most sophisticated target marketers understand the limitations of too wide a scope for their multinational constituencies. A crucial component of their staff training is to develop an awareness of the complex intraethnic variations among both the Hispanic and Asian segments and to pass this knowledge on to their clients. For instance, although both Cubans and Mexicans are classified as Hispanic by virtue of their common language, in reality their sociocultural histories and patterns of settlement in the United States are quite divergent and demand differentiated marketing approaches. When marketing specialists at the Bustelo coffee company determined that Mexicans and Central Americans, compared with all other Hispanics, preferred instant coffee to espresso, they developed television commercials depicting their instant varieties to broadcast in the Chicago and the Bay Area, urban centers with substantial Mexican-American communities. Bustelo's market research is so refined that the company has even tracked how tastes in coffee drinking change when people relocate. For example, Mexicans who move to Miami or to New York tend to pick up on the espresso and specialty coffee trends, and subsequently their consumption of instant coffee declines.

Unlike Hispanics, among the diverse Asian populations—Chinese, Japanese, Filipino, Korean, Vietnamese, Cambodian, etc.—language (other than English) is not even a common ground on which to base communication strategies. To reinforce the absurdity of lumping all Asian Americans together, in one of his ethnic marketing training sessions, Elliot Kang of Kang & Lee Advertising quipped: "If your father is Japanese and your mother is Korean and you lived in Taiwan and then your parents got divorced, moved to Los Angeles and your father took up with the Filipino woman next door and married her—well, that's almost like being Asian American."[3]

Yet despite all the research into the shades of diversity, one other unexplored multicultural frontier still exists. Marketing specialists to date have failed to recognize the growing intracultural variety *within* the nation's conglomerate black population. With increasing numbers of non-Hispanic Caribbean consumers of both British West Indian and Haitian descent, not to mention the array of new arrivals from various nations of the continent of Africa itself, clarification of the nuances of African-based ethnicities, of the distinctions among Haitian, Jamaican, Ethiopian, or African-American cultures become more and more relevant in the marketplace and beyond.

One of the most elaborate of the differentiated corporate marketing specialists is Florida-based Market Segment Research and Consulting (MSR&C), a firm that has put itself in the forefront of the demassification trend by attempting to fill what it identifies as an information gap concerning the country's changing demographics. An Ethnic Market Report published by MSR&C in 1996—in collaboration with the U.S. Census Bureau, Geoscape International

TYPE OF SNEAKER/ATHLETIC SHOE
PURCHASED IN THE LAST 12 MONTHS

	General Market	Total Anglo, %	Total African-American, %	Total Hispanic, %	Total Asian, %
Casual sneakers	56	57	49	60	48
Exercise walking	33	35	30	22	21
Basketball	26	26	41	19	14
Outdoor	21	22	27	8	16
Cross training	16	17	23	7	12
Aerobic/step	14	16	14	10	9
Jogging or running	14	13	17	11	17
Hiking	11	12	9	3	12
Tennis	11	9	12	26	10
Golf	3	4	1	0	2
Bowling	2	2	2	2	2
Soccer	1	1	0	7	2

Example of a comparative table from the 1996 MSR&C *Ethnic Market Report*

(specializing in mapping demographic shifts), and Information Resources, Inc. (to help answer the question of who is buying what)—goes a long way toward closing that gap. Entitled *A Portrait of the New America*, the compilation provides the most up-to-date information about ethnic consumers' cultural, demographic, and behavioral patterns. The report had broad corporate sponsorship from such leading firms as Procter & Gamble, Pepsi, Anheuser-Busch, and General Mills.

The primary survey data was based on five thousand telephone and face-to-face interviews in major cities across the country, which used native-language speakers as interviewers so that respondents could answer in the language they preferred. National random sampling was mixed with samples that reflected a cross section based on variation in population density. Of the five thousand interviews, two thousand were conducted with Hispanics and one thousand each with the Anglo, African-American, and Asian segments, covering the subject areas of media usage, shopping behavior, views on social and political issues, leisure activities, product information, and financial services. Examples of the kinds of questions asked include number of hours spent watching TV, listening to the radio, and reading newspapers and magazines in English and native languages; frequency of grocery shopping, coupon use, catalog mail-ordering, and purchase of recycled products; attitudes toward gays and lesbians, drugs, government, and immigration; types of movies preferred, number of greeting card purchases, car ownership, kinds of medical insurance, and incidence of various types of bank accounts.

In the most fascinating and informative section for marketers and social scientists alike, the results of the same interview questions that were posed to each segment are compiled in comparative charts so that the reader can easily see the differences between general market, Anglo, African-American, Hispanic-American, and Asian-American consumers in all categories. Finally, the volume includes reprints of the U.S. Bureau of Labor Statistics 1994–1995 Consumer Expenditure Survey as applied to Hispanics and African Americans and the 1992 Economic Census Surveys of Minority and Women Business Ownership.

What sets this report apart from earlier MSR&C publications is the incorporation of the software technology of Geoscape International. The book is illustrated with visually incisive and user-friendly "geodemographic profiles" that map market landscapes across the country, including levels of media coverage, to create an entirely new field of marketing topology. For example, for the six megametropolitan centers of Chicago, Houston, Los Angeles, Miami, New York, and the Bay Area, Geoscape diagrams distribu-

AGREEMENT WITH STATEMENTS CONCERNING
EATING AND GROCERY SHOPPING (AGREE COMPLETELY)

	General Market	Total Anglo, %	Total African-American, %	Total Hispanic, %	Total Asian, %
I prefer to use sugar rather than sugar substitutes	52	49	56	69	50
I enjoy baking	40	39	40	57	23
We're mainly a meat & potatoes family	39	38	34	59	21
I collect recipes	35	36	32	37	27
No matter how busy I am I make sure I eat the right foods	35	30	36	65	48
I exercise regularly	34	33	34	43	31
I'm worried about becoming overweight	28	24	27	62	28
I often overindulge	20	19	22	33	18
One way to limit the amount of sugar I use is by using sugar substitutes	24	22	24	38	14
I feel guilty eating foods I like	18	15	17	39	16
My family and I eat a lot of fast food	11	8	19	27	12

Example of a comparative table from the 1996 MSR&C *Ethnic Market Report*

tion of the primary multicultural aggregations, where Hispanics, African Americans, Asians, or a combination of these groups make up 25 percent or more of the neighborhood's population on a map that also indicates the size and location of all the shopping centers in the area to make the parameters of each micromarket segment clear. Other illustrations highlight more scattered population densities, labeled hot spots, in states that are not usually associated with this type of ethnic diversity. The purpose here is to furnish companies with the tools for microtargeted advertising initiatives that will save them having to cover an entire region to reach more localized concentrations of potential customers. Indeed, the whole thrust of these mappings is to reduce the guesswork involved in target marketing, whether the focus is on foreign-language use, retail site segmentation, outdoor advertising campaigns, the design of sales districts, or tracking telecommunications networks.

The other collaborator, Information Resources, relies on what is called an InfoScan service that brings together data from over twenty thousand grocery, mass merchandise, discount, and drugstores to expand considerably the documentation of ethnic purchasing trends. If a client wants to know which ethnic group buys more pickles, antifreeze, or foot care products in any particular locale, the answer is immediately available. Indeed, even more specific preferences are tabulated, such as whether chicken noodle or tomato soup is favored by African Americans or Hispanics. Sometimes explanations are given for differentials in ethnic consumption; e.g., the higher Hispanic birth rate (twenty-two versus thirteen per thousand among Anglos) is offered as the reason that diaper sales have soared in Hispanic neighborhoods. But for the most part, the findings are presented without further analysis. Thus the *1996 Ethnic Market Report* brought together the methods of more traditional social science data-gathering, such as surveys and in-depth interviews, with the latest techniques of consumer research, including detailed population profiles, zip code, census tract and block group breakdowns as well as precise measurements of media signal quality and product sales, to determine the universe of potential buyers. Employment of a multilingual staff polishes this comprehensive approach to marketing dynamics.

Some ethnic marketing initiatives do use foreign-language advertisements, especially as a strategy for reaching the Hispanic population, since Spanish remains by far the most popularly spoken non-English language in the United States. (Seventy percent of Hispanic residents were born abroad; an equal percentage speak Spanish at home.) French, German, Italian, and Chinese are the next most frequently spoken languages, but German and Italian are declining in popularity, whereas the number of Chinese-speaking households is rapidly increasing, along with Korean, Vietnamese, Farsi, and Hindi speakers. For example, in Los Angeles, the Korean-speaking population is large enough to support the circulation of *three* daily native-language newspapers. According to Maria Dias, marketing manager at AT&T Language Line Services, the three industries in which language resources are becoming increasingly essential are utilities, health care management, and financial services; the languages most in demand include Arabic, Cantonese, French, Haitian, Japanese, Korean, Mandarin, Portuguese, Russian, Serbian, Spanish, and Vietnamese.

Language Line Services was started in 1990 to assist 911 operators in responding to non-English-speaking callers. By 1998 their over-the-phone interpretation service to various segments of the business community had expanded to provide access to professional interpreters twenty-four hours a day in one hundred forty languages. For GTE telecommunications, attention to the Asian-American segment has become paramount in recent years. There has been an emphasis on marketing in the Chinese language—both Mandarin and Cantonese dialects—and in Korean and Vietnamese. Since this customization began, the company has seen significant growth in those sectors.

The demographics in certain sections of the country are so compelling that even car manufacturers have begun to design foreign-language advertising. In 1999 the Ford Motor Company produced its first Asian-language advertising to market its minivan and sports utility models. The promotion includes TV and newspaper ads in three languages—Chinese, Korean, and Filipino—to appear in newspapers and on cable news programs throughout California. In addition, the company has set up an 800-number consumer hot line staffed with operators fluent in the three languages. Although other car makers have targeted Asians by dubbing English-language commercials, Ford is the first to create specific in-language spots. The new ads also feature actors representing the three nationalities.

Imada Wong Communications based in Los Angeles has been particularly successful in campaigns to reach new-immigrant consumers. One of their most innovative promotions was the design of a booklet welcoming immigrants to the United States and filled with practical advice, such as how to turn on the gas, open a checking account, or use an ATM. Called *The Newcomer's Guide*, it was co-sponsored by corporations from several industries, including Bank of America, AT&T, Pacific Gas and Electric, GTE, and New York Life. The first twenty-five thousand copies published in Chinese and in Spanish were snapped up in a couple of weeks.

Bank of America and AT&T also say that ethnic consumers are responding to the in-language commercials they air on the Spanish-language Telemundo and Univision networks. The vice president of Ethnic Marketing at Bank of America, David Bland, echoes the overarching philosophy of all such industry efforts when he says that "We feel it is not just a good thing to do in the social consciousness sense, but it is a good thing to do in the business sense." For in-language spots on television, marketers can "add the cultural nuances, music, and other cultural cues that make the message much more memorable," explains Fred Teng, district manager of marketing communications at AT&T. YAR Communications also concentrates on diverse domestic foreign-language campaigns. Yuri Radzievsky reasons that "You're talking about a marketplace equal to a good-size European country that can be reached with non-English media within the U.S."[4] Shopping in one's native language is also catching on in the burgeoning frontier of e-commerce with such alternatives as *www.espanol.com*, an on-line marketplace designed for the Spanish-speaking world and specializing in the sale of books, music, and videos.

As companies are investing in a wide variety of foreign-language promotions, they also must address the possibility of more than one language spoken among a particular ethnic population or even multiple dialects within a shared-language group. When Kang & Lee runs ads in Chinese, they design them in both Cantonese and Mandarin versions. Determining exactly which foreign-language media will be most effective, which dialects are most appropriate, and whether to advertise in English as well to capture the majority of foreign-language speakers who are bilingual are all important issues for the ethnic marketer.[5]

Even if the actual ads are not in the first language of the target group, the research that an ethnic marketing firm undertakes is likely to be more accurate if it is conducted in the respondents' native tongue. Kang & Lee does all of its survey and interview research in the first language of immigrant consumers. Its studies showed that close to 80 percent of Koreans, 98 percent of Vietnamese, and 85 percent of Chinese interviewed preferred to speak their own language at home. The lowest rate, at 30 percent, is among Japanese because they are the most assimilated subset of the Asian segment. The marketers are quick to point out, however, that this does not necessarily mean that those surveyed do not understand English. In fact, it is likely that their jobs require that they speak English during the day, but when they are home, their preference is almost always to receive messages in their own language. Erlich Transcultural Consultants, a California firm, uses both quantitative and qualitative methods to specialize in studies that are conducted in-language. One such research effort, a strategic qualitative study of Filipinos in the United States and the Philippines conducted for U.S. and Hong Kong banks, garnered the company a 1996 industry award for the best non-English advertising.

In addition to corporate research, a sprinkling of studies dealing with immigrants as consumers has begun to appear in academic and professional publications. Earlier investigations tended to compare Mexican consumption patterns to those of Anglos. The findings resembled those of the corporate experts; e.g., Mexicans prefer to shop at stores where Spanish is spoken and are more brand-loyal than their Anglo counterparts. Lisa Penaloza's 1994 article on Mexican immigrants in the *Journal of Consumer Research* is a departure from that comparative model, addressing instead the question of how these newcomers adapt to the marketplace once in the United States. She demonstrates how recent intensive initiatives by corporate America to target the Latino market have influenced Mexican immigrant consumption patterns. The combination of a well-established Mexican-American community and the systematic strategies already in place to market to this population eases the transition to their new surroundings because it means there is considerable continuity in buying patterns. Most obviously, many of the same foods consumed in Mexico are now conveniently available in the United States, but, in addition, familiar health and beauty products, household goods, religious artifacts, and items of clothing can readily be found in their new surroundings. Furthermore, the globalization of American businesses means that many of the immigrants are probably already acquainted with popular franchises and brand names such as McDonald's, KFC, Nike, Levi's, and, of course, Coca-Cola and Pepsi, all of which have a foothold in Mexico. This study showed that immigrants from urban areas had an easier time adjusting than their rural counterparts, since as city-dwellers, they had more exposure to a consumer culture resembling that in the United States.

However, Penaloza's conclusions go further than simply crediting the marketplace with facilitating adaptation; they suggest that, in powerful ways, marketers both validate and perpetuate the maintenance of a vibrant Mexican culture in the United States. Invisible in most other contexts of their adopted country, Mexican immigrants as American consumers have been recognized and even sought after by marketers, who make concerted efforts to reach them through the Spanish-language media. Marketers offer specially tailored merchandise and services that support the continuation of Mexican cultural forms while at the same time providing the vehicle through which the newcomers are introduced to the mainstream consumer world.[6]

The YAR Communications agency systematically differentiates between long-standing and emergent ethnic communities in the discourse of their promotional literature and in the design of their campaigns, referring to these recent immigrant target groups as New American Pioneers, a title that includes all non-English-speaking people arriving in significant numbers, such as Iranians, Koreans, or Russians, no matter what that population's racial makeup. Actually YAR is the only agency to have gone so far as to develop promotions pitched specifically to *Anglo*-Americans, cleverly featuring emblematic British customs and idiosyncratic turns of phrase in ads created for AT&T's international long-distance service. They recognize that the impetus to want to identify with shared cultural roots is universal in America today. Newcomers and old-timers, white and nonwhite ethnics alike, become strategic targets. The result is a common psychology of advertising.

YAR's communications strategies take into account the way length of residence in a new country affects variation in consumer demand. Yuri Radzievsky explains:

> As much as these newcomers love America, they remain equally rooted to the cultures of their homelands. Marketers that can bridge these two influences will create a dynamic new generation of brand loyalists. Rebuilding lives and households, they will consume goods and services on a scale unprecedented in the modern era . . . The marketer who speaks to the unique blend of old and new for each of the New American Pioneers will win their acceptance—and their business.
>
> Immigrants have this bond with their roots. They may live in their ethnic communities or they may move out of their communities because their income allows them to buy better places in better geographical locations but inevitably most of them come back. Not physically but come back in the sense that when they open the *New York Times* the first thing they are

The Humane Approach
to Savings from AT&T

"Well I never, bach. Now you can save up to 50%* on direct dial calls to Llanfairyneubwll, Rhosllanerchrugog and the rest of the UK with AT&T World Savings. There's generous for you."

"I say, that's absolutely splendid news old boy. Only 50 cents a minute every single time one makes a call to Blighty. Awfully decent of those chappies at AT&T, what?"

"Ere cop hold of this, me old china. These savings, which are truly mega I'll 'ave you know, they're not just to a few phone numbers either..."**

"Unlike some other dog and bone companies we could mention, know what I mean, squire, say no more. And the hours are a real treat."

"Just think, great savings from 3pm to 8am, Monday to Friday, and 24 hours on weekends. But please, try not to wake my sister."

"Aye, with AT&T thee can ring all thy family and mates in t' British Isles and still save a bundle. Eee that's right champion."

"And darlings, until January 31st, you can save over 35%* on calls to just about anyone, anywhere in the world. Whether it's Daphne in Davos or Nigel in Nairobi. Okay yah?"

"Och, can ye believe it? All for a wee $3 monthly fee."

"So come on all you lazy ex-pats, cohabiting with those Yanks over there. Look sharpish, get on the blower, and ring AT&T right this very minute on 1 800 367-9806 ext. 853."

Focusing on Britain's great love for dogs, this ad features English breeds talking about the benefits of AT&T.

Save 25% on English Language Refresher Courses, Courtesy of AT&T.

This is your golden opportunity to rediscover that jelly is jam, a diaper is a nappy, the subway is the tube, the tube is the telly, an English muffin is pure invention, and a WASP is simply a winged insect with rather a nasty sting.

Because with AT&T *Reach Out*® World Savings, you can save an average of 25%* on AT&T direct dialled calls to the British Isles, as well as to over 50 other countries and areas worldwide. No matter how many numbers you call.

And the hours are convenient enough to suit everyone's body clock. All day Saturday and Sunday, and from 3 pm to 8 am, Monday through Friday, for calls to the UK (so you can ring up the minute Coronation Street ends). All for a meagre $3 dollar monthly fee.

But our generosity just doesn't stop there. From September 1st until the end of October, we're offering special 24-hour, 20%** savings on AT&T direct dialled calls to a further 150 countries and areas.

So if you don't have *Reach* Out World already, call 1 800 367-9806, ext. 600 today, and start brushing up on your English.

Then, with all the bucks you can save on AT&T International Long Distance calls, you'll be quids in on your next trip home. AT&T *Reach Out*® World Savings. Just another part of *The i Plan.*℠

Playing on the differences between British and American expressions, AT&T caters to the British in America who miss their "native tongue."

looking for is, "What happened in Russia yesterday?" or "What happened in Cuba yesterday?" They go back to the neighborhoods where their cultures live to go to the restaurants and the cultural events. The connection is much more than language and geographical location.[7]

Although typically more concerned with the psychology of the immigrant experience in general, social scientists have concurred with YAR's more pragmatic analysis that new immigrants are likely to be avid shoppers. Consumption can provide a means of creating a new identity in America, particularly when upward mobility occurs or is anticipated. Some newcomers eagerly look to migration as an opportunity to alter their identity, but even those for whom the experience of relocation has been more jarring, consumer goods can serve as a means to reconstitute new cultural identities.

In many respects, immigrants are the ideal consumers. The "need-everything" generation arrives without refrigerator, stove, washing machine, television set, or automobile. They buy what they can afford, but as they adapt and move up the economic scale, they upgrade these items so that both the need and frequency of purchase is greater than in the general marketplace. Moreover, as Radzievsky points out, there is often an overcompensation factor: they tend to make up for all the years in which acquisition of such an array of material goods would have been unthinkable. One of the few systematic studies of new-immigrant buying patterns confirms this point. Among the young, upwardly mobile Punjabi population, the accumulation of high-status possessions is a key marker to signify successful assimilation into American society, signs that they actually fit in.[8]

Although some newcomers, such as Mexicans, arrive already familiar with American labels through the export of American popular culture and have been shown to carry brand loyalty with them across the border, Radzievsky, nonetheless, looks at new immigrants as consumers who are wide-open targets for advertising campaigns:

What a fantastic opportunity! What an audience—a brand-blind audience. They come willing to learn, willing to experiment. They don't have preconceived notions of loyalties to other brands. All you need is to become the choice of the community. Because the opinion swell of the community is more powerful than any rational reason. You come and you ask your neighbor what to do. You do what others do. This is virgin territory. There are no preconceived choices. And advertising to them is not more expensive than advertising through the mass media channels. It's just more targeted—less wasteful.[9]

Actually, the newest multicultural marketing niche is what sociologists term the 1.5 generation—individuals who straddle the immigrant generation (usually referred to as the first generation—born outside the United States) and the children of immigrants (born in this country and known as the second generation). The 1.5 cohort is made up of those who arrive in the United States as young children, under eighteen years of age. They come to their new country with their parents or as part of family units, not by their own choice. As a result, their patterns of assimilation and the ways in which their native language and culture are manifest may differ from either the immigrant or second generation. Some may adapt very quickly, as if born in the United States themselves, speaking English without an accent and exhibiting cultural preferences that are representative of mainstream American culture, whereas others may more resemble the immigrant generation and still hold strong ties to native traditions. Marketers now realize that they need to pay attention to such nuances of behavior among this growing sector. This is especially true among the burgeoning Asian-American segment because this not only is the fastest growing population in every age cohort, but also ranks highest of any group in the United States in average household income and level of education.

Another approach to ethnic marketing is represented by Hallmark's highly successful Common Threads collection, which was discussed previously. Rather than trying to target a particular segment, this line was intended to broaden the ethnic market by appealing to consumers who appreciate cultural diversity. Hallmark's Ethnic Business Center oversees their popular Mahogany (African Americans), Primor (Hispanics), and Tree of Life (Jewish) lines, but the Common Threads collection is not under its auspices. The unity cards are not reflective of a specific culture; nor are they directed at a particular ethnic group. Instead, messages are chosen to represent shared truths found in poetry, proverbs, and lyrics drawn from a variety of the world's cultures, emphasizing a philosophy of global community and diverse cultural expression. After qualitative research determined that consumers are more likely to be aware of and interested in bringing multiculturalism into their daily lives, Hallmark created this product line to accentuate commonalties, not differences. "Common Thread is eth-mix, not ethnic," explained one design manager. Executives at Hallmark think that there is a strong possibility that historians will look back one day and label this era the "Age of Multiculturalism."[10]

Although it was anticipated that African Americans, Hispanics, or Asians might make up a small portion of those who would choose a Common Threads card, Hallmark focus group data revealed that primary interest came from the white or Caucasian market. These were the same buyers who reported ownership of multicultural clothing, jewelry, or decorative items for the home and who sought out goods they considered unique, inspiring, meaningful, or creative. Hallmark developed the collection to feature inspirational messages and colorful artwork drawn from a mixture of many different cultural backgrounds. On the back of each Common Threads card or specialty product, the underlying philosophy is spelled out: "Every culture enriches our lives with its own unique beauty and wisdom. Yet we all share the same hopes and dreams, the same need for love and home and kinship. These are the common threads that bind us together as one family in one world."

Companies such as Hallmark are cognizant of the profits to be made by marketing to the "New America." Moreover, they understand that a significant proportion of white America is ready to embrace these changes as well. As the largest maker and seller of greeting cards in the world—the company holds 47 percent of the American market alone—Hallmark has been dubbed the General Motors of emotion because of its close attention to social trends. Thus, Common Threads has not only cashed in on multiculturalism but also banked on the likelihood that its clientele will respond positively to other liberal appeals, such as the promotion of global awareness and cross-cultural understanding. Indeed, the theme of Patricia Nelson Limerick's presidential address, "Insiders and Out-siders," at the 1996 meeting of the American Studies Association, an annual conference for academics in the field that happened to be held that year in Kansas City, Hallmark's hometown, was a call for the membership to seek commonalties after years of accentuating differ-ences. Her scholarly conceptualization of the state of American cul-tural dynamics matched Hallmark's own corporate assessment of the pluralism of contemporary social trends.[11]

After only a few months on the market, sales tallies confirmed that the Common Threads idea was a sound one. Not surprisingly, the line sold particularly well among students and teachers, but what was especially noteworthy was that demand was strong in almost all areas of the country, not just in major metropolitan cen-ters. Nonetheless, what could not be alluded to in such a utopian representation of multicultural harmony was any suggestion of the harsh inequities inherent in the transnational labor market. Although the reality of the production of Hallmark greeting cards is itself relatively benign, imported merchandise that gets catego-rized as ethnic chic, especially garments and home furnishings, often results from escalating levels of worker exploitation. By the time global goods produced by local labor end up in the hands of cos-mopolitan American consumers, the process can have been a decid-edly inharmonious one.

Another way that the demographic revolution has touched cor-porate America is that executives are beginning to understand the potential of capitalizing on the diverse cultural backgrounds of their own employees to improve the quality of the goods and services produced. Similar to the process in the wider society, the ethnic composition of the business sector is also shifting, albeit more slowly than some would like to see, and firms that market ethnicity are able to use ethnic resources within their own ranks. As one design manager at Hallmark described it, "Artists and writers drew from their own ethnic heritages—which, in this studio, are particularly diverse. But we decided early on that they should have the freedom to express any cultural theme that they cared about and wanted to study." To illustrate, he pointed out a gift bag in the Common Threads line that reflected an African-American style but had been designed by an Asian staff member.[12] By giving him encouragement to follow through on his interests in "the other," the corporation was practicing the very philosophy that its product line promotes. Similarly, whether Jewish or not (and most are not), members of the design team for the Tree of Life division, a collection geared especially to appeal to Jewish consumers, are enrolled by Hallmark in Hebrew and Judaism classes and are frequently sent on trips to Israel, all for the purpose of cultivating the highest levels of cultural sensitivity in the creative process.

Among multicultural marketing firms, the diversity of in-house staff is often crucial to the company's success. Admerasia, a multicultural communications agency headquartered in New York, and its partner company, Cyverasia, highlight in their print ads the extent to which their multilingual and multiethnic employees expand the firm's overall cultural knowledge and learn from one another. On one side of a two-part spread, a white male holding a laptop computer is pictured with the transgressive and attention-grabbing line "He's not just Asian" printed across his obviously Caucasian body. The fine print, however, reads: "Jeff was just American, until he joined Admerasia. Now he's immersed in Chinese, Korean, Japanese, Vietnamese, and South Asian cultures, and he's running our multicultural interactive company." On the opposite page, the reader sees Zan, an Asian male, with children playing in a tree house as the backdrop and the words "He's not just American" in front of him. "Zan was just Asian, but he had a dream of coming to America. Now he's built a tree house just for his kids and a multicultural advertising agency called Cyverasia that bridges two cultures, Asian and American." At the bottom of the ad, the fine print explains that "Jeff and Zan work at Admerasia—the creative, market-driven advertising agency we created five years ago . . . for clients with interactive and telemarketing needs."

One of the main selling points of YAR Communications is that the professional staff represents some eighty different nationalities, speaking as many different languages. Radzievsky observes:

> We often tell our clients that we are the markets that they are trying to reach. We are representatives of these markets. We have French-Americans, German-Americans, Greek-Americans, Hispanic-Americans, Asian Americans working right here. We are a kind of reflection of the multiculturalism of the society.[13]

A central component of YAR's philosophy is the belief that "Brands that best embody cultural roots and values build the strongest bonds with consumers." The employees have been immersed in the very cultures that their clients are most eager to penetrate. Personnel are carefully organized into management teams called cultural circles, which at their best operate as groups of skillful ethnographers with an insider's perspective because they are natives of the markets they serve. As a result, many of their media and design ideas grow directly out of their own cultural experiences. The combination of first-hand cultural knowledge and American marketing savvy gives them a competitive edge. At the same time, they are much less likely to commit cross-cultural marketing blunders.

For example, ads for Mack Trucks featuring the well-known bulldog symbol presented a considerable challenge when the company decided to expand into the Chinese market, since dogs do not carry positive associations within Chinese culture; in fact, they are viewed as an inferior species. Linking the image of a dog to the product being sold would do much more harm than good. Thus, for Chinese-language TV stations in this country as well as for the Mack Truck campaign in China itself, the YAR team redesigned the piece, replacing the bulldog with the more highly regarded horse as the logo, an innovation that had the added advantage of alluding to the force of the trucks' horsepower. With another client, Merrill Lynch, it wasn't a bull*dog* but their trademark bull that caused problems when the brokerage firm wanted to begin placing ads in the Russian-language press in the United States. For Russians, the image seemed to trigger thoughts of food rather than finance and it needed to be reworked to achieve the desired effect. Indeed, in the global marketplace, it is no longer enough simply to specialize in knowing one other foreign culture well, as illustrated by the case of the Mitsubishi corporation wanting to name one of its new car models the Pajero. The YAR staff did a comprehensive search and found that in some parts of Latin America *pajero* is a slang term for compulsive sexual behavior! Needless to say, Mitsubishi made a quick switch and introduced the car as a Montero instead.

These were all cases where knowledge of appropriate cultural translation supplanted a literal one. The two kinds of expertise, foreign-language proficiency and thorough cultural comprehension, go hand in hand. Emphasizing the importance of grasping the nuances of distinctive cultural detail from facial expressions and gestures to modes of dress, Anna Radzievsky, YAR's executive vice president, stresses that, "It matters which way you close your kimono . . . and what color you wear for mourning."[14] Whether dealing with language, logos, visuals, or packaging, the cultural context is intrinsic to YAR's strategy.

Having a workforce that is representative of the ethnicities of the primary target audiences not only helps to ensure that cross-cultural marketing campaigns succeed but also adds greater credibility to the business, particularly concerning issues of authenticity. The InterTrend Communications firm, based in California and specializing in the Asian market, uses just such a cross-cultural blunder to promote its own services in a print ad that shows a bowl of rice

If this picture offends you, we apologize. If it doesn't, perhaps we should explain. Because, although this picture looks innocent enough, to the Asian market, it symbolizes death. But then, not every one should be expected to know that.

That's where we come in. Over the last 7 years Intertrend has been guiding clients to the Asian market with some very impressive results. Clients like California Bank & Trust, Disneyland, GTE, JCPenney, Nestle, Northwest Airlines, Sempra Energy, The Southern California Gas Company and Western Union have all profited from our knowledge of this country's fastest growing and most affluent cultural market. And their success has made us one of the largest Asian advertising agencies in the country.

We can help you as well. Give us a call or E-mail us at jych@intertrend.com. We can share some more of our trade secrets. We can also show you how we've helped our clients succeed in the Asian market. And that's something that needs no apology.

InterTrend Communications
19191 South Vermont Ave., Suite 400
Torrance, CA 90502
310.324.6313   fax 310.324.6848

OOOOPS.

with chopsticks plunged vertically into its contents and the word "OOOPS" written above it. The lead-in narration reads: "If this picture offends you, we apologize. If it doesn't, perhaps we should explain. Because, although this picture looks innocent enough, to the Asian market, it symbolizes death. But then, not every one should be expected to know that. That's where we come in." InterTrend goes on to promise to share more of their trade secrets with interested clients. Indeed, even within the company itself, there was considerable resistance to the design by some Asian staff members who were appalled at the idea of a promotion that used such a disturbing image.[15]

From the very beginnings of international marketing endeavors, the need for cross-cultural awareness and sensitivity has been evident. When International Harvester began advertising to foreign markets in the early years of this century, a Chinese salesman warned the company that red should not be used in the ads because it represented mourning and would be offensive. Similarly, by 1913 the Armour company realized that it had to make changes in the traditional blue-and-yellow color scheme of its labels when it began to sell its products in Norway because those were Sweden's national colors.[16] Although such dangers have challenged the business sector since the advent of world marketing campaigns, it is only in the last several years that specialists have appeared on the horizon of corporate America to obviate such problems.

Interviews conducted with individuals involved in ethnic marketing reveal a consistent pattern of passionate commitment to their work. To be sure, they hold the conventional goals of increasing market shares and profits in the business world, but they are motivated also by the emotions associated with expressions of personal identity. These professionals are able to find meaning and inspiration in the workplace by building on their own cultural strengths. Furthermore, they typically carry an enthusiastic sense of purpose about their niche in corporate America. When Gary Berman, president of Market Segment Research, Inc., clarifies concerns that are central to his firm—the questions of what, if anything, differentiates any ethnic group from the general market and which media will make a significant impact—he quickly adds, "And then the issue is how does one reach them in a culturally meaningful and respectful manner?" Anna Radzievsky puts it this way: "Multicultural marketing means approaching consumers through their

complex cultural affinities—the various symbols, core values, traditions, political nuances, and passions. It means that, by your knowledge of what is important to them, you are not merely an interloper
who is trying to make money from them, but a kindred spirit who
knows their hearts—and is really one of them."[17]

Oftentimes, ethnic marketers are involved with the manufacture
and promotion of goods and services that they and their families
want and do consume themselves, products that were unavailable to
them in an era of mass consumption. Amy Hilliard-Jones, an African
American who now heads her own ethnic marketing agency in
Chicago, began her specialization by asking a simple question of the
Gillette corporation in Boston when she was first hired in 1980 after
graduating from the Harvard Business School. She wondered if they
had a shampoo for women with hair like hers. She asked not only out
of interest in the company but also because of personal concern
about her own hair care. That inquiry led to her development of the
highly successful White Rain Shampoo and Conditioners line and to
Hilliard-Jones spending the next ten years with Gillette. In the early
1990s she moved on to Pillsbury, where she created their targeted
marketing division. Hilliard-Jones is a multicultural marketing
authority who feels most proud of her work when it takes her clients
to whole new levels of cultural awareness.[18]

Some entrepreneurs may find that what they produce fills an
important affective gap in the lives of their customers. Phil Okrend,
the founder of MixBlessing, a family business that markets interfaith holiday cards, believes they are doing much more than merely
selling stationery. The clientele reports that the merchandise—
items such as the Chanukah/Christmas greeting card displaying the
scene of an inviting hearth decorated with both a menorah on the
mantel and Christmas stockings hanging from it—provide an emotional resource and a means of engagement among a population that
may no longer feel a sense of belonging to either the Jewish or the
Christian community because of intermarriage. The Okrends are
definitely on to something. Their small company is only in its sev-
enth year, yet its sales top more than 200,000 cards annually.[19]

At Mattel, Deborah Mitchell, the product manager for girls' toys and developer of the Shani line of black dolls, pragmatically stated: "You can't say we're just in it for the money, and you can't say we're in it just for public relations. We're looking at it both ways, and you're going to see a lot more companies move the same way."[20] In today's marketplace, even those who are clearly driven solely by the bottom line must still *appear* to be genuinely interested in the workings of diverse cultures and may discover that in the process they have learned something meaningful about the behaviors of both their own cultural group and that of other ethnicities.

Like anthropologists, ethnic marketing specialists are paid to be conscious of cultural nuances and will usually introduce their specialty with a personal narrative, demonstrating how their own cultural background relates to their current projects. At the "Marketing to a New America" conference for corporate training in outreach to ethnic consumers, attended by managers representing such big-name companies as Procter & Gamble, Pillsbury, J. C. Penney, and Cellular One, the presenters began their sessions with anecdotal and personal accounts of themselves, their families, or their communities. Thus, the training began from the moment the workshop leaders took the podium. The audience might have seen an Asian or Hispanic face, but before stereotypical responses could set in, the speakers revealed and, thus, individuated themselves through autobiographical speech. They talked about their families or told a safe ethnic joke to immediately personalize their expertise and to affirm that, despite perceived ethnic or racial differences, they shared much in common with those in attendance.

At one session, after a glowing introduction by the white male chairperson and president of the organization, Gary Berman, which included nothing short of crediting the next presenter with revolutionizing the marketing strategies of the entire U.S. Postal Service, the African-American head of ethnic marketing at the Postal Service, who was conducting the workshop, began by taking nearly ten minutes of his forty-five-minute presentation to introduce himself and his family, replete with slides and sound effects. Since the conference was being held in New York City, the speaker cleverly used the location as the pretext to show slides of a recent family vacation in the Big Apple. He then effortlessly segued into the substance of his talk—the charts and the figures—beginning with "The Postal Service is a newcomer in this field." His carefully thought out prefatory remarks and the amount of time devoted to them served to demystify and dilute stereotypes of black men. The specialist is an approachable, suburban, middle-class family man—his son, the African-American equivalent of Macaulay Culkin—and the family experienced typical adventures in the big city that would be familiar to almost anyone. The introduction also served to demonstrate and model cross-racial workplace rapport, first with Berman's enthusiastic comments about the speaker, but even more effectively later with the speaker's own depiction of easy socializing at a previous conference.

Though handled with subtlety, such concerted attention to combating racial stereotypes has probably not been overdone. In conversation exchanged prior to his formal presentation, the speaker talked about the core resistance to ethnic marketing at the U.S. Postal Service, particularly at the senior management level—not surprisingly since this is a cohort made up primarily of white males over fifty. He attributed Gary Berman's success as a trainer partly to Berman's being a white male like them, someone with whom they can identify more readily. Personnel have generally responded positively to Berman and tend to be less threatened by the changes his strategies suggest. Although Berman's more mainstream identity profile is an asset for reaching such occupational groups as Postal Service managers, since he is the chief consultant at an ethnic marketing firm, it is equally important for him, at the same time, to clearly establish his multicultural credentials. At the New York Ethnic Marketing conference, he accomplished this right from the start of the day's events as he introduced the conference agenda, setting the tone and modeling the autobiographical approach.

However, unlike the other workshop leaders representing various minority groups who followed him and who attempted to debunk assumptions based on ethnic stereotyping by creating self-portraits that highlight their commonalities with the corporate managers in the audience, Berman, instead, showcased his multiethnic versatility as a way to legitimize his authority on the subject. In the midst of a slide-lecture filled with sophisticated tables, geographic mappings, and numerical breakdowns of the size and growth of diverse ethnic segments, he threw up a slide showing his wife and two daughters, indirectly conveying in a deliberately light-hearted tone that his wife has Hispanic origins by telling the audience that half the time she speaks Spanish to the kids, and always to her friends and family, and that one of their daughters uses the Spanish spelling of her name.

Perhaps the riskiest segment of Berman's presentation was his discussion of the racial implications of shopping patterns related to razor blade consumption. Preliminary findings revealed that African Americans have a lower incidence of purchase, a pattern that has been tentatively linked to data showing that this population suffers more often from the painful condition of razor bumps, making it harder for them to shave and, thus, less likely to shave as frequently. Berman went on to report that Hispanics rank very high in razor blade use, but not necessarily because they shave so much more often but rather because there is a strong belief in the culture that you should shave with a razor only once. Consequently, they buy the disposable variety, discarding them after each use. Finally, and most cautiously, he got to the Asian segment to suggest why they too rank lower than the norm, qualifying his assertion that "it is not because they suffer from razor bumps but rather, on balance, making a sweeping generalization here, Asian Americans have less facial hair almost from a genetic or biological standpoint." And he added quickly, "This is just one piece of data from which we have thousands. There are so many stories, at least hypotheticals, that you should at least think about."

When the specialist on advertising to the Asian-American market came up to the lectern immediately following Berman's talk, he picked right up on the razor blade analysis, diffusing its controver-

sial quality and getting the audience to burst into laughter by jok-
ing, "I just want to support Gary's data on the razor blade issue.
Tomorrow's my shaving day. It's true. I shave a lot less than some of
the women." Next he started to teach the assembled group a few
Korean words, beginning with the Korean ways of saying "hello"
and "how are you," then gave them a phrase that translates into "I
like Elliot!" (the first name of the speaker). The audience broke out
into even more laughter, to which the speaker responded with self-
satire, "As a typical shy, introverted Asian male I need that support," putting the stereotypes lightly out on the table but allowing
the audience to join him in looking at them afresh. Considering that
only in the last couple of years have Asians been seen alone in product advertisements, such multiracial consciousness-raising is no
waste of an afternoon. Prior to 1996, if Asians were portrayed at all,
they would be featured in ads as only one of several hues in a rainbow assortment of faces. Today they can be seen by themselves buying and selling Parker pens, UPS delivery, or IBM Thinkpads.

The YAR Communications agency describes its approach as one
that links "the *commonalities of consumption* with the *similarities of culture*" (italics theirs). Big business, while recognizing the profitable
possibilities of the ethnic marketplace, is at the same time borrow-
ing the language of cultural anthropology to elucidate its aims. The
head of a Chicago multicultural marketing firm even refers to herself as a "marketing anthropologist," while the director of ethnic
marketing at AT&T declared that "Marketing today is part anthropology." It is in this sector of the economy that both business
acumen and knowledge of culture meet. Sometimes the combination
can have chilling implications, as in the case of a luncheon session
sponsored by MasterCard at a multicultural marketing conference
in New York, in which the organizers promised that MasterCard
would "unveil the *real* values and attitudes of the Hispanic, African-
American, and Asian-American markets" (italics mine). In this arena,
marketing experts become accomplished ethnographers mapping
out the subtleties of cultural preferences and the demographics of
multiethnic communities. At best, when such ethnic marketing

events provide the right balance of sales information and cultural sensitivity training, those in attendance can return to their home offices not only with the tools to implement new segmented marketing strategies but also with a model of communications for operating in increasingly diverse workplace settings.

Four

The Romance of Ethnicity

In *Lost in Translation*, her memoir of eastern European émigré life in the United States, Eva Hoffman, the Polish-Jewish literary critic, concludes that for Americans,

> It's a problem of identity. Many of my American friends feel they don't have enough of it. They often feel worthless or they don't know how they feel. Identity is the number-one national problem here . . . "Identity," for my Polish friends, is not a category of daily thought, not an identity etched in their minds in high relief. My American friends watch the vicissitudes of their identity carefully: now it's firm, now it's dissolving, now it's going through flux and change.[1]

Although ethnic tensions have been a cause for concern in select urban areas of the United States, prompting local politicians to give such friction serious attention, within a comparative international context, the nation today is enjoying a period of relatively minimal blatant ethnic conflict. Ethnicization has itself become normative, a part of the Americanization process. Immigrants no longer simply become Americans; they become *ethnic* Americans so that there is little contradiction between assimilation and ethnic particularity. This is ethnicity-lite, a harmless form of ethnic identification that demands little and carries few costs. In his theory of symbolic ethnicity, Herbert Gans was the first to conceptualize (in 1979) the notion of a low-level ethnic identification based more on symbolic structures that represent a nostalgia for traditions than on communal demands or organizational affiliations that require a more intensive commitment. Symbolic, or voluntary, ethnicity is, above all, comfortable and usually manifest as a form of leisure activity expressed in entertaining festivals and fairs; cultural spectacles of music, art, film, theater, and dance; and samplings of a smorgasbord of both traditional and nouvelle cuisines where diverse groups can coexist in harmony rather than put the focus on histories of social inequities, interethnic tensions, entrenched notions of cultural superiority, and anti-immigrant bias.[2]

Alicia Svigals, a member of the Klezmatics musical group, explains it this way: "Coming from generations that tried and tried to assimilate, we realized that we're pretty happy that we're still sort of unassimilated. We've got something that is not quite American. It's its own thing." Another American-born Jew in her sixties reflects that, "It's OK to be Jewish now. And when I was a little girl it was *not* OK. And even in the '40s and '50s, it was just beginning to be OK. Now it's kind of chic. When everybody is eating bagels and everybody has Yiddish in their conversation." In her study of Armenian-Americans, aptly subtitled, "From Being to Feeling Armenian," Anny Bakalian found similar attitudes. Results of her questionnaire to Americans of Armenian descent residing in metropolitan New York and New Jersey showed that although they had undergone considerable assimilation, including the loss of the Armenian language, the majority of those surveyed continued to fiercely cultivate their Armenian identity, primarily through leisure-time activities. Among Polish-Americans, the fervor of the ethnic revival was so great that a 1972 survey by U.S. Census Bureau interviewers found that over a million more individuals were identifying themselves as Polish-Americans than had done so only three years earlier.[3]

At the 1997 dedication of the new Yiddish Book Center complex, Aaron Lansky, founder of the organization, told the story of his grandmother's arrival in the United States as a young girl of fifteen. She brought only one suitcase, in which she had packed her few belongings, including several family photographs. Her much older brother, who had already been in this country for several years, met her at Ellis Island, and the very first thing he did was to throw that suitcase into New York Harbor, telling his sister that she was an American now and that she had to leave the Old Country behind. As Lansky recounted,

> My grandmother never saw her parents again, and she lost the photos of them as well. Somehow within my family that story had always been a secret. I only learned of it myself a few years ago. It always carried with it the sense of terrible embarrassment and shame. But of course, my family was not unique; they were emblematic of every Jewish family in America. Because the truth is that cultural abandonment, throwing away the past, jettisoning one's own culture was perceived as the price of admission into America. And although my story may serve as a metaphor, the truth of the matter is that in one way or another it is the experience of us all.
>
> But times have changed . . . It is a new day in America, a day when we can begin reclaiming our baggage, our luggage, our cultural specificity, and bring it back into the American whole. I do not believe there is a person here who would argue that America is not the richer for its diversity. We can safely affirm that now, and our affirmation gives us the permission to reclaim what was lost.[4]

Similarly, Yuri Radzievsky, a Russian émigré, assessed the shift this way: "Those families who entered the United States 60, 70 years ago, what were they telling their kids? Study English, get rid of the accent, be an American, try to become as American as you can be, blend in. Today it's not so. It's OK to be Polish-American, Russian-American, Japanese-American; it's OK to be a hyphenated American. It's even sexier in some ways."[5]

Conversely, such levels of tolerance and mutability leave many feeling lost in the sea of possibilities and unhappy with the inevitable superficiality of the daily interactions that often result. Once the reality of imagined community is cast into doubt, ethnicity offers tangible markers and potent symbols of ascribed commonality. The preoccupation with exploring ethnic culture and the desire to cling to a more personal identity persists as a response to the fragmentation, ambiguities, and rapid pace of change inherent in the postmodern world. As one thirty-something professional woman put it, "absorbing all I could of Yiddishkeit was a way to satisfy my yearning to belong to something larger than myself but smaller than the human race."[6] Despite the fluidity of ethnic categories today, identifying with a particular ethnic group becomes the home base, a point of orientation that serves to satisfy the yearning to belong. Furthermore, in the absence of other taken-for-granted affinities, ethnicity delimits possibilities of trust. When individuals look alike, speak the same language or dialect, come from the same place, worship God in the same way, or claim the same descent and history, they naturally feel less strange with one another and are more readily able to see themselves reflected in the eyes of the other, a recognition that can bring about some measure of shared meaning and interest.

The new ethnicity appears to hold appeal for men and women alike. Although traditionally women have been the culture-bearers on the homefront, whether by preparing ethnic foods or ensuring that traditions such as holiday celebrations continue to be observed, in the recent revival, male and female roles are blurred. Just as the masculine domain, in general, has broadened and become feminized, it has become more acceptable for men to actively participate in the perpetuation and reclamation of ethnic identities. Men are returning to their roots not solely for filiopietistic purposes and to trace patrilineal heritages but rather to express the same longings as women to find a sense of place, to domesticate and turn inward toward family and community. One woman who wanted to resuscitate her sense of Jewishness first considered learning Yiddish since it had been spoken by both her parents and her grandparents, but she decided, instead, to learn Hebrew. Meanwhile, her husband, who is also Jewish but had no such Yiddish infusions in his own upbringing, quite unexpectedly made a decision to learn Yiddish himself. In the end, he became much more absorbed in the language and culture than his wife did, changing his name from Jim to Yisroel and leading the entire family to participate in four days of Yiddish celebration at the 1996 *Mame-Loshn* Conference—the term means "Mother Tongue" and is used to refer to the Yiddish language.[7]

Findings of survey interviews conducted with five thousand Hispanic, African-American, Asian, and Anglo consumers by one ethnic marketing research company showed that the great majority in all segments, but with Anglos somewhat less in agreement, felt strongly about the importance of ethnic pride within their value system. Similarly, most firmly agreed about the need to sustain their heritage with ethnic traditions and symbols, although once again only 40 percent of Anglos subscribed to this point of view. All considered commitment to family of primary importance in the category of factors essential to preserving their ethnic culture, while language preservation was also of great significance for Hispanics and Asians. Among African Americans, religion ranked almost as high on the list as family, and among Asians, respect for elders carried a great deal of weight. Each of these components—commitment to family, language, religion, and respect for elders—was seen as more notable than music, foods, or holidays in the maintenance of a group's cultural heritage.[8]

Yet when asked specifics about how this type of vicarious ethnicity is manifest in their daily lives, respondents in a range of interview settings mention cuisine, holiday celebrations, or musical traditions as often as family cohesiveness, religious affiliation, or language use. Typical of an explanation for the role and significance of ethnicity in one's life is this Armenian-American's description:

> Ethnicity has had a definite impact on my life. . . . I attended
> the Armenian church and Armenian language school through-

out my childhood. I live in the suburbs and did not have the benefit of having a lot of Armenians in my neighborhood. So like my father, I ended up with mostly non-Armenian friends. I always resented that I had to go to Armenian school on Fridays. My complaints found a deaf ear everywhere except amongst my Korean friends who had to go to Korean school and Korean church. I wanted to go to Catholic church. . . .

Yet, at the same time, I relished the tightness of my Armenian family. I loved how on holidays, and particularly Thanksgiving, we all got together. And as much as I hated that my church was different, I loved it. I loved the church picnics, the bazaars, the fact that almost all my parents' friends were there. I loved how it seemed like anywhere we went, if we found an Armenian, an instant friend was found. That ethnic bond was so strong. . . . All I needed was people around me, in my immediate area, to appreciate it with me, to let me know it was okay to like these things that were so culturally different.[9]

The postmodern ethnic revival takes myriad forms—from a Jewish motorcycle club known as Yidden on Wheels (YOW), which members say allows them to ride their Harleys free of the anti-Semitism that they have experienced around other bikers and gives them the freedom to, in a sense, come out of the closet as Jews who like touring on their "hogs" (with the nonkosher nickname, no less), to children lining up in Savannah, Georgia, on St. Patrick's Day to drink the green (mint-flavored) milk customarily offered by the local dairy.[10]

It's a phenomenon that has encompassed a resurgence of interest in tracing genealogies as well. Prior to the publication of Alex Haley's hugely popular *Roots* and the television miniseries that followed in the 1970s, genealogical study was largely the domain of the most long-standing American families, typically descendants of Anglo-Saxons. Haley's epic family history provided the model and inspiration for members of any ethnic group, no matter how obscured by political or socioeconomic circumstances, to delve into the archives and attempt to reconstruct their distinctive heritages. Such cultural detective work has proven to be amply suited to convenience ethnicity.

Arthur Kurzweil, the author of a popular guide to Jewish genealogy, has explained that "Genealogy is not a heavy trip. . . . We're not asking people to give money, or keep kosher or the ultimate—make *aliya* [permanently relocate to Israel]. This is a nonthreatening way for people to feel more connected."[11] Indeed, thirty years later, *Roots* continues to be the archetype for exploring cultural legacies. During an interview in 1999 to promote his new film, *This Is My Father*, an Irish family's story, actor and co-producer Aidan Quinn explained: "It's primarily a love story, but it's informed by the search for family and the search for your roots. It all really goes back to *Roots* and [Alex] Haley, and Frank McCourt with *Angela's Ashes*. It's out of that same tradition. James Caan's character needs to know who his ancestors were, who his father was, who his family is, hoping that will make him better understand who he is."[12]

Another lightly construed manifestation of the revival was the widespread appearance in the 1970s of hundreds of ethnic community cookbooks published in limited editions from small presses and sold as fund-raisers for local associations, societies, and church groups. Published in English, no matter what type of cuisine was the focus, the recipes typically reflected an interest in achieving a synthesis of old and new, of preservation and innovation, suggesting the latest techniques and time-saving methods of preparing grandma's favorites but for the convenience of modern women on the go.

Formerly, such compilations did not even begin to appear until a generation or two after a new immigrant group had settled in, since the more recent arrivals could still rely on hands-on experience in the family kitchen or oral tradition to pass along the special ingredients and culinary techniques that distinguish ethnic dishes. Sometimes the very process of collecting the recipes—the memories and memorabilia that resurfaced in assembling the cookbooks—served as a catalyst for even more active involvement in the celebration and reinvention of ethnic identities during this period. The popularity of the new ethnicity cookbooks and their local sales success did not go unnoticed by the mainstream press, prompting the publication of a wave of commercial imitators that have also profited nicely from the consumer side of the ethnicity craze.[13]

At times the awakened interest in heritage retention is demonstrated by people throwing their energies into revitalizing already existent ethnic organizations that have languished in the decades of assimilationist thinking. In other instances, entirely new group activities have been initiated to meet the needs of individuals searching for meaningful ways to express their ethnicity. Such was the case when Jim Berry, a third-generation Irish-American, started the Boston Police Gaelic Column in 1992. The Boston Police Department brought in an Irish band from New York to play at a funeral. Berry and others in attendance asked themselves why, with such a large contingent of Irish in Boston, they needed to import musicians from out of state and quickly responded to that query by forming their own sixty-member band. Within weeks the new band was asked to perform at another officer's memorial service. This was their public debut, an earlier and more solemn event than they had planned. Since that time, they have marched in parades in and around Boston, including, of course, the big St. Patrick's Day celebration, although given their line of work they find themselves all too often playing at funerals and memorial services.

Berry grew up with a certain sense of Irishness in a family with a definite, if understated, pride in its heritage, though little explicit attention was paid to this Irish background, nor was it consciously celebrated. He himself had very little interest in his heritage well into his thirties, and it was not until the early 1980s, when he married an Irish enthusiast, that his own awareness was piqued. Still, it took a few more years and the reports from his brother's honeymoon trip to their family homestead in West Cork to animate him. He began to devour books on the history of Ireland, to trace his family's genealogy, and to reacquaint himself with the music and folklore of his youth, culminating in the first of three pivotal trips he has taken to Ireland in the last several years. When asked "Where is home?" his response of "Ireland" is swift and in a tone that implies an "of course." Berry reflected on his transformation in this way:

> One of the proudest achievements that I have today is as a policeman and an Irishman. I started the Boston Police Gaelic Column. It was to celebrate an Irishness that we were lacking in the police department, which has a great Irish-American history in Boston. . . . I've celebrated the music. I've brought the music, I think, to the public level.
>
> I want people to enjoy what I have; the realization, an awakening. I can't say enough about that experience of going back to Ireland. It was a religious experience for me, not in a Catholic Church type of way. It's something that touched my soul. It sparked something in me I just wasn't aware of. . . . When I first got into that town, I can't tell you how I felt inside. It was incredible, just that anticipation. . . . Here were the roads my grandfather walked.
>
> I never experienced anything like that before and it has made me read and research my history. My appetite just can't be satisfied. I've gone from not reading at all to being able to read three and four books in the course of a week. That's unbelievable. Now I want everybody to be able to do just that, I want everybody to be able to go back and say, "This is where your people come from" because your destiny lies in your past.[14]

Even though the Gaelic Column has a sprinkling of Italian- and Scottish-American members, most are of Irish descent, and Irishness is central to the band's identity. This became an issue when the group had to agree on a uniform and it was decided that their kilts could not be tartan because the Column was Irish not Scottish. They chose a solid color instead—navy blue because they were policemen and solid because they were Irish. Since the members wanted the organization to be more than a band and to have an educational function as well, they decided to produce a monthly newsletter and designated one of the group as their official historian. A couple of times a year, they sponsor family get-togethers.

Like James Berry, Eileen Leahy, a second-generation Irish-American from Boston, is passionate about her Irish identity: "I don't know how to explain how important it is to me to hold onto the Irish culture, the heritage, to understand what they went through and to really remember often, what it felt like growing up in an Irish home." In 1990 Leahy's already vital connection to her ancestry got an extra boost when she won the Boston Rose of Tralee pageant. Local contests are held for young women of Irish ancestry, aged eighteen to twenty-five, in countries around the globe, and the winners then compete for the worldwide title in the town of Tralee in County Kerry, Ireland. Although the original Boston pageant began in 1959, it was discontinued a short time later. However, as with so many other aspects of the renewal of ethnic consciousness, in the early 1970s efforts were made to revive the event and it has become a focal point of Irish-American cultural life ever since. Local chapters of Irish organizations such as the Ancient Order of Hibernians or area churches sponsor contestants, and the winner receives a free trip to Ireland courtesy of Aer Lingus. "It's amazing," Leahy recalls. "Their biggest celebration of the year. I think it's equivalent to our Miss America, but it's not a beauty pageant. There's no bathing suits. But it's the highlight of the year. . . . There's a parade through Kerry and when my float came through, the crowd just roared. They just love Boston." When asked what brought her to the Rose of Tralee contest in the first place, Leahy replied, "I guess when you're growing up in such an Irish home, there are certain things that are kind of always a part of you. You either do Irish step-dancing or you play a fiddle, or you're a good singer. So I was the dancer in my house."[15]

Although nostalgia forms much of the emotional texture of movements for ethnic heritage retention, another resonating factor among certain groups has been oppression as a basis of shared identity. An important element of a renewed ethnic consciousness can be the revelations of the hardships and indignities that one's ancestors may have suffered. James Berry used this approach to console a relative who was going through hard times:

> I had a brother-in-law who, back in '89, lost his house. He had a hardware store up in New Hampshire and it just did miserably. His collateral was his house. He lost the business, he lost his house, he lost everything. And I thought, "What do you say to a guy like that?" I sat down and said that you are two generations away from people that have suffered through having their farms taken away. They were tenants on their own land. Even though they were farming it, they were paying rents to other people. And those rents had to be paid. If they weren't paid, they starved. They were thrown off. Their buildings were taken down, and the lands went to someone else. So I said you think about that, and the survival that was in your own family to bring you to the States today. So yeah, you've had a setback. But is it as horrible as what your people have faced before you? I don't think so. You'll survive this.[16]

A population that had previously distanced itself from its ethnic background, the Irish-Americans in particular are finding relevance in multicultural America by connecting to a legacy as victims of British oppression. Numerous programs, including special exhibits, symposia, and commemorations, have been launched in the last five years to mark the 150th anniversary of the Irish famine, the "Great Hunger" of 1845–1850, when more than a million Irish died of starvation and disease and another 2 million were forced to emigrate, the great majority coming to the United States. Some 100,000 of the émigrés arrived in Boston, where a century and a half later, the city is erecting a memorial to honor those who died or fled their homeland. To be located on the historical Freedom Trail, it is expected to be visited by a million people a year. It will cost $1 million; the organizers plan to use the remainder of the $2.1 million they have raised to establish a Famine Institute dedicated to fighting hunger throughout the world.

Such initiatives use a language of comparative oppressions, likening the famine to shameful historical episodes of genocide and extremes of human exploitation, especially the Holocaust. At the Museum of the City of New York's 1996 Gaelic Gotham exhibition mounted to coincide with the 150th anniversary of the famine and covering the 300-year history of the Irish, the potato blight was specifically referred to as "our holocaust." In a review of *Michael Collins*, a bio-pic of the Irish revolutionary leader, the commentator likens the movie to Spielberg's Academy Award-winning Holocaust film, *Schindler's List*, and to Spike Lee's *Malcolm X*, concluding that "*Collins* is a milestone for Irish America, not because it proves our box office prowess but because it confronts Irish-Americans with a piece of their own history that has never before been confronted on such a bold and massive scale."[17]

Another strategy has been to push for inclusion of curricula on the Irish famine in the public schools. Again, this approach is based on the model of Holocaust studies that have been introduced as an educational resource in recent years. The most controversial aspect of turning the famine into the Irish holocaust is the conceptualization of the mass starvation in Ireland from 1845 to 1850 as an act of genocide. Equating a disaster that most would agree was caused by a complex mix of natural and political factors with the premeditated and systematic annihilation of European Jewry is highly problematic. Nonetheless, in 1996 an Irish famine curriculum was adopted to be made available for teachers in New Jersey to use at their discretion. It was included as one of several options besides the study of the Holocaust, such as the Armenian genocide, slavery, the treatment of Native Americans, and the Cambodian genocide; and although in early 1999, the U.S. Postal Service issued an Irish immigration stamp, efforts to win approval for a commemorative famine stamp were turned down.

In an exhibit of the American-Irish Historical Association lam-

basting the British and titled "So the World May Know," one critic
used the term "manufactured outrage" to describe the phenomenon
of fifth-generation Irish-Americans getting so exercised at Britain
for its role in the famine. The questions raised by the possible political and commercial aspects of the new-found famine industry reflect
more general intragroup tensions among proponents of Irish-
American ethnicity, revolving around the issue of what is considered to be superficial "shamrock pride"—Erin Go Brah-less jokes
and green beer—as opposed to more profound expressions of the
Irish cultural legacy. The support of a sense of Irishness steeped in a
heritage of oppression obviously calls for taking such identifications
seriously.

Another group that emphasizes its historical victimization as a
rallying point is the Armenian-American population. The organizers of the Armenian Cultural Festival and Block Party in Watertown, Massachusetts, the hub of the Greater Boston Armenian
community, feel that the primary reason that second- and third-
generation Armenian-Americans stay so closely tied to their ethnic
community is the collective historical memory of the 1915 massacre
of one and a half million Armenians by the Turkish government.
Christine Manavian, a twenty-three-year-old Watertown resident,
explains, "It's because we were challenged and there was a chance for
our language and lives to be lost. From day one you're taught to
learn your language and preserve your culture. If I don't speak
Armenian with my brother, my parents just start with us."[18] When
discussing the significance of ethnicity in his life, another young
Armenian-American of college age said:

Like my father, in college I find myself liking more and more
about my ethnicity and disliking less and less. I think that this
is more than mere coincidence. The more education a person
receives, the easier it becomes to see the value of one's ethnic
identity . . . there are very few Armenians on this campus, yet
rather than view that fact as a negative, I thrive on it. I jump at
every chance I can get to talk about being Armenian, Armenia,

or the genocide. It seems that today whenever an ethnic group gets together, the majority jumps on it as an excuse to say the group does not want to assimilate. These groups are needed because ethnicity is a vital part of a person's identity. For Armenians in particular, this struggle for recognition and distinction is vital. The genocide shattered the Armenian community into fragmented populations worldwide. The remembrance of these events, as for the victims of the Nazi Holocaust, is critical to the survival of the Armenian people. As long as my name is Raffi Ara Ishkanian, whether I want to be part of the Armenian ethnic community or not, my name will associate me with it, be it good or bad. And I am proud.[19]

At times, hyphenated Americans who feel strongly about their homeland heritages are challenged to clarify their loyalties. Charles Sahasian, a World War II veteran who was wounded in the Battle of the Bulge, explains:

You know people have often asked me about how I can be so Armenian and be American, too. I said I have enough love for both countries, don't worry. The questions are asked in such a way as, would I subvert America? Would I not go to bat for America? My answer to that is don't worry, I've gone already. I've shed the blood. I've got my purple heart. If you think for a minute that I would hesitate for my ancestral homeland, I'd do the same.[20]

Karen Kazanjian, a twenty-one-year-old, fourth-generation Armenian-American, addressed the issue in this way:

Someone asked me once if Armenia and the United States were playing each other in the World Cup, who would you root for? I still ponder that because the entire world would know about this little country that's trying to get as much help as possible. But then, on the other hand, I have an American flag and I'll wave it because this is where I'm from and I feel as though I'm American. I stand for what goes on here.[21]

Whether tracing their family trees, contributing to ethnic cookbooks, or creating new ethnic organizations, individuals are intent upon finding ways to personally express their ethnic identities. Perhaps the most common public display of this romance with ethnicity, however, has been the increasing popularity of the ethnic festival. Typically the outcome of a combination of commercial, civic, and cultural resources, in recent times, these festivals have become paradigmatic events to celebrate cultural diversity. In the market world of the ethnic festival, it is not at all unusual for corporate, small-business, penny-capitalist, and nonprofit interests to be brought together for the enjoyment of locals and tourists alike. The ethnic festival is an opportunity for co-ethnics to celebrate their cultural heritage and reconnect with their roots. It also raises public awareness of their group, giving outsiders a chance to learn more about the background of a culture different from their own. Usually they are organized to attract people of all ages, with special activities for children, teenagers, and adults; as a result, they are often multigenerational affairs. At their best they function to raise money and multiethnic consciousness simultaneously.

Although such festivities have become especially popular in recent years as manifestations of the ethnic revival, they are not an altogether new phenomenon. The Tulip Festival in Holland, Michigan, began in 1929 to celebrate the Dutch heritage of the community's original settlers. Tulip Time is still a flourishing event today, drawing upward of 500,000 visitors. Because this celebration has become so essential to the local economy through the years, town shopkeepers have gone so far as to renovate their storefronts in keeping with the design of a traditional Dutch village, thus appealing to the tourists who flock to the festival seeking an authentic Dutch experience. The more elaborate Franco-American festivals of today are an outgrowth of local church bazaars of the past, which were held regularly as a way of raising money for both charity and regular upkeep. In 1941 the Swedish community in Lindsborg, Kansas, held its first Swedish Pioneer Festival, introducing the smorgasbord as the centerpiece of its celebration. But since the 1970s, such happenings have sprung up all across the country, from national multicultural extravaganzas such as the Smithsonian-sponsored Festival of American Folklife in Washington, D.C., to neighborhood events that highlight several different heritages at once, such as New York's Lower East Side Festival, to even more-localized festivities organized around a single group or region, such as Chicago's Rizal Day (named for the Filipino nationalist hero José Rizal), the Armenian Cultural Festival and Block Party in Watertown, the West Indian Carnival in Brooklyn, or New Bedford's Cape Verdean Family Festival.[22]

Actually the largest of the Yiddish festivals, a biannual extravaganza known as Ashkenaz, is held outside the United States, in Toronto. The festivities go on for eight days. In 1997 some fifty thousand people attended the ninety different cultural events, which included film, visual art, theater, music, dance, and other kinds of performances. Although the primary aim of Ashkenaz is to showcase contemporary Yiddish artistic production, much of it experimental, a participatory atmosphere prevails, and the festival also features a huge and colorful costumed parade, a mouth-watering array of food for sale, imaginative crafts displays, and a full children's program. The artistic director, David Buchbinder, describes it as "a huge container for magical, perhaps even ecstatic connections between people." As with Aaron Lansky's National Yiddish Book project, the organizers of Ashkenaz are mindful of the limitations of looking at the remnants of prewar Yiddish culture as simply artifacts of a bygone era. Instead, they see the gathering as an opportunity to use the Yiddish past as a vehicle to inspire not only the present but a vibrant Ashkenazi future. Says Buchbinder, "This is a festival that has at its center a vision of Yiddish culture as something that is being renewed, that is alive again. It's not about nostalgia; it's not about looking fondly back at what's past. The center of the festival is presenting work that's highly personal, from artists who found their voices within traditional Yiddish culture or are using the beautiful raw material of Yiddish culture for their own artistic explorations."[23]

Los Angeles' Yiddishkayt! Festival was initiated in 1998. Promotional literature referred to the nine-day event as "The New Face of an Enduring Culture" and emphasized both the richness of the Yiddish cultural legacy and the ways that heritage inspires contemporary artistic expression. The organizers of Yiddishkayt! hoped to offer "a new look for a thousand-year-old tradition" and to "carry a storied past into the vibrant present." One way to achieve those goals was to recognize the multiethnic character of their location by highlighting cross-cultural collaborations. An evening of "Music from East Side Labor Traditions" recalled that the area that was once the center of Yiddish culture and Jewish labor organizing, where the painters', carpenters', and bakers' unions known as the "Hebrew locals" were based, is now the heart of Los Angeles' Latino community. On another night, the 1953 movie *Salt of the Earth*—a pioneering collaboration between Latino workers and blacklisted Jewish filmmakers from Los Angeles—was shown, and although Yiddishkayt! was born to celebrate the Yiddish culture and language, Spanish translation of the film was provided. A festival exhibition, "Thrills and Shpiels: Visual Responses to Living in LA," featured the work of six contemporary artists from the Jewish, Chicano, and Korean communities depicting their explorations of the realities of everyday life in the city from both the native and immigrant points of view. Finally, the world premiere of "Viva Klezmer-L'Khayim Mariachi" brought the rousing beat of two disparate musical traditions together on center stage.

Los Angeles is home to the world's third largest Jewish population. Another objective of the festival was to reintroduce Yiddish into the educational system by launching a pilot program of a one-week curriculum for fifth-graders in ten religious, secular, and public schools. In cooperation with various art and community centers, libraries, and bookstores, Yiddishkayt! events were held at a wide variety of venues in neighborhoods located throughout the city. It culminated in a day-long Family Festival held at the Watercourt on downtown Los Angeles' California Plaza. The celebration was replete with an abundance of Jewish food, music, storytelling, crafts, and goods for sale but took such festivities to another level with its grand finale, a mock *shtetl* wedding featuring giant bride and groom puppets. Plans are to hold the Yiddishkayt! festival every two years. In between, the organizers hope to mount events such as "Yiddish Blitz," a one-day intensive Yiddish language and culture program.

The three-day Irish Festival held every June at Stonehill College outside of Boston gets more and more elaborate every year. The latest gathering brought more than thirty bands, a street marketplace of close to a hundred vendors of Irish goods, a panoply of activities including cultural exhibits, a parade, a Giant Dublin Horse Show, the Emerald Pony Jumping Classic, Irish and Scottish breed dog shows, a step-dancing feis and a Ballinasloe agricultural fair—and record-breaking attendance totals. Corporate sponsorship of this extravaganza expands yearly as well, and now ranges from big-name international companies, such as Pepsi and Budweiser, to those based in Ireland, such as the Irish Tourist Board and Aer Lingus, to local players, such as the *Boston Herald* and Star Market.

As popular as this Boston event has become, New York's Guinness Fleadh, a two-day Irish music fair held in June 1997, was billed as the largest festival ever organized outside of Ireland. *Fleadh* is Gaelic for festival and the main sponsor of the festivities, the Guinness Import Company, is headquartered nearby in Stamford, Connecticut. This gathering featured sixty bands, twice the number heard in Boston, with such superstar Irish entertainers as Van Morrison and Sinéad O'Connor on the bill and with American headliners such as Natalie Merchant and the Neville Brothers. The goal was to showcase both traditional and contemporary music and to reach a multigenerational audience.[24]

Sponsorship of ethnic festivals is becoming more and more common as corporate strategy to reach the inner-city groups that represent some of the fastest-growing consumer segments. Carnival Miami, a week-long celebration along Calle Ocho, the most famous street in Little Havana, is a raucous and hugely popular gathering with numerous parades, concerts, sporting events, and cooking contests. In recent years multinationals such as Coca-Cola, Pepsi, Budweiser, AT&T, and Colgate-Palmolive have run promotions and sampling booths. During New York's Korean Chusok Festival, Colgate-Palmolive contacted Korean-American store owners with a direct-mail piece written in Korean. In 1994 the Bank of America Corporation decided to capitalize on the Lunar New Year with special promotions to reach Asian-American consumers. They set up booths at the Chinatown New Year Street Festival in San Francisco and at the Chinese Flower Market Festival in Monterey Park. People who opened checking accounts at that time were entered into a contest to win free trips to Singapore and Ho Chi Minh City; Bank of America also offered a choice of special checks with artistic designs by an Asian painter. This was so successful that the following year, Bank of America promoted specialty checks with Diego Rivera works at Cinco de Mayo celebrations.

Especially in California, where the largest number of Asians are concentrated, many marketers have taken systematic steps to become involved in Asian-American cultural events, particularly lunar festivals and harvest and prosperity ceremonies. The telecommunications and financial services industries have become especially interested in being present at these festivities. This demonstrates their respect for the cultures represented and also serves as an entrée into a booming market segment that includes a significant entrepreneurial sector of both small-business owners and multinational executives who make frequent trips to Asian countries. Perhaps the largest such event is the two-day Asian-American Expo, a cultural and marketing extravaganza that has grown steadily since it first began in 1985. Timed around both the Chinese Lunar New Year and the traditional Tet celebration, it currently draws as many as 100,000 people from diverse Asian populations. Formerly known as the Chinese Expo, the event was designed primarily to attract Chinese consumers. However, with the broader Asian-American umbrella, the cultural and commercial offerings reflect the growing numbers among the Vietnamese, Japanese, Korean, Filipino, and Indian communities who also participate. As attendance figures have grown steadily, so has the number of corporate sponsors. Thus, besides an array of live entertainment, Asian-food vendors, a street fair, and a parade, corporations set up hundreds of booths to promote merchandise and offer product samples and sign-ups.

One of the leading sponsors of the Asian-American Expo is GTE, which in 1998 tied in its on-site booths and displays with its "Sweet Rain" advertising campaign targeting Asians and emphasizing prosperity by using the symbol of an orchid. However, since GTE has made targeting the Asian-American segment in California such a priority, its presence at the Expo is just one of the several local cultural initiatives in which it has become highly involved. It also sponsors the Chinese-American Athletic Association in San Jose, an annual Tet Festival for Vietnamese in Garden Grove, a major Chinese New Year parade in Alhambra, and a flower celebration in San Francisco. In the past, major firms would have been indifferent to such local community events, but the need to reach burgeoning minority and new-immigrant populations creatively has brought them directly into the ethnic neighborhoods and enclaves of the foreign-born.

Besides providing gathering places for compatriots to celebrate their cultural roots, ethnic festivals can also serve to educate outsiders who participate. The two-day First Americans Festival in Canastota, New York, featuring Native-American artists and craftspeople, as well as dancing and drumming competitions, is designed with precisely that goal in mind. Brenda Bush, an Oneida clanmother, explained: "We want to introduce outsiders to our history and we also want them to see us as people living in modern society . . . we want this to be an authentic experience." Native-American festivals across the country draw tens of thousands of visitors every year.[25]

Organized tours of ethnic neighborhoods are also increasingly popular. By taking such excursions, the new urban tourists are propelled by the same nostalgic sentiments and sense of contemporary displacement that characterize other aspects of the ethnic revival. They hope to get a glimpse of an idealized past when everyday life seemed more colorful, connected, and meaningful because it was carried on within the context of ethnic communities. However, these are people of the late twentieth century, and according to Jennifer Gates, who studied ethnic tourism in New York City, they see

> ethnic neighborhoods—and sometimes their residents as well—as a commodity, a series of goods to be perused, assessed, compared to their expectations, then ultimately accepted, validated, photographed, purchased or rejected. However, in contrast to earlier tourists in ethnic neighborhoods, today's visitors are savvy consumers trained to evaluate what they buy, whether by reading *Consumer Reports*, comparison shopping, or taking cues from popular culture. Thus, tourists are also constantly making judgments about what they see: its "value," its uniqueness, its interest, its desirability.[26]

In her study of Italian-Americans in California, Michaela Di Leonardo discusses the ethnicity of San Francisco's "Little Italy" as a commodity in and of itself, "a kind of local color or atmosphere, like cable cars or fog, to be consumed by tourists."[27] This is just what two young men, one Jewish and the other of Irish descent, who were then doctoral candidates in American Ethnic and Urban History, set out to capture when, in 1991, they founded Big Onion Walking Tours, of New York City. Their brochure tells us that long before it was dubbed the Big Apple, New York City was called the Big Onion by those who knew the city. Many of the neighborhood tours are designed to peel back the layers of the Big Onion's ethnic past. Walkers can select an eclectic excursion "From Naples to Bialystock to Beijing," through "Immigrant New York," or take the popular "Multi-Ethnic Eating Tour," or they can choose to specialize instead by signing up for the Irish New York, Chinatown, Jewish Lower East Side, Little Italy, or Historic Harlem tours. Big Onion also arranges customized Irish, Italian, or Jewish tours of Ellis Island. It now employs sixteen guides, who host more than thirty different tours that are available year round; and the walks are not booked just by tourists; locals take them as well. Indeed, the most popular trip of the year is on Christmas day when five hundred people stroll through the Jewish Lower East Side. In fact, the company's inaugural walk in 1991 was this particular excursion. When almost everything else in New York is shut down for the holiday, Jewish people have found this a fitting and enjoyable way to spend the day, and some are already making it an annual outing.

Although it offers the most varied ethnic walking tour menu, Big Onion is not the only organization in New York providing such activities. On weekends from April to November, the Lower East Side Tenement Museum also gives guided tours, called "The Streets Where We Lived," through six immigrant neighborhoods, and NYC Discovery Tours features an "Immigrant Heritage Eating Tour" and their newest walk through "Jewish Greenwich Village." Chicago also offers programs for those interested in exploring the metropolitan area from an ethnic perspective. By pressing a button at Philadelphia's official Visitors' Center, individuals can select any ethnic identity and receive a computerized itinerary to guide them through the streets and sites.

Multiethnic marketing within the domestic tourist industry has not been limited to the big cosmopolitan cities known for their rich immigrant histories and still vibrant ethnic communities, however. It may not be surprising that there are organized walking tours of the ethnic neighborhoods of New York City; more remarkable is to find the same type of pitch being used by the tourism board of Missouri, right in the middle of America's supposedly bland heartland—an indication of just how pervasive the ethnic appeal has become. At every major hotel and at the tourist bureaus throughout the state, the visitor can find *The Multi-Cultural Travel and Tour Guide*. This slick eighty-page publication, produced by the departments of Economic Development and Tourism and endorsed by the governor, features chapters on Missouri's African-American, Hispanic,

Native American, and Asian heritages. With a special pullout calendar of events, it encourages visitors to spend their tourist dollars by attending ethnic festivals or powwows, to feast on authentic cuisine, and purchase artifacts from ethnic vendors. Kansas City's annual multicultural fair is listed as an "Ethnic Enrichment Festival." Indeed, in this way, tourists simultaneously "enrich" both their cultural understandings and Missouri's local coffers.

One of the earliest examples of emphasizing the ethnic heritage of a particular locale to stimulate tourism and commerce is an initiative based in the Midwest as well. In the late 1950s, the town of Frankenmuth, Michigan, originally settled a century earlier by German immigrants from Bavaria, fell victim to Eisenhower-era interstate highway construction. Traveling salesmen and other visitors who would usually make stopovers, often to dine at the restaurant in the Fischer Hotel, known for its "all you can eat" chicken dinners, were passing right by. In 1958 the owners of the Fischer decided to remodel and adopt a Bavarian look. They changed the name of the hotel to the Bavarian Inn, leading the way to the revitalization of the local economy. Soon the entire downtown business community had reinvented itself as a German village, with the aromas of strudel and schnitzel emanating from bakeries and restaurants, Bavarian music piped into the streets and a glockenspiel chiming every hour, buildings adorned with gingerbread towers and Bavarian flags, and even bilingual street signs. Now Frankenmuth, a veritable Bavarian theme park, is one of the biggest tourist attractions in the state with three million visitors a year. Karen Zehnder, the manager of the Bavarian Inn, calls Frankenmuth "a very themed town. You know, Disney does a wonderful job with theming . . . it is so important these days. People like to experience different themes, ethnic themes . . . we try to be as authentic as possible."[28]

In general, the ethnic revival and its marketplace manifestations are no longer the domain of inner-city neighborhoods, where immigrants have traditionally made their homes. Not only are some of the foreign-born themselves relocating to more affluent suburban areas but American-born people interested in accentuating their cultural heritages reside throughout the country in rural and suburban areas, in cities big and small, in distinctive ethnic enclaves and nondescript dispersed aggregations. Hence, new malls are springing up that cater to foreign tastes and exotic niches, and ethnic marketers can now think in terms of a national consumer base. Indeed, with the advent of the Internet and telemarketing, retailers need not be based in a particular ethnic community at all. Increasingly, regional differences have become harmonized and American society has come to be characterized by a placeless market economy.

Such portable ethnicity has also manifested itself in recent years through the evolution of cyberspace. The emergence of high-tech global communications makes it possible for those who remain geographically dispersed to no longer be isolated from one another. Indeed, geography becomes but a quaint affectation. Stephen Forstein, the only ordained rabbi in South Dakota, helped ameliorate the problem of isolation for small-town Jews by starting a Web site called *Olam Katan* (small world), aimed at what he terms the "Jewishly isolated." Similarly, the Memorial Foundation for Jewish Culture has created an on-line pilot program for Jewish parents who have felt cut off from Jewish community resources or have had negative experiences in the past with Jewish education. Aptly named *Mishpacha* (family), it is a Web site where participants who may be uncertain about their Jewishness, geographically isolated, or too busy to get involved in classes or activities outside the home can explore their identity, chat with others in similar situations, or take an on-line course called "A Community of Learning for Jewish Parents." *Mishpacha*'s educational director, Dianne Cohler-Esses, explains, "The Internet is the most accessible, safest context for a Jew who feels ambivalent. Our goal is to create on-line communities for people who don't have [Jewish] communities where they live." Because the organizers seek to get beyond the ephemeral, they have decided to restrict applications for their classes to parents only, reasoning that the goal is not only to enhance one's Jewish life in the present but to pass these revitalized traditions on to the next generation—or should it rather be said, to pass traditions on to the *virtual* next generation?[29] Such experiments certainly throw into question the fundamental meanings of community and of ethnic enclaves. Nonetheless, for the first time in history, co-ethnics are able to stay in daily contact without physical proximity.

Advances in telecommunications may also contribute to strengthening ethnic solidarity. At a 1996 conference on the Portuguese-American experience, Joseph Machado, director of the Portuguese Historical Museum of California, cited financial investments from real estate, development of the former dairy farms, and the emergence of the high-tech electronic, global communications industry in the Silicon Valley as key factors to explain why Portuguese-Americans in California were doing so much better both politically and economically than their Massachusetts counterparts. He went on to conclude that "although the Portuguese communities of California remain geographically dispersed, they are no longer isolated from each other or their homeland. The California Portuguese communities are becoming electronically integrated."

Machado also pointed to increasing openness to neo-ethnicity on the West Coast as compared to the more entrenched attitudes toward long-standing immigrant communities back east.

> There's a greater acceptance of the new immigrants. The Portuguese community [in California] does not suffer the same perception problems encountered [in Massachusetts]. The post-'60s revitalization of Portuguese ethnic identity in California has resulted in a vibrant cultural fluorescence of festivals, bands, soccer teams and folklore groups. There has also been an accompanying renewal of the Portuguese language and pursuit of academic achievement.[30]

Festivals and tours are some of the most visible public displays of portable ethnicity to have grown out of the ethnic revival, and although it is often a subtext, they are also examples of cultural forms grounded in economic interests. Sometimes, however, the commercial dimension plays a much more centrally orchestrated role. In *Sponsored Identities: Cultural Politics in Puerto Rico*, anthropologist Arlene Dávila looks at how companies that market such items as tobacco, liquor, and food through corporate sponsorship of the many cultural festivals that punctuate island life there end up transforming such globally identified products as Winston cigarettes or Budweiser beer into brands that appear to Puerto Rican consumers as distinctly representing their culture alone. Evidence of just how embedded in the local culture these brands have become can be heard in the words of one of the organizers of the Festival del Burén, a celebration of Puerto Rico's African heritage in the coastal town of Loíza (a *burén* is the iron sheet traditionally used in cooking), who explained, "We decided to seek Budweiser as a sponsor. After all, Budweiser is *cosa de aquí* (from here)."[31]

The next chapter will explore an array of business ventures, large and small, that have sprung up in response to the renaissance of interest in ethnicity, where, as in Puerto Rico, economic self-interest is not the backdrop but a driving force. In most cases, the cultural and commercial dimensions are so intricately woven into the very rationale of the enterprise that to speak of a dichotomy between the two elements would indeed be to make a false distinction.

Five

Ethnic by Design: Marketing to a "New America"

For generations in America, ethnic enterprises, a sector of the economy characterized by small-business ventures run by immigrants and their families, have modeled the fusing of commerce and culture so fundamental to today's corporate segmented marketing approach. Arthur T. Gregorian Oriental Rugs, Inc., an Armenian-American family business located in Massachusetts (its logo reads, "A Little Part of Persia in Newton Lower Falls"), has been successfully operating since 1934. It perfectly exemplifies how intrinsic culture can be to business expertise in a local ethnic enterprise. Although extensive knowledge of Armenian rug-making traditions has always formed the basis of the company's rationale, in recent years recognition of a widespread demand for authenticity especially among middle- and upper-class consumers in combination with an increasing appreciation for local knowledge has led the owners to highlight the richness of their Armenian legacy in their advertising, including pitches that emphasize cultural education as an extra bonus when customers do business with Gregorian's.

In its third generation, the founder Arthur Gregorian has turned business operations over to his son John, the current president, so that he can concentrate full-time on the educational goals of the company. In addition to publishing learned books on Oriental rugs, he delivers lectures on the topic and on the history of Armenian culture. His granddaughter, Melissa, has also taken up the role of educator. In radio ads for the store, after letting listeners know of the breadth of selection and the quality of their merchandise, John Gregorian proudly announces his daughter's expertise and her availability as a speaker who offers training in rug-making and the Armenian heritage for children in elementary school. Consumers are encouraged both to shop at Gregorian's and to take advantage of the educational opportunities that come with it. While Arthur writes for the serious art collector, Melissa has penned a children's story and designed a coloring book about how rugs are made. The store itself has become an educational site as students from the youngest grades to adult education classes visit on field trips.

In the process of teaching the history of rug-weaving, the staff at Gregorian's provide information on the making of Armenian culture with the underlying objective always, of course, to generate sufficient interest for the curious pupil (or family member) to ultimately turn customer. The Gregorians have adapted to the contemporary craving for material representations of authentic cultures by becoming more than simply rug dealers. They are also scholarly authorities who make a contribution to multicultural education through their teachings, not only about the art of rug-making but also about the little-understood history and culture of the Armenian diaspora, narratives that are literally woven into the very merchandise that they are selling.[1]

In another small-business venture, even the pocketbooks that carry one's money are being created with particular cultural meanings in mind. Metro Handbags, designed by New Yorker Zoe Metro, are lined in red with reproductions of nineteenth-century Chinese coins. Both the choice of color and the use of coin imagery are said to attract money and peace of mind alike. Small rectangular envelopes, the purses are designed to be just big enough to carry a cell phone, a credit card, and a lipstick—the essentials for the contemporary woman—held in a cushion of traditional Chinese good luck symbols. Metro, who studied ancient Asian art at Princeton University, has translated her knowledge of Chinese culture to the marketplace. Her celebrity customers clamor for her custom-designed pouches and for her charm bracelets, which were purportedly inspired by ancient Chinese prayer bracelets that carry with them the four traditions of fortune, wealth, long life, and happiness. In a flare of either city chic or urban kitsch, depending on how you look at it, Metro packages the charm bracelets for sale in the standard wire-handled Chinese take-out containers![2]

Ethnic marketing has become so widespread that, in some cases, it goes far beyond local enterprise to transform entire industries. In the areas of food retailing and wedding planning and throughout the arts and entertainment world, consumers are asking for and receiving goods and services that heighten their ethnic consciousness and reflect their desire for tangible evidence of a distinctive ethnic identity.

Nothing is more universal as an expression of ethnicity, or more accessible, than food. For many, eating ethnic dishes may be the only way that they manifest their cultural backgrounds. In a 1983 interview César Chavez, late leader of the United Farm Workers Union, reflected:

> When I was a kid, our identity was strong within our own group. We hid our tacos and our tortillas. Today we promote them. Today identity means getting more professionals into good jobs. It means getting more influence so others can get breaks. Yes, the Hispanics are going to become more like the majority. Their families will be smaller, better educated, more traveled. Roots will be lost. Language will be lost. Food will be the last to go. We will be eating tacos and tortillas for a long time to come.[3]

Even if food is a last vestige of cultural origins, it can still trigger the taste of nostalgia in powerful ways. New York's Hungarian-owned Paprika Weiss Importing Company says it well in their company brochure. Its "family business has always operated to sell pleasant memories." Both Mary Waters, in her study of suburban third- and fourth-generation white ethnics, and Richard Alba, who looked at ethnic identity among a similar population of inland New Yorkers, demonstrate that food, especially cooking for holiday celebrations, is often the most significant marker of ethnic identification. Interestingly, both authors found that the salience of cuisine in the preservation of culture was especially pronounced among their Italian-American respondents.[4]

When not consuming the flavors of one's own ancestry, eating may well be the only way people expose themselves to a culture different from their own, since trying out foreign foods is typically a nonthreatening and pleasurable way to sample a new ethnicity. Particularly in the last twenty years, urban neighborhoods have become so ethnically diverse that it is not unusual to find restaurants of many different cuisines in storefronts right next to one another being patronized by local diners of equally varied ancestry. In a two-block stretch of the Brighton area of Boston, you can find an Irish pub, a Greek pizza parlor, a Chinese take-out, a Brazilian café, and Thai, Russian, Italian, Indian, Japanese, Korean, Mexican, and Vietnamese restaurants—a display of international choices replicated in cities across America and in the food courts of sprawling suburban malls as well.

Since the 1970s, coinciding with the booming ethnic revival and with the soaring increases in immigration from ever more diverse societies around the globe, interest in ethnic foodways has been steadily on the rise. A blitz of ethnic cookbooks appeared in the 1980s, a trend that is still going strong today. From the proliferation of restaurants with distinctive ethnic fare to the panoply of international foods available in grocery stores large and small, business has responded to the craze. The ethnic foods market has grown at an average rate of between 5 and 7 percent each year. Food service providers have been the catalysts in fueling the consumer demand for more wide-ranging ethnic choices on the supermarket shelves. The president of the Mexican-American Grocers Association (MAGA), Steve Soto, has predicted that within the next couple of years, there will be no "general market here in Los Angeles, so people will either have to figure out how to do business with the ethnic market or else they'll be busy figuring out another business to do period." Some customers are shopping for the ingredients that make up their own culture's cuisine, whereas others are seeking the seasonings of the new and exotic from another culture. Oftentimes, the same clientele, typically well educated, urban professionals interested in natural and health foods, includes those who want to try out ethnic foods as well, whether foreign or native to their palates.[5]

Grocery stores in southern California have been the pioneers, having catered to Hispanic and Asian populations for some time; in recent years the range and availability of these specialty foods have broadened significantly. Niche food marketing is no longer solely a West Coast phenomenon. In addition to major grocery chains expanding their Latino or Asian selections, entire megamarkets specializing in one type of ethnic food are springing up. The hugely successful Mi Bandera (My Flag) Hispanic supermarket, located near the Lincoln Tunnel in Union City, New Jersey, draws as many as eight thousand customers every weekend. Opened in 1992, it now includes a global phone center, a travel agency, and a restaurant. Many shoppers come from as far away as Philadelphia and Delaware, presumably driven by longings to purchase familiar foods if they are of Hispanic origin or to savor the exotic foods, if they are not. The Cuban-born owner, Abel Hernandez, who is well aware of the diversity of the clientele, decorates his store with *banderas* from all the different Latin American countries as well as the flag of the United States.

Besides stocking Spanish foods, these supersized bodegas are often laid out differently from mainstream groceries, accommodating the particular shopping patterns of their Hispanic clientele. For instance, since Hispanics tend to buy more fresh fruits and vegetables than non-Hispanic customers, the produce section in a Latino supermarket will most likely take up a larger percentage of the overall space. At the La Placita supermarket in New Rochelle, New York, the proprietors have also added a catering component to their business, where they help their patrons figure out what to serve for weddings, *quinceañeras* (the traditional celebration of a girl's fifteenth birthday), or Christmas dinner. Although studies show that the percentage of Hispanic households owning microwave ovens is significantly lower than for the population as a whole, the data also indicate that as Hispanic newcomers assimilate, they frequent fast-food restaurants in dramatically increased numbers. Recognizing this trend, the owners of La Placita have responded by expanding their business further to produce time-saving, ready-to-eat items, such as vegetarian empanadas for sale to restaurants and delis.[6]

Even long-standing ethnic businesses, such as Hispanic-owned Goya Foods, which was founded in the mid-1930s, are now facing the challenge to diversify. Based in Secaucus, New Jersey, the company originally targeted the Puerto Rican and Cuban communities of the New York metropolitan region. With the presence in pockets throughout the country of increasingly significant numbers of potential customers from other Hispanic nationalities, especially Mexicans and South Americans, the firm has stepped up its advertising appeals to these segments while at the same time trying to court the non-Hispanic consumer. Managers at Goya, who are also keenly aware of the need to compete in the arena of convenience foods, have introduced such products as frozen guacamole and other fast-food items for an ethnic-conscious and on-the-go clientele.[7]

The fierce product loyalty of its diverse Asian clientele is what has led the Chinese-owned 99 Superstores to deal with hundreds of different import suppliers so that they can carry such a plethora of choices. Their floor plans repeat merchandise categories in several areas of the store to provide brands sought by each segment of the Asian customer stream. The same items are put on the shelves in different sections because the Vietnamese customer's favored brands of canned quail eggs or pickled vegetables may be different from those preferred by the Chinese shopper. Thus, the owners satisfy the distinctive needs and wants of their patrons and manage to convey an atmosphere of abundance and prosperity. Supermarkets such as Mi Bandera or the 99 Superstores are marketing to the broadest clientele by raising the banners and carrying the foodstuffs that appeal to all their composite consumer populations—and as at Mi Bandera, customers come from near and far to shop at 99.

Grocery stores are also designing appeals to consumers of other ethnic foods. The biggest supermarket chain in the greater Boston area, Star Market, has recently initiated a specialty store-within-a-store called Morrissey's of Ireland, on Morrissey Boulevard in Dorchester, an area with a large Irish-American population. Advertised with the clever lead "Take a Walk Down the Emerald Aisle," its shelves are stocked with what the company claims to be the largest selection of imported Irish foods anywhere in the United States. Developed jointly with the Irish Food Board, a government agency in Ireland, Morrissey's also offers an assortment of nonfood merchandise: perfume, sweaters, jewelry, books, and music. Staff member Kathy Ferguson explains: "What we are trying to do is to put every piece of Ireland that people would want into one place." Under a "World Market" umbrella concept, Star also has plans to renovate another of its stores located close to the large Armenian-American communities of Watertown and Belmont to include a shop specializing in Armenian groceries and goods.

Throughout the country the bigger chains have long had an international foods section for groceries from several foreign cultures, usually a combination of Chinese, Mexican, and Jewish foods for general consumption. But by devoting an entire discrete section to one type of cuisine pegged to the ethnic composition of the surrounding neighborhood, grocers are taking the ethnic foods market up a notch.

Executives at Star Market and other chains are also hoping to attract the increasing number of consumers who like both mainstream American and ethnic foods, the typical American of convenience ethnicity, by having regular groceries and ethnic specialty foods available under one roof. For those who still actually cook at home, Star Market even brings in ethnic chefs for demonstrations.

The extent to which initiatives such as Star Market's Morrissey's can be threatening to local proprietors of ethnic specialty shops is still in question. There are now fifteen or twenty Irish-themed retail stores in the Greater Boston area, and Mary Devlin, owner of one of them, A Taste of Ireland, worries that "It's going to affect a lot of businesses that have been here for years and years. How does anybody compete with Star Market? I do hope this is a long-term commitment. What happens if, in a few years, they're not getting the return they expected and they decide to abandon the idea? Meantime, all the Irish stores will have gone out of business." Yet, alternatively, despite the growth of supermarkets like Mi Bandera, it is estimated that Hispanic families in New York still spend over half of their food dollars in local bodegas. Their neighborhood locations, familiar ambiance, and willingness to set up shop in low-income areas helps to ensure the bodegas' competitiveness.[8]

The American kosher market is a rapidly expanding segment of today's food business, with promotional campaigns that rely on sophisticated market research. In every year since 1990, approximately 1,200 new or newly certified kosher items entered the marketplace, so that by 1997 there were over 8,000 companies producing more than 36,000 different kosher comestibles. Ranging from small businesses manufacturing a single kosher product to multinational corporations such as General Mills that sell processed kosher foods or Marriott Hotels that offer kosher food service, industry domestic sales together reached $3.25 billion in 1997. At approximately 12 percent, annual growth in the kosher market far surpassed the overall food industry, which typically sees only a 2 to 3 percent rate of increase each year. For example, when the results of a survey conducted by Dannon concluded that Jews were particularly fond of yogurt, the company made an all-out effort to get their products upgraded from the generic "K" for kosher to the more stringent "OU" (Union of Orthodox Jewish Congregations) certification, with impressive results. Dannon initially spent less than $125,000 to implement these modifications yet increased its sales by more than 25 percent to the Jewish segment. Indeed, the kosher craze has meant that the certification business itself is flourishing. In 1998 there were a whopping 304 different agencies or individual rabbis with identification symbols guaranteeing kosher ingredients; a third of these had been authorized only since 1996.

The demand for kosher products is so widespread that national chains, such as Kroger's and Albertson's, have begun to incorporate kosher meat departments, bakeries, and delis within selected stores beyond the traditional New York, Miami, and Los Angeles hubs. Residents of cities such as Atlanta, Seattle, and Dallas can now conveniently buy kosher food as part of their regular grocery shopping. But for those who observe *kashrut* and live in remote areas, there is another solution, an on-line kosher supermarket that was set up in January 1998. Although the Web site was not yet making a profit by the end of its first year, the number of users was increasing rapidly. For some items, such as fresh poultry, the demand was so great that orders could not be filled.[9]

Some manufacturers are further capitalizing on related trends among health-conscious consumers who assume that kosher means higher quality or greater purity as well as signifying that the ingredients do not contain pork or pork by-products. Thus, by targeting vegetarians and even Muslim customers, they are coming up with scores of innovative varieties from kosher gazpacho to kosher imported artesian springwater. On the sixtieth anniversary of what it used to sell door-to-door as seltzer, the Brooklyn Bottling Company redesigned its Best Health brand of kosher bubbly in 1997 by renaming it Best Health Gourmet Soda, adding diet options to their classic Black Cherry and Vanilla Cream flavors, and giving the bottles snazzy art deco labels that feature nostalgic images of Ebbets Field and the 1955 World Champion Brooklyn Dodgers. A central part of the its new marketing campaign is its claim to be the only major company whose entire line of sodas is OU-approved.

Marketing studies show that most of those who purchase kosher products are nonkosher customers and, furthermore, that it is the growth in popularity of these foods among non-Jews that accounts for the boom of the last several years. Estimates show that a total of seven million people buy kosher fare in the United States today. The enterprising Fleischmann's brand has jumped into this sector full-force with its Dairy with a Difference campaign, which offers dizzying combinations of certified kosher health foods, such as its unsalted, kosher, lactose-free, cholesterol-free, *parve* (nondairy) margarine (*Mmm, sounds delicious*).[10]

But it is not only kosher dairy that is thriving. Not to be outdone by the bonanza of new vegetarian choices, vendors of such unlikely delectables as kosher venison and kosher buffalo products set up shop right next to their herbivorous competitors at Kosherfest '96, the industry's annual trade show. In *Boychicks in the Hood: Travels in the Hasidic Underground*, Robert Eisenberg offers a fascinating portrait of a Lubavitcher family relocated from Crown Heights to the hinterlands of Postville, Iowa, to corner the kosher meat business:

> In three short years, entrepreneur Aaron Rubashkin and two of his sons have tapped into the glittering motherlode of the *glatt* kosher market, an industry that is expanding almost exponentially as its traditional customer base continues its demographic explosion.[11]

Even producers of foods that are inherently kosher, not requiring a rabbi's certification, want the kosher *hechsher* on their products as a way to appeal to the Jewish consumer and to stimulate overall sales. For instance, except during the Passover holiday, beer is considered to be an intrinsically kosher drink, but that has not stopped major brewers such as Coors from displaying the kosher seal, and with good results. The newest "Jew Brew," however, comes from a small microbrewery based in San Francisco, which broke into a glutted market to debut with raucous success both because it zeroed in on a ready niche and because of the creative gimmickry of its name and logo. After realizing that although there were Jewish wines and Jewish food, there was no Jewish beer, twenty-eight-year-old Jeremy Cowan founded the Schmaltz Brewing Company, calling his new product He'brew—The Chosen Beer. (One can easily imagine that feminist pressure might push Cowan to introduce a "Her'Brew" or "She'Brew" alternative.) Jews had never before been specifically targeted for beer sales, so Cowan stepped right in, specializing in high-quality ales that taste good when consumed with meals. "It was designed to go well with food," his simple reasoning goes, "because obviously you can't have anything for Jews that does not go well with food." Cowan named his first "creation" Genesis Ale and intends to follow that up with batches of Messiah Stout—"the beer you've been waiting for."[12]

While Cowan incorporates ethnic humor into his promotional strategy, another newcomer to the kosher alcoholic beverages market is being called "the biggest in-joke in the wine business." The Abarbanel Wine Company of southern France is touting its Beaujolais Nouveau, sold primarily to meet the demands of American-Jewish consumers who insist on kosher wines, as the world's first kosher Beaujolais. Wine critics call it a "caricature of regular Beaujolais" since it is made from grapes of much poorer quality, the fermentation time is drastically reduced, and the filtering and bottling process so hurried that within six months the wine turns to vinegar in the bottle. But the demand is there, the per-bottle profit margin sizable, and easy money flows for winemakers and merchants alike. Proclaims one critic about the inferior quality of the product:

> It doesn't matter much. What matters is that kosher consumers now have the chance to participate in this utterly modern marketing bonanza the Beaujolais have developed with what can only be described as genuine American chutzpah. That's something to dwell on the next time you pour yourself a glass of this year's Beaujolais Nouveau—or as the French sometimes call it, *le vin Americain*.[13]

An adorable, robust, and bright-eyed baby looks out at you from the Beech-Nut corporation's print ad hawking its more than eighty certified kosher varieties of baby food. But this is not a pitch directed solely at the traditionally patriarchal orthodox Jewish family. The accompanying text reads: "You want what's best for your baby. And you want to feed *her* Kosher [italics mine]." Meant to catch the consumer by surprise, the use of the feminine possessive reveals that the creators of this campaign are trying to appeal as well to followers of *kashrut* with a feminist consciousness, where gender equality and the unsettling of an assumed male subject can be appreciated and engaged. The ad goes on to assure parents that the Beech-Nut brand contains no additives, including no chemically modified starch or extra sugar. Once again, the audience being tagged is one concerned not only with proper religious form but also with the ever-growing health-conscious wave of nutritional correctness.

Similar sensibilities are being tweaked in ads for Kosher Gourmet Goodies, featured at the Kosher Cellar groceries' three New York City locales. The specials on organic mesclun salad mix and imported French Brie point to an upscale clientele, most likely the same discriminating shoppers who would dine out at the Theater District's trendy Le Marais restaurant, where in addition to nouvelle kosher cuisine, patrons can enjoy jazz on Monday nights and an expensive stogie any night of the week in its private cigar bar (except Friday, when the restaurant closes for the Sabbath).

Nouvelle kosher perfectly exemplifies the recombinant style and the vicissitudes of convenience ethnicity. What could be more traditional than the ancient dietary laws of *kashrut*? Yet what could be more novel and user-friendly than kosher baby food, kosher-for-Passover taco shells, or kosher ravioli plucked right out of the freezer case and popped into the microwave? One company, Galilee Splendor, Ltd., purveyors of gourmet *matzo*, the unleavened wafer eaten during the Passover holiday in remembrance of the Israelites who had to flee Egypt so quickly that there was no time to wait for their bread to rise, markets its product as "the original fast food"(!). Innovative items, such as fake crab, faux caviar, and "Jewish bacon," actually promote greater orthodoxy because they allow consumers to readily circumvent ritual prohibitions, making it easier and more appealing to adhere to strict eating practices. Moreover, whether dining on sushi or spicy curries, the consumer can try out the cuisines of many different cultures as long as the ingredients and

preparation fall within the format of Jewish dietary regulations. As a version of modern-day alchemy, kosher marketing is currently so successful because it satisfies the simultaneous though seemingly contradictory desires among so many to be able to consume the old with the new.[14]

Even if consumer trends were not providing enough evidence to convince big companies to offer kosher options, the supermarket chains themselves are making this demand of those firms that manufacture products sold under their in-store labels. Information gleaned from the checkout scanners, as well as direct inquiries from shoppers about the availability of kosher foods, has made stocking such items a priority in the intensely competitive grocery business.

Although eating habits are the most common manifestation of new ethnics' desire, no matter what their background, to maintain their distinctive heritages, other popular venues for varied cultural expression are special occasions, such as holiday celebrations and weddings. Again, since these events occur intermittently, they are highly conducive to part-time ethnicity. As illustrated in chapter one, not only has the buying and selling, even the export, of certain American holidays become a central feature of the ethnic market-place but the lucrative wedding industry has also been sparked by dramatically shifting demographics and the keen interest in ethnicity. Throughout Midwestern cities, Marshall Field's department stores provide ethnic training for bridal consultants "to help couples incorporate culture in an updated way," reports Susan Pershke, the regional coordinator for gift registry and tabletop, by using bilingual registry forms and brochures on the customs of ethnic gift-giving. Then there are regional fairs such as the 1995 Hispanic Bridal Show sponsored by Burdine's of Miami, in which more than 50 percent of the population is Hispanic. Similarly, Macy's now participates in locally sponsored events, such as the African Brides of Distinction Fair and a Greek Bridal Show.

Independent wedding coordinators claim that they need more ethnic-specific background information to successfully carry out their services, and marketing specialists oblige them with such findings as the tendency of Asian families to be generous givers of cash and jewelry, with the older generation preferring money to other gifts. In response, businesses are targeting the younger Asian cohort, who have evinced more interest in gift registries. Monika Hickey, the manager of the custom bridal salon at Saks Fifth Avenue, explains that "Second- and third-generation Americans are rediscovering their heritage. They want a wedding like it was in the old days in the country. If Italian, they want mandolins strumming Neapolitan love songs and the guests around a ring doing the tarantella." A recent New York bride who was intent on planning a Russian-Jewish-imbued wedding in authentic detail echoed Hickey when she stated that "My mother commented on how it's like a circle—the people who immigrated two generations ago were doing everything they could to assimilate, and now my generation wants more ethnicity." One enterprising start-up business has gotten into the act by marketing personalized *chupahs*, the cloth canopies symbolizing the home that shelters the bride and groom in a Jewish wedding ceremony.

Perhaps it is the skyrocketing expense of putting on a wedding

today more than a return to the ethnic that has brought the traditional "Money Dance" back into fashion at Polish, Ukrainian, and
Cajun receptions. The guests give cash to the bride either by pin-
ning it directly onto her gown or slipping it into a purse dangling
from her wrist for the privilege of a dance or, better yet, a kiss. Similarly, "La Bursa" (the purse) to hold donations intended to help
cover costs has made a reappearance at Italian-American weddings
inspired by scenes in the *Godfather* films. Indeed, the Reverend Peter
Refrano at Our Lady of Mount Carmel Church in New York's East
Harlem, who in his fifty-eight years as a priest has performed hundreds of Italian-American nuptials, credits the movies as much as
the ethnic revival for the resurgence of such customs, declaring that
"no doubt whatsoever there is a trend for bridal couples to go back
to their roots, but . . . often now it's more Hollywood than Italian."

African Americans started the ethnic wedding vogue more than
a decade ago with the introduction of Africanisms in the choice of
musical accompaniments and clothing for the wedding party made
with kente cloth and cowrie shells or woven hairstyles with elaborate beading and braids. Another current trend is the revival of the
"jumping the broom" ritual. *Bride* magazine did a recent photo-
essay showing imaginative ways to decorate the broom. In *Jumping
the Broom: The African American Wedding Planner*, Harriet Cole writes,
"Our ancestors didn't have any legal rights, including marriage.
They chose the broom, a universal household symbol, to declare
their commitment."

Now there are entire magazines devoted to ethnic wedding
preparations, such as *Latina Bride* published in Pasadena, California,
which touts its regular inclusion of articles devoted to the planning
of *quinceañeras* while also focusing on marriage rituals. The editors
claim that their publication is unique in being the only one in the
United States that showcases the fifteenth-birthday celebration and
that overall they make a singular connection with their readership
by offering bilingual feature articles and using Latina models. The
creators of *Latina Bride* emphasize the culture-related subject matter regularly addressed in each issue, describing the magazine as

"more than just ads for pretty dresses," and combining "a contemporary perspective with a respect for tradition." Once again, the appealing formula of drawing on the old and mixing it with the new forms the basis for targeted marketing.[15]

Finally, a vast and rapidly expanding arena where culture and commerce meet, where occasional ethnics are using their leisure time to find meaning and resonance while savvy segmented marketers seek ways to capture such desires, is that of arts and entertainment. In the intensive competition for entertainment dollars, whether the medium is film, music, or the visual arts, these initiatives span both popular culture and the traditional fine arts. With the ever-present concern of the possible harm that market forces can do to cultural creativity, however, it is still an uneasy partnership.

A clear-cut example of collaboration between commercial and cultural interests that serves both well is based on one of Hallmark's newest lines of greeting cards, called Imagining a Better World: Reflections of Love, Hope and Courage. Part of Hallmark's Tree of Life division established several years ago to attract Jewish customers, the thirty-six cards reproduce pictures by Holocaust survivor Nelly Toll, painted when she was just eight years old and in hiding. Hallmark has pledged to donate a percentage of the sales to the Museum of Jewish Heritage in New York, thereby offering a concrete demonstration of its expressed commitment to fostering world tolerance. Museum administrators are grateful, Hallmark profits, the educational or emotional value of the merchandise is meaningful to card-buyers, and the artist herself benefits. This, then, is the win-win and, perhaps, even win again scenario of successful cultural marketing. As Ms. Toll told a reporter from the *Forward* newspaper, "Creating this art inspired me through a difficult time. I hope these cards send messages of human tolerance and joy."[16]

In a 1998 review of the new fall television line-up, the critic declared, "Break out the corned beef and beer! The Irish are taking over the tube! This is a season of Hibernian overkill. There's trashy Irish (the now canceled *Costello*) and feisty Irish (*To Have and to*

Hold). Don't forget *Legacy*, a saga disguised as an Irish Spring soap commercial. And now there's *Trinity*, a virtual St. Patrick's Day parade of ethnic stereotypes." Irish literature, film, and theater are everywhere: the hit performances of *Riverdance* and its spin-off, *Lord of the Dance*, have been enjoyed by sold-out audiences nationwide, and Irish-style bars are popping up alongside long-standing establishments in commercial centers and neighborhoods of all kinds. In the quest for authenticity and to claim itself as literally "of Ireland," a recent addition to the pub scene located in downtown Boston boasts that the wood-paneled interior was built by carpenters in Ireland, shipped across the Atlantic, and reassembled in its new home across from City Hall. Carmel O'Reilly, artistic director of the Boston's Sugan Theatre, observed that "There's been a shift of wealth, and Irish culture is for sale. There hasn't been much to buy besides Waterford in the Aer Lingus catalog. Now you can go to *Riverdance*. You can look at *Angela's Ashes* or *My Left Foot*. And you can say 'Look how far we've come.' "[17]

With all the blitz of Celtic chic, Irish-Americans no longer have an excuse for what Pulitzer Prize–winning author Frank McCourt sees as their penchant for forgetting about the past, quipping that they suffer from "McAmnesia." McCourt's blockbusting best-seller *Angela's Ashes* can be credited with helping to remedy the syndrome, as thousands of readers devoured this Irish-American memoir. The book, which sat on best-seller lists for more than two years, spawned a related enterprise as tourists began flooding into McCourt's hometown of Limerick, hoping to spot the various sites he mentions in his story. In collaboration with a New York entrepreneur, Limerick's Irish Trade Board began to arrange "Angela's Ashes Tours," five-day excursions, costing $1,250 a person, of which a $50 fee is donated to the St. Vincent De Paul Society, which brought the McCourt family through its hardest times by providing them with food and clothing.[18]

In 1998, at the height of the vogue for all things Irish, PBS released its sweeping documentary *The Irish in America: The Long Journey Home*. Unlike the scrounging for funding and the need to make more out of less that are the staples of nonprofit broadcasting projects, the backing for this series, which cost about $4 million to complete, a sum at the very high end for documentary filmmaking, was always flush. Once more, the product tie-ins included a collector's video set, a glossy companion coffee table book, and a CD of the soundtrack that features the voices of Sinéad O'Connor, Van Morrison, the Chieftains, and Elvis Costello. All this was possible because the project had been originally commissioned by Disney, a private corporation, for which the budget was a drop in the bucket. Roy Disney, nephew of Walt, is passionate about Irish history and enthusiastically sought out the collaboration with PBS.

Initially, there was much concern about the potential for corruption when a door is opened to commercial backing of public television, and the project's producer, Thomas Lennon, was quite apprehensive: "To say I was skeptical is putting it mildly. Why would this big commercial company want to do the work that I do?" Yet, in the end, Lennon felt that Disney gave him:

> creative support, no creative interference. . . . Do you see Mickey Mouse in that series? No, you don't. My feeling is that commerce is great as long as it doesn't affect the central piece of the work. If Disney wants to market the hell out of those videocassettes and recoup a large amount of money, that's great. If we can get Sinéad O'Connor and Elvis Costello and people see it because they're involved, then hallelujah. But you have to be clear that you don't start shaping the product around that, and I was never pressured to do that.

With spectacles like *Riverdance* selling out giant auditoriums wherever they play and the huge popularity of films like *Good Will Hunting*, the story of a young Irish-American from south Boston, some of the success of the documentary can be attributed as well to its having been aired at a time when, as Lennon puts it, "Irish and Irish-American culture is hot, hot, hot."[19]

So hot, that even the World Music scene was taken by surprise when traditional Celtic music began to sizzle. The decade known for its revival of Celtic music was the 1970s, but it was the 1990s that saw Irish music become part of the cultural mainstream. As one critic put it,

A compilation of all the World Music charts from *Billboard* magazine gives some inkling as to who and what sells . . . but one trend seems to have come out of nowhere. In March 1995, the label Narada introduced *Celtic Legacy: A Global Celtic Journey*, which debuted at the number two position . . . remained on the charts for fifty-two weeks and appeared on *Billboard*'s list of the top ten World Music albums of 1995.

Moreover, this recording was only one of more than a dozen Celtic albums to make either the World Music or New Age charts by 1996. Irish-American recording artist Seamus Egan, whose sound track for the 1995 box office hit *The Brothers McMullen* reached number five on the World Music charts, reflected that

It's a very strange time. Irish music is entering the marketplace. That's fairly phenomenal and a little scary. It's creating new opportunities, but it's also making it much more of a business. Because suddenly people can make money off it. And that was never something that anyone ever said about Irish music. . . . It's a new phrase in our vernacular.

Enthusiastic sales in this niche prompted one of the major labels, Atlantic Records, to start a new line, which they called Celtic Heartbeat, to appeal specifically to Irish-American listeners. Moreover, the music has so caught on in the mainstream—it was even featured on the sound track to *Titanic*—that many who have no Irish ancestry at all have become devotees. During the 1998 pledge drive at WGBH, a Boston public radio station, more calls came in per hour during *The Celtic Sojourn*, a weekly program of traditional

Irish music, than any other program except Garrison Keillor's ever popular *Prairie Home Companion*.[20]

Because it is so commonplace, traditional Irish music has not been widely supported in Ireland itself, except when artists cross over to mainstream pop. Curiously, however, with the economic upswing in Ireland, recent emigrants are turning around and returning to their homes. While they were living in the United States, many found themselves for the first time seeking out Irish bands, attending concerts, and buying traditional recordings. Thus, they arrive back in Ireland as enthusiastic new fans of their own musical heritage, a passion that they would perhaps never have developed had they stayed at home.[21]

The popularity of Celtic music is so widespread that it is being tapped to sell other merchandise. In 1993 Volkswagen developed a television ad for their Passat model that used background music from the Irish group Clannad. Thousands of people responded to the ad's 800 number, not only to inquire about the Passat but also to ask the name of the featured band and how to obtain a copy of the music. Indeed, there were so many inquiries about Clannad that the company revised the commercial to include the names of both the song and the band, boosting sales of the album dramatically. Equally dramatic was the increase in sales of the automobile itself, up by 25 percent. Tower Records, a leading music retailer, jumped in, promoting the album with the slogan "Shift Gears with Your Ears" and a nationwide drawing in which the Passat was the grand prize.

Folger's coffee has capitalized on the *Riverdance* phenomenon by using step-dancing in their TV commercials, and Seamus Egan can also be heard with fiddler Eileen Ivers in an IBM ad, this one featuring two Irish goatherds promoting software. From film sound tracks to commercials for banks, the sounds of Irish jigs and reels have permeated American consumer culture. Though cautious about the effect of the traditional music's broadening appeal, Egan is nonetheless optimistic about the possibilities. "It's showing that you don't have to do something that sounds like mainstream music to create something the mainstream will buy and that's encouraging. It proves that when the mainstream lets the music get out there, people who hear it will want to buy it. The interest is there."[22]

Another genre of World Music whose popularity has soared is so-called neo-klezmer. Like so many aspects of the ethnic renaissance, klezmer music represents a blending of the old and the new. In their attempts to revitalize Ashkenazi Jewry, some bands are simultaneously crossing genres, generations, and cultures to produce musical mixes derived from American forms that have been colorfully labeled "intergalactic Jewish funk," "polkadelic klezmer," "diasporic rock-and-roll," "psycho-Semitic sounds," or "postmodern garage klez." Beyond the festival circuit, klezmer music is drawing listening audiences at folk coffeehouses, at classical venues such as Tanglewood, on World Music tours, and at jazz clubs. "A lot of people are wanting to call it Jewish jazz, not just the critics but some of the bands themselves," remarked Klezmer Conservatory Band director Hankus Netsky. "It's an easy way to market it in this country. But to me, that sells it short."[23]

Although few ethnic marketing firms are directly targeting immigrants themselves, one enterprising company has made the clever link between the current vogue for World Music and the burgeoning population of the foreign-born in this country. Intercultural Niche Strategies or INS(!), founded in 1996 by two veterans of the music industry, Anita Daly and Holly Poirier, assists major record labels such as BMG, Polygram, and Atlantic in tapping the more than twenty-six million immigrant consumers residing in the United States, a population that is often overlooked in the music business. Certainly all the big-name record companies that INS represents already have well-developed in-house marketing operations in place, but these departments are concerned solely with reaching the widest sector of the mainstream listening audience. INS functions as an adjunct, focusing instead on the music-buying potential of particular new-immigrant and ethnic groups, populations about which in-house marketers may be unaware and, furthermore, would not know how to reach even if they could identify such segments.

Employing a multiethnic and multilingual staff, INS creates grass-roots promotion, advertising, public relations, and tour campaigns aimed at particular niche groups, and finds alternative retail distribution outlets such as Asian-Indian spice shops, Japanese bookstores, or Irish gift shops for their clients. Another key strategy of the firm is to participate in ethnic community festivals and street fairs across the country, where they sell records, conduct contests, and open up additional distribution channels to ethnic restaurants, coffee houses and cigar bars, spas, and pubs. At another level, they also turn to a category of contacts they call tastemakers—people who are influential in their ethnic communities who represent more official agencies, such as the Irish Trade Board or the Italian-American Federation. Tastemakers are found at the consulates, embassies, cultural centers, or historical societies of various nationality groups.

The grass-roots approach of INS has led to some highly successful marketing campaigns for individual ethnic artists, such as the Irish music of *Riverdance* and the Chieftains, Native American vocalist Buffy Sainte-Marie, Asian-Indian performer Ravi Shankar, Chinese violinist Vanessa-Mae, and Japanese jazz pianist Akiko Yano. One of the company's most challenging undertakings, but one that worked out very well, was their promotion of the Chieftains' *Santiago*, released by RCA Victor. Although the Irish group is a world beat favorite, this album features traditional music from Galicia, a region in the northwest of Spain. More than twenty years earlier, the Chieftains had discovered that there were strong Irish links to Galician culture, particularly through music, and wanted to explore that connection.

Indeed, Galicia was once described as "the world's most undiscovered Celtic country," but how to reach beyond the audience of loyal Chieftains followers to the Hispanic and Portuguese markets? As Daly wondered, "Who would have thought a Spanish-speaking audience would want to listen to the Chieftains? But they're buying it." One important hook was the collaboration with Galician artist Carlos Núñez, who performs on the bagpipes for the album. But, in addition, INS mined their extensive ethnic database, determined that there were some 350,000 Galicians living in the United States and, since Galicia itself borders Portugal, decided to target the Portuguese-American population as well. They used the local press, direct mailings, and a blitz of flyers to reach members of both ethnic communities. It worked so well that Daly and Poirier went on to try their hand at the reverse, marketing Núñez's solo recording *Brotherhood of the Stars* to Irish-American listeners as well as to the more obvious Spanish-speaking target groups.

When marketing *Santiago*, the INS staff found a large Galician community in Newark, New Jersey, and as is typical of the firm's approach, they sought an alternative avenue of exposure for the release, sending complimentary CDs to all the Galician restaurants. When they did a French record, in addition to participating at a New York Bastille Day festival by setting up a booth selling records, they sent records out to all the French Connection clothing stores around the country. Researching the possibilities for successful promotion of La Banda—traditional wind music from Italy—Poirier recalls:

> I was making some initial calls to some of my tastemakers in the Italian community to see if we should take this project on, and one woman—she's out on Long Island, and has this Italian show on the radio—said, "You know, my father was a banda musician and every town in Italy has a village square and every village has a banda band and, oh my God, this brings back such memories." You knew right there you had to take this project on and eventually we found all these people across the country that felt the same way about this recording, that it reminded them of somewhere in their distant past, about this village life that they had in Italy.

Research for INS clients can bring the staff to odd nooks and crannies on the American scene. One of their most fascinating projects was the promotion of *joik* music, the chanting of Sami peoples, European Indians indigenous to the circumpolar region. After first learning that there were Samis living on the West Coast, they dug a little deeper and found a U.S. Sami Foundation. Poirier explains that

> they estimate that there are forty thousand people of Sami descent and that they came in the early 1800s from Finland. They settled in the Continental United States and Alaska—they were reindeer herders but they couldn't keep the reindeer because they weren't Americans. When the reindeer were taken away from them, they migrated to the Seattle area and that's where they are now. Research like that is the kind of fun thing we do.

Such an approach goes beyond usual marketing practices and is the hallmark of the young company's promotional strategy.

The project that Poirier and Daly are perhaps most pleased with was marketing the teenage violinist Vanessa-Mae's release *China Girl* to the Chinese-American community. Born in Thailand of mixed Chinese-British descent, Vanessa-Mae was a child prodigy in the classical world. *China Girl* is a celebration of her Chinese roots and features the Happy Valley Overture, a piece she created for the Hong Kong reunification festival in 1997. Indeed, Vanessa-Mae was the only Westerner—and she is considered to be a Westerner—to perform at the momentous event. Poirier described the role of INS in promoting the record.

> Our client, EMI records, asked us to market this—to do our magic with it. Above and beyond what they are doing. They're taking Vanessa-Mae to CNN or they're taking her to *Time* magazine. Whatever they can get. But there are 1.8 million ethnic

Chinese living in this country. No one knew how to get to them. The music industry has never targeted the Chinese. Ever. They [ethnic Chinese] currently get their information from Chinese media and Chinese television; they buy their cassettes and CDs from Chinese stores that import them from Hong Kong or Taiwan. So we hired a product manager who is not a music industry person. She's a Chinese marketer—has her degree in marketing from China. We put together a list of publications and television shows and radio stations that feature Chinese music and we also crossed over to other Asian programs.

There are a lot of journals for young Asian out there, for example, that are going to second- and third-generation Americans who want to go back to their Asian roots. There's a very popular one right now called *A Magazine* that reaches eighteen- to twenty-five-year-olds. Vanessa-Mae was a winner for them. They put her on the front cover. Not only did we get press on the album release, we set up interviews and we created print and video advertising in Chinese—both Mandarin and Cantonese.

Although, overall, the Vanessa-Mae campaign was a success, it was not without its cultural stumbling blocks and communication glitches. Attempts at marketing within ethnic communities demand a nuanced understanding of the economic culture of each population. The INS staff recognized that Chinese record stores abound in certain areas: in New York's Chinatown alone, a neighborhood that is only about ten blocks long, they counted a dozen. Thus, a primary goal was to try to establish a Chinese distribution source. They looked carefully at the pricing structure in this channel. Poirier observed:

We happened to be fortunate in that a pricing issue is not a problem in the Chinese community because they are currently buying their music from Taiwan and Hong Kong, very high-priced compared to us. It was different when we had Ravi Shankar. Try to sell in Asian-Indian retail and you're competing with prices coming out of India—$5 a cassette—there's no way we can sell a cassette at retail for $5—at wholesale, they don't even sell at that price—so each ethnic group presents its own challenge for us and our clients.

Despite having a Chinese marketer involved, however, misunderstandings occurred and mistakes were made. Community members were suspicious and unaccustomed to the company's approach. After much careful negotiation, INS finally acquired a Chinese distributor who put the product into all the major Chinatowns throughout the United States. It worked for a while, but then the distributor spotted a newspaper ad from Coconuts, a major record chain, featuring *China Girl* at a lower price than his. Since INS has no control over what releases record stores will decide to discount, there was nothing they could do about it, but no amount of explanation satisfied the distributor. He felt betrayed and terminated his agreement with EMI. Although this was a low point in the *China Girl* promotion, in the end the campaign was enormously successful. EMI received a great deal of press and inquiries from many different sectors. People who had never heard of Vanessa-Mae before fell in love with her. All this coverage culminated in a huge promotional event. In conjunction with EMI, David Tang, a designer as well as a very high-profile Hong Kong financier, held a grand opening of his ritzy new Madison Avenue boutique, Shanghai Tang, that featured a performance by Vanessa-Mae. The streets were blocked off, a stage was set up, and INS arranged for a torrent of television coverage for the ethnic community.

After three years in operation, INS has targeted the Japanese, Irish, Hispanic, Native American, Russian, Chinese, Asian-Indian, Italian, African, and African-American populations. As with YAR, the founders of INS recognize that at the same time as the foreign-born are assimilating, they are also maintaining cultural roots and certain aspects of their hyphenated identities, including their purchasing preferences. Both firms look at this vast, seemingly unreachable population of immigrants and ethnic minorities as a marketing challenge and an opportunity that will take more than a comprehensive mailing list and a multilingual staff to successfully target.

Marketers also need to understand how each ethnic group operates in the business world and to learn the culture from the inside, taking what YAR has termed an "in-culture" approach. For example, when the INS staff was marketing Buffy Sainte-Marie's *Up Where We Belong* for Angel Records to American-Indian retailers and casinos on reservations, they discovered that cassette recordings were preferred over compact discs. They convinced Angel to produce more audiocassettes of the album, and the result was an increase in initial sales of *Up Where We Belong* by seven thousand units, a number that was 36 percent higher than its anticipated totals.[24]

It is clear that participation at the grass-roots level, whether by working with the local ethnic media or setting up shop at an ethnic festival, pays off even for the larger corporate entities. Moreover, the approach works whether the product is music or fine art, as evidenced by the tactics employed by New York's Metropolitan Museum of Art to promote its *Glory of Byzantium* exhibit in 1997. The marketing staff decided to aggressively woo the Armenian, Greek, Russian, and Ukrainian communities. Ancestors of these ethnic groups had created the art of the Byzantine culture that peaked from the ninth to the thirteen centuries, and publicists reasoned that an ethnic-based appeal to this cultural and historical legacy would boost attendance. The strategy was also innovative because these are populations that even the most sophisticated ethnic marketers do not typically target. The museum ran commercials on Greek and Russian radio outlets throughout the metropolitan area and full-page ads in the Armenian, Ukrainian, Greek, and Russian press. The ads were customized to best represent each of the cultures being targeted. For example, an illuminated page from the thirteenth-century Zeyt'un Gospels was used to advertise to the Armenian-American community, whereas the publicity designed for the Greeks showed a mosaic of Saint Andrew that came from the

Archaeological Museum in Serres, Greece. Touting the exhibition as a pioneering effort, Harold Holzer, the museum's vice president for communications, explained: "We are living in a community that is a mosaic of cultures in which such marketing is ideal. . . . This show gives pride of place to a number of ethnic groups whose treasures have been gathered together here for the first and only time."

Although appeals to Armenians, Greeks, and Russians may be brand new, this was not the first time that the Metropolitan Museum had run a successful ethnic marketing campaign. In 1996 they specifically courted the Asian-American population for their *Splendors of Imperial China* show; as a result, attendance by Asian Americans was as high as one in five visitors, and overall totals were the largest of any art exhibit in the world that year.[25]

Although it has been a long time coming, Hollywood is finally beginning to court Latino moviegoers. This trend is not surprising, since, according to the Motion Picture Association of America, in just one year, from 1996 to 1997, ticket sales to Latinos increased by a formidable 22 percent, making them the fastest-growing ethnic group among domestic film audiences. Furthermore, Hispanics tend to be concentrated in the leading urban markets, where most movie tickets are sold. For example, one recent Nielsen study showed that in Los Angeles 45 percent of the prime moviegoing age cohort, those from twelve to thirty-four years old, were Latino. The head of publicity at Dreamworks, Vivian Mayer, explains: "Specifically including the Hispanic audience was once the marketing exception. For us at Dreamworks, it is the rule. Our marketing campaigns not only reflect but respond to this diverse moviegoing audience. It makes both cultural and fiscal sense." Simultaneously making fiscal and cultural sense is precisely what ethnic marketing is all about, no matter what the category of merchandise.

For the most part, however, studios have been disinclined to invest in tracking Latino viewing habits; as a result, they are far less sophisticated in their outreach strategies when trying to target this population than with their general promotional appeals. Typically, studios would put effort into attracting a Latino audience only when the film had clear-cut Latino themes, such as the 1997 hit *Selena* or the earlier box office success *La Bamba* (1987). Even then their efforts were limited to a few Spanish media outlets. The Spanish newspapers would often complain that advertisements for upcoming films would run only for the opening weekend.

Recently, some production companies have become more aggressive in their bid for Latino audiences. Two films released in 1998 by Columbia TriStar, *The Mask of Zorro* and *Dance with Me*, were widely promoted in Spanish print, TV, and radio outlets and at Latino events and festivals nationwide, including New York City's lavish Puerto Rican Day parade. Even more unusual was the promotion of another 1998 film, *Out of Sight*, co-starring George Clooney as an escaped convict and the Latina actress of Puerto Rican descent Jennifer Lopez (the star of *Selena*) as a federal marshal. The movie does not carry Latino themes, nor is there any attention given in the story line to the Lopez character's ethnicity. Indeed, the film has no Latino content at all, but because Lopez commands a popular following in the Latino community, Universal Pictures departed from the norm and developed special trailers for Spanish-language TV stations, distributed posters at hundreds of shops in Latino neighborhoods, and advertised widely in Spanish publications. The possibilities for marketing both mainstream and Latino-themed films to the Hispanic community has led to the formation of at least one movie-marketing company. Headed by Santiago Pozo, the Arenas Group specializes in targeting the Latino audience.[26]

The desire to capture the Latino market has led some businesses to experiment with new initiatives, including the use of movies to reach audiences. In what is believed to be the first instance of a financial services company drawing on Hollywood star power, Banc One, the country's tenth largest bank, spent close to $1 million to couple its product with *Selena*. Following the strategy of soft drink, tobacco, and automobile companies, its hope was to attract the legions of fans of the beloved Tejana performer by paying for prominent product placements in key scenes, such as the opening shot of Selena singing to a sold-out crowd while Banc One banners wave throughout the concert hall. Bank representative John Russell explains: "We serve a large Hispanic customer base in the West and Southwest, so it seemed a very logical move to imprint our brand. The Latino markets are growing faster than the mass market. This is an opportunity for a Midwestern bank to gain recognition and generate favorable feelings in areas where it already has a large presence."[27]

Key players in the marketing of Latino culture, particularly the Cuban connection, filtered through the music world are the husband and wife team of Gloria and Emilio Estefan. Superstar Gloria, who has ten multiplatinum albums to her credit, and Emilio are the CEOs of Estefan Enterprises, a Miami-based business dedicated to showcasing Cuban culture through recordings, restaurants, hotels, and television programming. The company was worth more than $200 million in 1998 and has some seven hundred, primarily Cuban-American, employees. The Estefans own Crescent Moon Studios, out of which they publish music, create movie sound tracks, and manage Latin talent. They are also the proprietors of Larios, a Miami Beach restaurant that brings in long lines of diners every night, and of Bongos, a 500-seat restaurant recently opened at Disney World. In keeping with their goal of spreading Latino culture beyond Latin America, they have negotiated a deal with Universal Television to produce TV programs that will dub South American soap operas into several languages. Emilio Estefan points to a general blossoming of interest in Latin food and culture as the reason for their decision to branch out beyond the realm of the music industry and says that he feels a responsibility to present Cuban culture accurately to the world. "It's not about money. We make money, but at the same time it's important that they see the flavor of the culture."[28]

Not that the Latino music industry isn't mushrooming in and of itself, particularly the latest wave of Latin pop, which brought such crossover artists as Ricky Martin, Marc Anthony, and Jennifer Lopez to the top-ten charts in 1999 with releases that sprinkle Spanish into the lyrics untranslated (such as Martin's megahit "La Vida Loca") or are sung completely in Spanish. Alex González, drummer for the band Naná, whose *Sueños Líquidos* album sold over six million copies, enthusiastically reports: "We've managed to get non-Spanish-speakers to listen to our music." Latin music is so trendy that in 1998 the magazine *People En Español* came out with a special issue devoted to the music and its star performers, and plans are in the works for the first Latin Grammy awards scheduled for September 2000. When the American Women's Soccer Team played its championship World Cup game in Pasadena during the summer of 1999— the sold-out crowd was the largest ever to attend a women's sporting event—Jennifer Lopez headlined the pregame entertainment extravaganza. Christy Haubegger, publisher of *Latina* magazine, sees these young performers not as outsiders who have made their way into the mainstream but rather as the mainstream of America itself: "Haven't Jennifer Lopez and Ricky Martin embodied the future of America in some ways? These bilingual, bicultural kids, isn't that America? They are amalgams of all kinds of ethnic influences. They are mirrors. I'm not sure if they are projecting or reflecting, maybe both."[29] This is a population that is not only bilingual but completely bicultural. Gloria Estefan put it quite simply when she was asked about her identity during an interview for the *A & E Biography* series: "I am not Cuban and I am not American. I am both."

The rage for the Hispanic sound and tallies that showed that sales of Latin music for the first half of 1999 soared by 54 percent over the same period in 1998 and that this market is growing faster than overall mainstream totals have led major music retailers to make serious bids to capture this lucrative sector. Wherehouse Entertainment has established a separate operating division known as Tu Musica (Your Music) to appeal to Latino consumers. It has also opened ten stores in California that sell a wide range of genres, including the crossover artists as well as ranchera, grupo, and salsa music. These stores also carry Mexican, Cuban, and Puerto Rican favorites. The latinization of American music has spurred both the

Musicland Stores corporation—whose retail outlets encompass the Sam Goody and On Cue chains—and Trans World Entertainment—the parent company of Coconuts, Record Town, and Strawberries, among others—to take steps to reach Hispanic customers. Plans are in the works for new ads and promotions, Spanish in-store signage, and increased hiring of Spanish-speaking sales staff in locations with a high percentage of Latino customers. The interest in Latin music is so great that a twenty-four-hour Spanish-language music television network has been initiated.

As for television, Hispanics have the already well established Univision and Telemundo networks catering to this ever-growing population. Recent efforts by Telemundo, whose parent company is Sony, have included the creation of original TV programming for children and the presentation in Spanish of some of the Nickelodeon network's morning favorites, such as *Rugrats*. Studies show that 12 to 15 percent of Americans speak a second language at home, so it is not surprising that the viewing of foreign television stations is on the rise. Cable television and satellite services enable immigrants to watch programming from their homelands, giving them news and entertainment in much the same way that ethnic newspapers function in the maintenance of hyphenated identities.

The desire of ethnic groups, especially those of the immigrant generation, for access to programming from their countries of origin is what led the Russian-born Pavel Paley to found the Ethnic-American Broadcasting Company (EABC), which began as a radio station in 1987. Paley expanded into television, catering to Russian immigrants who craved local news, political gossip, and an infusion of Russian culture brought right into the living rooms of their adopted country. In 1991 he sold the small company to an investment banker, David Moro, who immediately enlarged and diversified the scope of the network to include Arabic, Indian, Chinese, Filipino, Korean, Greek, Italian, Polish, and Ukrainian programming. According to Moro, for viewers the station "was an umbilical cord connecting them to the culture and language in their home country. And just as important, it became the voice of their community here. . . . What we help do is keep alive their culture and language in the broadcast medium." In addition to the news, coverage of both the home country and the immigrant communities themselves, the most popular shows—old movies and vintage TV series—fall into the category of nostalgia programming.

The underlying design of EABC is an appeal to the homesickness of the nation's newest citizens and to the more mellowed nostalgic sentiments of those who are slightly more settled. Plans are afoot to open a corporate headquarters in Fort Lee, New Jersey, where it is expected that twenty different channels will be in operation within the year. A twenty-four-hour network that typically has four commercial breaks an hour, EABC is now attracting major advertisers such as AT&T, Metlife, and Western Union. Since the manager of national advertising at the network approximates the buying power of non-English-, non-Spanish-speaking populations in the United States at $250 billion, a cohort that has not been systematically targeted until now, this constitutes pioneering territory for marketers. Indeed, EABC's print advertising to the business sector runs with the lead, "There's a $250 billion market waiting to hear from you . . . *only you're not speaking their language.*"

Even more narrowly defined in-language television promotions are bringing worthwhile results. Geffen Records, which typically is more concerned with targeting by age group rather than ethnicity, tried out an advertising campaign on the Filipino Channel, a division of the ABC/CBN network. Geffen ran commercials for the music group Kai, most of whose members are themselves Filipino. Given the band's ethnic composition and the fact that they are based in San Francisco, a city with a high concentration of Filipino residents, Geffen executives made the gamble and won, even though TV advertising to specific non-Spanish, non-English groups is the exception in the industry. Asian programming, in general, may soon mirror the extent of Spanish-language TV, since Asian American is the fastest growing ethnic group, with over 60 percent of Asian-American families speaking a non-English language at home, and this sector indexes higher than other ethnic groups for average TV viewing on all days of the week.[30]

The link between economic self-interest and cultural dynamics has always been the basis of immigrant and ethnic entrepreneurship in this country. Until the last two decades, however, this business approach has largely been carried out on a small, localized scale by new immigrants selling merchandise and services to co-ethnic consumers. Since the onset of the ethnic revival, however, these petty entrepreneurs and family businesses have been joined by both megacorporations and a range of mid-level ventures, whether ethnic-based or not, in the quest to win consumer dollars. They have expanded well beyond the immigrant enclave, selling to ever-widening markets, and have found particular success in areas such as food consumption, special occasion events, and leisure-time activity, where it is possible for the new ethnics to practice a level of cultural expression that is convenient, portable, intermittent, and symbolic. The following chapter will take a more in-depth look at how these dynamics are carried out among three different ethnic groups.

Six

A Rainbow Coalition of Consumers

Although there have been many examples throughout this volume of marketing to Latinos, to American Jews, and to Irish-Americans, what follows is a closer look at the some of the specific ways that consumer culture has intersected with ethnicity among these three populations. In each case, whether nonprofit or for profit, whether at the corporate, small-business, or community level, the dynamics illustrate the paradoxical role that commercialism plays, simultaneously enhancing and commodifying ethnic identities and cultural meanings.

The Hispanic Connection

In the mid-1950s, before targeted marketing, Judith Ortiz Cofer recalled how important the local Latino-owned shops were to her family and neighbors in the Puerto Rican community of Paterson, New Jersey:

> These establishments were located not downtown but in the blocks around our street, and they were referred to generically as La Tienda, El Bazar, La Bodega, La Botánica. Everyone knew what was meant. These were the stores where your face did not turn a clerk to stone, where your money was as green as anyone else's. . . .

Though father preferred that we do our grocery shopping at the supermarket when he came home on weekend leaves, my mother insisted that she could cook only with products whose labels she could read. Consequently, during the week I accompanied her and my little brother to La Bodega—a hole-in-the-wall grocery store across the street from El Building. There we squeezed down three narrow aisles jammed with various products, Goya and Libby's—those were the trademarks that were trusted by her *mamá*, so my mother bought many cans of Goya beans, soups, and condiments, as well as little cans of Libby's fruit juices for us. And she also bought Colgate toothpaste and Palmolive soap. (The final *e* is pronounced in both these products in Spanish, so for many years I believed that they were manufactured on the Island. I remember my surprise at first hearing a commercial on television in which "Colgate" rhymed with "ate.") We always lingered at La Bodega, for it was there that Mother breathed best, talking in the familiar aromas of the foods she knew from Mamá's kitchen.[1]

Although they may not be aware of the marketing possibilities in nostalgia associated with the way Spanish-speakers in earlier decades were accustomed to pronouncing their product labels, the Colgate-Palmolive company today is one of the leading corporate entities to be systematically courting the urban Hispanic consumer. A cleverly designed approach has been implemented in recent years whereby Ajax cleaning products and cash grants are donated by the parent company, Colgate-Palmolive, to clean up public spaces in selected cities, such as Baltimore and Atlanta, in a program they have called the Ajax Clean Sweep Promotion. The funds are used to employ hundreds of inner-city kids in summer jobs, while exposing them to an array of Colgate-Palmolive consumer goods. Another initiative targeted at Hispanic youth is the Bright Smiles, Bright Future promotion. A Colgate van circulates through inner-city neighborhoods dispensing free dental checkups and free samples of

Colgate toothpaste and toothbrushes. "There's no question about it: Ethnic consumers respond to promotions aimed at them," says Henry Nisimblat, market development manager, who himself hails from South America. "We are leveraging that. These events aren't just charity. We're establishing contacts with future consumers."[2]

Beginning in 1970 the growth of the Hispanic sector in the United States started to outrun significantly that of the general population, so that by the early 1980s systematic studies were already being undertaken to determine how best to capture the potential of the Hispanic market. These early reports predicted a dramatic rise in buying power, concurrent with expanded advertising budgets directed at the Hispanic population; an increase in the number and types of Spanish-speaking and Hispanic-oriented media outlets; and because of the comparative youth of the Hispanic population, a trend toward targeting young consumers. Indeed, the forecast was accurate. At century's end the Hispanic population in the United States, slightly over thirty million, equaled the entire population of Canada, growing by 17 percent over the course of the 1990s as compared to an 8.2 percent growth rate for the population as a whole. If the approximately four million Hispanics living in this country illegally are added, as well as the nearly four million Puerto Ricans on their island, the total is even higher. Moreover, the youth of this sector is definitely a factor: 35 percent of Hispanics are under eighteen years of age and another 31 percent are between the ages of eighteen and thirty-four, according to 1998 tabulations. Such figures have prompted ethnic marketers to hold trainings specifically focused on reaching Hispanic teenagers, such as "Latino Youth Power," a corporate conference that uses case studies from companies like Coca-Cola, Target Stores, and MTV to teach business executives how to go about winning the Latino youth market.

Currently estimated at $380 billion, the purchasing power of Hispanics in the United States is said to exceed the GNP of any one Spanish-speaking nation in all of Latin America. This figure represents a 66 percent increase from 1990, and it is projected to nearly triple by the year 2010. Furthermore, the Hispanic population is concentrated in key cities so that targeting this market is relatively easy to implement. When the Social Security Administration released the rankings of the most popular baby names for 1998, Michael still topped the list for boys nationwide, but in California and Texas, two of the most populous states, José was the winner, evidence of the Hispanic cultural turn.

With a population of this size and degree of diversity, however, there is always the danger of stereotyping. At Hispanic Market Connection (now called Cultural Access Worldwide), a consulting firm in Los Altos, California, the staff attempts to determine general distinguishing characteristics of Hispanic consumers, what the company's president, Isabel Valdez, terms the "cultural axis." The trick is to be able to recognize both the overarching features and the differing elements that represent a specific nationality or socioeconomic class within the wider Hispanic rubric. Gary Berman of the Florida-based Market Segment Research and Consulting firm (MSR&C) uses the mundane example of beans to illustrate the necessity of nuanced ethnic marketing strategies to stay competitive. All surveys show that as a group Hispanics eat more beans than do non-Hispanics, but Mexicans prefer refried beans, Cubans are more inclined to cook with black beans, and Puerto Ricans consume the red variety. Berman is convincing in demonstrating that for those who sell beans, knowledge of this breakdown could be the key to its successful marketing.

Findings from MSR&C show that it's not just beans; of the four groups surveyed—African-American, Asian, Anglo, and Hispanic—the Hispanic population spends more on weekly groceries in general. Analysts have come up with two different hypotheses to explain the data. One is demographic: that with higher than average birth rates and larger families, Hispanics simply have more mouths to feed. The other is related to consumer habits. This sector tends to be more oriented toward brand-name and consequently slightly higher-priced products. Hispanics are also viewed as more conservative and traditional in their purchasing preferences and, thus, less likely to switch brands. The staff at MSR&C believe that a large part of this brand loyalty, however, is related to the number of products this segment is exposed to either in Latin America or in communities within the United States. This also includes the extent to which brands are marketed in the Spanish language. Preliminary findings demonstrate that as the number of exposures increases, a population stereotyped as conservative in their shopping patterns will try out other products and may even switch brands—that is, their so-called brand loyalty is simply a function of lack of exposure. Other data showing that Hispanics are not likely to use grocery coupons, a primary means by which companies induce consumers to try out new items, corroborate this interpretation. Since Hispanics do not generally read the English-language newspapers, where these coupons are found, they are not exposed to the same incentives as the general population to try something new.

Indeed, the Latino market is unique in that another language besides English is often used to facilitate marketing, either in the advertisements themselves or by using a Spanish-speaking sales force. In marketing to other American ethnics, such as the Irish or Jewish populations, except for a sprinkling of Gaelic or Yiddish expressions, the English language is used. This also holds true for targeted promotions to other components of the "New America." Since African Americans are English-speaking, they do not require language-specific strategies, whereas Asian Americans speak too many different tongues for language to be successfully incorporated, in most cases, into a general marketing design, although more and more initiatives directed to specific Asian populations are appearing. But with Latinos, whether of Cuban, Caribbean, or Mexican background, the same language is understood and can be used effectively.

The dramatic growth in the Hispanic population and the impact of Latino culture on the United States have led Hallmark, a company that had first entered the Hispanic market in the 1980s with its Primor line of greeting cards, to launch a rehauled and expanded Spanish collection in 1999. The updated "en español" line features more than three hundred new designs. Unlike the earlier offerings, most of the new selections are written entirely in Spanish with English translations of the sentiments provided on the back of each card.

Companies are so eager to get it right with their promotional appeals to the Hispanic market that some have gone so far as to try out new ideas in Puerto Rico before launching a full-scale campaign at home. The head of one such venture explained that "Puerto Rico is the first step to explore a new market in a stable territory. It is different from standard U.S. markets but not as exotic or different from them as a Latin American country."[3]

AT&T's involvement with the Hispanic community includes a range of initiatives to buttress the arts, education, and the humanities at a time when government support for such endeavors has been steadily waning. Since 1993 the corporation has funded fellowships for college and graduate students to assist the Hispanic Division of the Library of Congress, an archive for the study of Latino language, culture, and history that has been in operation for almost sixty years. The fellows produce bibliographic tools, develop computerized listings, transcribe recordings, and conduct research on a variety of Hispanic topics.

Over the last twenty years, AT&T funding has been one of the principal resources to sustain the Spanish-language theater company, Repertorio Español. Based in Manhattan, the troupe primarily performs *zarzuelas* (musical comedies), operas, and musical anthologies by Hispanic playwrights. A third of those who attend the performances are public school children on field trips from the Bronx and upper Manhattan who are studying Spanish. The first money the theater company ever received from AT&T was a $1,000 donation; more recently the corporation contributed $25,000 to support a series called *Voces Nuevas* (New Voices). Because theater is such an expensive art form and because of drastic cutbacks from traditional sources of funding, cultural programs such as the Repertorio have increasingly come to depend upon corporate support for survival.

Some of AT&T's outreach to the Hispanic community is filtered through their Hispanic Association of Employees (HISPA), a professional development organization. For example, revenue generated by the mail-order sales of *Buen Provecho*, an illustrated cookbook of Hispanic recipes from all over the world developed by the New Jersey chapter of HISPA, is allocated for college scholarships to needy high school students under the auspices of the National Hispanic Scholarship Fund. AT&T's Minority and Women Business Enterprise program (MWBE) is often another conduit to support Hispanic initiatives. An MWBE grant is what started Marta Camacho off on a new career in Hispanic catering. She began by doing events for Latinos in the corporate world, developed a steady clientele of Latino organizations and individuals, and before long was catering parties for as many as a thousand people, as she did for the Puerto Rican Day Parade in 1997. The AT&T funding also helped Camacho to open her own café, Exotic Foods, in Ossining, New York. Its involvement in the Hispanic sector is so extensive that AT&T recently began publishing a quarterly newsletter, *Adelante con AT&T*, solely to report on its activities within the Latino community.

Ethnic marketing has permeated all aspects of the business world from corporations and firms of every size that devote a substantial portion of their manufacturing activities to producing ethnic merchandise to retailers, end-product brokers, suppliers, and distributors. For example, in 1974 a Cuban-American, New Jersey-based distributor of health and beauty care products began to sell "American" items, such as Crest toothpaste, Alka-Seltzer, and aspirin, to bodegas, the small grocery stores located in neighborhoods with significant Hispanic populations that cater to the community by selling the fruits, vegetables, and cuts of meats that Hispanics prefer. Usually bodegas are Hispanic-owned and, thus, the proprietors speak the language of their customers. Often the merchandise that this distributor supplied would be the only American products on the shelves. Twenty-five years later the company has made a complete turnaround. Now, instead of distributing American merchandise to Spanish retailers, it is supplying a wide range of Spanish products to major American chains, such as Walgreen's and Rite Aid, so that these stores can fill the ever-expanding *farmacia* shelf space needed to meet the growing demands of Latino customers and even some non-Hispanic crossover shoppers who have discovered the benefits of remedies and beauty-enhancing items that come from south of the border.

The transition came about when several Cuban-Americans, some of whom had formerly owned bodegas, bought a few independently owned supermarkets in a small chain and wanted to stock a mix of American and Spanish health and beauty products for their clientele. There was a particular demand for a line of shampoos and facial creams of well-known Cuban cosmetologist Marti De Peralas, who was based in Florida and who advertised heavily on the Spanish television network. The best way to get such merchandise into their stores was for the owners to switch to a Hispanic distributor who could supply them with both American and Spanish goods. "That's how we started distributing to a chain store," recounts one of the partners:

> By the 1980s, we were already heavily into the Spanish lines, going into the New York discounts and the New York pharmacies in upper Manhattan where there's a lot of Spanish people and a lot of Dominican clientele but the businesses were still largely Cuban-owned—people who had been here for a long time. So we were servicing, basically, the independently owned pharmacies and discounts.

By the late 1980s the company broke into distribution to big-name drugstore chains on Long Island and in Manhattan. One day the distributor just walked into a Walgreen's in a Manhattan neighborhood heavily populated by Puerto Ricans and noticed that although they did have a shelf labeled *farmacia* for Hispanic customers, the merchandise was from California and Illinois:

> Basically, I could tell that because the products were items that are consumed by the Mexican market. People think of the Spanish market as one homogeneous group, and it isn't. Every-

body consumes the product that they know from their own original country. So, when you look at the Spanish market, it's not a market that consumes—even the same types of foods. We cook differently. We have preferences for products according to where we're from.

Conversation with the store's manager revealed, not surprisingly, that the *farmacia* stock was not selling well. She told him,

"The problem is that you have the wrong mix." The manager then asked me to contact his district manager. I met with him, and he knew what I was talking about, because he had been in the Florida market and he knew that it was primarily Cuban and that there was a difference. So at least I was dealing with an American person that was aware that all the Spanish market was not the same . . . and he wanted to know if we had items like honey and Florida water. And I said, "Sure." Then he said, "Well, I need you to service our store." And that's how we started in the chain stores with an Hispanic plan-o-gram . . . There is a need. People know that if they are not capturing the Spanish consumer, they are losing business.

Of course, the immigrant and ethnic composition of the big cities in America has been shifting so rapidly in recent years that the original Mexican brands in this particular drugstore could well be the right mix today. The Mexican population of New York City has quadrupled since 1990, making it the fastest-growing immigrant group in the city, and the new arrivals bring a whole new blend of consumer needs and desires with them. Thus, one of the most critical aspects of successful ethnic marketing has been to find ways to accurately track the constantly changing settlement patterns of the country's immigrant and ethnic populations. This need is part of what has made ethnic marketing specialists, particularly those with sophisticated demographic training, such hot commodities.

Among the products that Hispanics might hope to find on the *farmacia* shelves is a variety of herbal teas that aid relaxation and digestion or combat insomnia or weight gain. These might well be found in a natural foods store but not in a traditional pharmacy. Also highly popular among Hispanic customers are baby care products, such as colognes and certain types of shampoos, that are not available anywhere else at all. They are not manufactured by the American beauty and health care industry, and neither the holistic alternative nor mainstream American stores carry such goods. But the Gerber company has introduced a line of baby food, bottles, and bibs called Tesoros (Treasures) that are very popular among Hispanics. The bright-colored bibs are decorated with sayings in Spanish and with tropical fruits, and the baby food varieties include a black bean soup.

Studies have shown that Spanish-immigrant consumers are highly brand-loyal, not only to the specific American brands they were first introduced to either in this country or at home but also to the Spanish labels that they were raised with and still consider to be the best. One way to obtain such items, if the newcomer still has close contacts back home, is to have the goods mailed to them, but this is hardly convenient. Another is to seek out favored products in an American drugstore. Thus, when Dominicans peruse the *farmacia* shelves in a Rite Aid in New York, they are looking for a label familiar to them from the Dominican Republic. Colombians search for a recognized brand from Colombia, and so forth. Consequently, Hispanic wholesalers supply entire product categories that cannot be found anywhere else, such as remedial teas and baby colognes, and also the particular brands of a host of different goods preferred by each nationality group. The New Jersey distributors will even try to find the original Spanish products manufactured in Spain and introduce these specialties to the mainstream pharmacies in the United States because this merchandise already has longtime, proven success among Hispanic consumers. Sometimes non-Hispanics will show an interest in purchasing certain of these lines, such as the

Maja brand of cosmetics imported from Spain. Other immigrant populations may also find themselves in the *farmacia* aisle, searching for products akin to their own cultural preferences. For instance, Indian immigrants regularly shop for baby care items in the Hispanic section.

Luis de las Mata, the Latino marketing director at the Bustelo Coffee Company (an enterprise begun in 1928 in New York City by Gregorio Bustelo, an immigrant from Estuvia, Spain, and then acquired by the Tetley corporation in the late 1960s), has a two-pronged promotional strategy. When marketing to the Hispanic community, the focus is on intragroup distinctions, and since the Bustelo name is already familiar to many Hispanic sectors, the sell does not need to be a hard one. Rather, the ads depict domestic scenes in which the Bustelo product is configured as simply another member of the Hispanic household. To further the image of being a part of the Hispanic family, the coffee company gets involved in community cultural events. At the same time, however, Bustelo is trying to win Anglo or crossover consumers, and as a result, one of its primary advertisements depicts a classic scene of European immigrants arriving in the United States; the voiceover narration of the company's founding is meant to imply that European and Hispanic immigrants are no different in the trajectories with which they have pursued the American dream.

Yiddish Remade

American Jews are no exception to the pattern of ethnic revival in the United States. Particularly in the last fifteen years, they have enthusiastically pursued the recovery of the language, literature, and culture of their Yiddish-speaking forebears. The explosion of Yiddishkeit goes well beyond increased enrollments in language classes. It encapsulates the resurgence of interest in the literature buoyed by the energetic recovery, restoration, and distribution of books and vintage films, as well as a booming revival of klezmer music and the Yiddish theater. Yiddish clubs, summer institutes, and curricula within Jewish Studies programs are also proliferating.

At one level, many find themselves celebrating and demonstrating their Jewish identity through conscious purchase choices—a gift mug, an apron, or a T-shirt with Yiddish sayings. One can even exercise in Yiddish by mail-ordering the video *My Yiddisheh Workout* (*Shvitz!* in Yiddish). Another possibility is to participate in a gathering such as the Lower East Side Festival, billed as a "voyage of discovery and rediscovery of cultural roots." The publicity flyer promises there will be "Hundreds of Vendors" on the premises, and visitors can spend their dollars on Katz's knishes, Guss' pickles, or Ratner's kosher ice cream, while taking in a performance by Tovah Feldshuh or tapping their feet to the music of the West End Klezmerim Band.

Under the auspices of the United Jewish Council of the East Side, preservation of this neighborhood became more systematic with the establishment of the Lower East Side Conservancy in 1998. Their advertisements implore potential donors to

> Come indulge your sense of nostalgia. Our grandparents grew up here. Played here. Prayed here. Became Americans here. It is home to our culture, our tradition. And today the culture and tradition live on . . . Take a guided tour of this historic neighborhood. *Kibbitz* with the old-time store-owners and get some great bargains to boot! You owe it to your culture and yourself.

The Yiddish revival has also inspired small-business ventures such as the cleverly conceived Mashuga Nuts label—"*mashuga*" is Yiddish for "crazy." Inventive as it is, the name doesn't quite carry over to their cookie line, so the manufacturers have included the annotation "Shortbread So Good It'll Make You Crazy" under the imperfect Mashuga Cookies logo. A pound of their cinnamon pecans sells for a cool $22 through the Bloomingdale's 1996 Holiday gourmet foods mail-order catalog. Another find for the Yiddish enthusiast is Einstein's toys, collectibles, and "museum with price tags" in downtown Philadelphia. The Jewish owners specialize in ethnic merchandise of all kinds, including Russian stacking dolls, African-

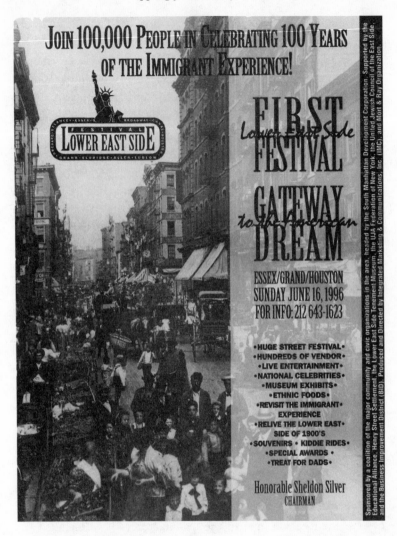

American toy soldiers, and rare ethnic artifacts from popular culture, such as playbills and posters. Playbills and posters are displayed in ethnically organized spaces in the second-floor gallery—a room for original Russian paintings, a Yiddish room, a wall devoted to Irish collectibles, and so forth. But nothing quite tops the board

game designed and produced by the proprietor himself, called "Look at the Schmuck on that Camel" with its accompanying cassette "Goys to Mensch," a take-off on the hugely popular black R & B group from Philadelphia, "Boyz II Men"—another item for which there is such great demand that Einstein's can't keep enough of them on the shelf.

But the marketing of Yiddishkeit is not limited to the commercial sector alone. One of the leading nonprofit organizations devoted to the preservation and revitalization of Yiddish culture is the Yiddish Book Center in Amherst, Massachusetts. In 1996, a new staff position, director of marketing, was created to facilitate the shift from an operating budget supported by charitable contributions to one in which two-thirds of the funding results from earned income. As Executive Director Eric Vieland explained:

> People no longer give for *tsedakah* (obligations of charity) alone. They want something for their money—something that appeals to their ethnic identity. People crave products that express their identity. The Book Center is going to try to corner that market, to specialize in challenging intellectual products. We ultimately are creating a community of members around the country who really feel that the Book Center is helping them make sense of their identity and make their identity useful to them. The fact of the matter is that the field is so wide open that we can offer products that are really loaded to the hilt with really rich, really substantial ethnic content and people will snatch it up. It's a classic win-win situation.

Ultimately, the center hired an attorney with expertise in intellectual property law to deal with the complicated issues surrounding the marketing of books, cassettes, or performance art rather than an advertising specialist. According the Vieland, "We don't need to promote and advertise. There is already a preexisting and hungry clientele. Essentially the merchandise sells itself."[4]

Opened in 1980, the Yiddish Book Center is the fastest-growing Jewish cultural organization in the country. In June 1997 an impressive new $8 million facility was dedicated. Funding came from private contributions and major foundation grants, including the Harry and Jeanette Weinberg, Kresge, and Steven Spielberg Righteous Persons foundations. Covering 37,000 square feet, the complex was designed to look like a nineteenth-century eastern European *shtetl*, and includes a book repository and processing center, exhibit galleries, an auditorium, outdoor amphitheater, a sound studio, conference meeting rooms, kosher kitchen, storytelling courtyard, and more. Although it was estimated that some fifty thousand people would visit in the first year alone, there is no admission fee. Instead, it is expected that the building's entire ongoing operating budget will come from the Visitors' Center bookstore sales. The shop is stocked with volumes in Yiddish and English, with posters, cassettes, CDs, and videos, and also includes "as many *chachkas* as they can think of . . . but tasteful." This is not an unrealistic goal. The recently opened Norman Rockwell Museum located nearby has a similar-sized gift shop supporting its own operation.[5]

When Aaron Lansky, the center's founder and president, was a twenty-three-year-old graduate student in Yiddish literature at McGill University in the late 1970s, he went in search of a book he needed for a course. In the process, he became aware that thousands of volumes of irreplaceable Yiddish works were being tossed away by the children and grandchildren of a once-flourishing immigrant generation because they no longer saw a use for them. Lansky singlemindedly set out to retrieve the priceless books, which were rapidly deteriorating from having been printed originally on acidic paper. He combed attics and basements and, in more than one instance, found himself making dramatic rescues from city dumpsters. What began as a one-man mission on a two-year project turned into a much more grandiose and long-term undertaking to recover an entire disappearing civilization. Lansky is acutely conscious of what he has referred to as the "miracle of timing" in these efforts. Just as the older generation was dying off, the younger one burst forth with an ethnic revival. "It was this perfect moment in time," he explained, "coming at the cusp of two epochs in Jewish history. If I had tried to do this fifteen years earlier, there would not have been sufficient interest. Fifteen years later, it would have been too late."[6]

Despite housing exhibits that honor the legacy of Yiddishkeit, the Yiddish Book Center has never been envisioned as an organiza-

The Yiddish Book Center Complex

tion that dwells on bygone days. Rather, it has been conceptualized from the beginning as a vibrant foundation on which to build a future. "Our intention is to help visitors move beyond sentimentality, nostalgia, and a lachrymose fixation on the past, and instead to understand the complexity and humanity of Yiddish culture—its relevance as a wellspring of contemporary Jewish identity."[7] Making use of the latest advances in communications and computer technology and with the support of another healthy grant from the Spielberg Foundation, the center is in the process of digitizing the more than thirty-five thousand titles in its collection so that the steadily decomposing volumes can be both widely accessible and preserved forever in cyberspace. Thus, by 2001 Yiddish will be one of the first languages to be entirely digitized. Furthermore, once the books are scanned, consumers will be able to shop for them on-line. At an astonishingly quick printing time of thirty seconds per volume, new books can be churned out electronically, this time-around on acid-free paper. Moreover, with a soft-cover binding, the volume will cost the customer less than $10.[8]

Although the center sponsors events and programs year round, its centerpiece is the Annual Summer Program in Yiddish Culture, which offers conferees five days of lectures, film screenings, and workshops focused on Ashkenazic history, Yiddish literary texts, Yiddish theater, and klezmer music. Knowledge of Yiddish is not necessary to participate fully. Indeed, on the first day of classes, Lansky poses several questions to the audience. He asks how many of their grandparents spoke Yiddish, and 98 percent of the hands go up. When he inquires about parents, the number decreases considerably, and by the time he asks about the hundred or so who are in attendance, the number of Yiddish-speakers in the group has fallen well below half. Finally, he wants to know how many have children who speak Yiddish, and then only a sprinkling of hands go up. Most telling, however, was when Lansky asked to see a show of hands of those who had read the Yiddish version of the previously circulated literary excerpts that had been photocopied in both Yiddish and

English: not a single hand was raised. The point made, it quickly recedes into the background; among those gathered, the atmosphere of excitement and passion about keeping the culture alive is so palpable, it takes right over.

The phenomenon of resurgent Yiddishkeit reaches beyond such grass-roots initiatives to the world of the multinational corporation. Perhaps the best example of marketing Yiddish at the for-profit level is illustrated by the enormously successful advertising campaign launched in 1995 by AT&T to appeal to emerging ethnic communities in the United States. Promotions aimed at the American-Jewish community include significant Yiddish content, such as the "With 50% Savings You Can Afford to *Kvell* All You Want" ad. Underneath a photo of *kvelling* grandparents at their grandson's Bar Mitzvah is written: "You're so proud you could just burst. After all, such an occasion you don't celebrate every day. So go ahead and call the whole *mishpocheh*," using not only the Yiddish terms *kvell* and *mishpocheh* (untranslated) but a Yiddish cadence and syntax. In a promotional brochure put out by the communications company that developed these campaigns for AT&T, *kvell* is defined for the reader in an accompanying note as to "beam with immense pride"; *mishpocheh* is not explained.

The ad titled "More Gab, Less *Gelt*" and showing Chanukah *gelt* (money) spilling out of two open hands was obviously developed for the holiday season. The accompanying text gives information about how to save money but does not carry on with the *Gelt* theme as does the *kvell* ad, presumably because it is a more universally understood representation that can stand on its own. However, the brochure does make sure to define *gelt*.

Another in this series that, with the exception of the 800 number to call, uses only text with Yiddish content shows a frontal view of a large pig wearing a hat and dark glasses, with the phrase "Something Here Just Isn't Kosher" in bold type above it. Underneath the pig is written "*Trayfe* Is *Trayfe*, No Matter How It's Disguised." In the fine print, the ad carries on with the "disguising *trafe*" motif, explaining:

WITH 50% SAVINGS YOU CAN AFFORD TO KVELL ALL YOU WANT.

You're so proud you could just burst. After all, such an occasion you don't celebrate every day. So go ahead and call the whole mishpocheh. With AT&T TrueWorld℠ Savings you'll get 50%* off all your calls to everyone in the one country of your choice, every weekend, for an entire four months. And you'll enjoy big savings to 250 other countries and areas worldwide.

Plus we've just introduced a domestic discount which offers you 20% off all your AT&T Long Distance calls within the U.S., 24 hours a day, 7 days a week.** So call AT&T and sign up for AT&T TrueWorld℠ Savings today. Then you can share all your naches without worrying about your bill adding up too quickly. And with AT&T it's a voice so clear you can feel it.

1 800 858-9027
AT&T. Your True Voice.℠

More Gab.
Less Gelt.

60% savings
on an entire month
of international calls.

Call now, collect later. AT&T will reimburse you 60% of the price
of direct-dial international calls on your December-dated bill —
that's a check of up to $100 just for keeping in touch.*

MCI is offering a 60% savings, but only to new customers. AT&T's
biggest savings is available to everyone. Whether or not you
already subscribe to AT&T **TrueWorld**℠ Savings,** simply call
to sign up for the 60% savings before September 30, 1994 and
talk all you want. The money will follow.

1 800 533-4735 ext. 611
AT&T. **Your True Voice.**℠

AT&T

Like the claims some other long-distance companies have been making. That they are doing you a *mitzva*, telling you how much you can save with them. Or put charts in their ads comparing their prices to AT&T prices. Meanwhile they are comparing their discount rates to AT&T's regular rates. Which is like comparing kugel to knishes. Bagels to bialys. It's just not the same thing. So make sure you always read the fine print. And if another long distance company calls, before they give you the whole *megillah*, just tell them to put their claims in writing. Remember when something sounds too good to be true, it's usually no *metsieh*.

In this case, none of the Yiddish references are defined, not in the ad itself nor in the promotional brochure. Plainly, shopping for a Jewish identity has become big business for contemporary consumer society.

The rebirth of interest in Yiddish culture has many sources, but one significant aspect of its appeal relates to the skyrocketing rates of intermarriage. Exploring one's Jewish heritage turns out to be far less threatening or foreign to non-Jewish partners than the kind of pressures that invariably arise when dealing with traditional interfaith relationships, particularly when religious conversion is contemplated. The stakes are simply less high. "You discover your roots, I'll discover mine, and the kids can explore both." Acceptance and participation on the part of a non-Jewish mate can be as facile as attending a klezmer concert or enjoying a dinner of blintzes and herring. This is part of the utilitarian nature of what some have labeled optional ethnicity. Whether an Ashkenazic Jew or not, one can approach Yiddishkeit from an intellectual curiosity and a level of social involvement that does not necessarily require having to renegotiate fundamental questions of faith and spirituality. Sometimes, rather than having a diluting effect, marriage to a non-Jew can result in a heightened sense of Jewish identity.

It is not just the twin factors of the soaring intermarriage and low fertility rates characteristic of Jewish demographics at century's end that challenge the vitality of the community, but analysis of the 1990 National Jewish Population Survey confirms that American Jews also demonstrate particularly high levels of geographic mobility. The findings of Sidney and Alice Goldstein's aptly titled volume *Jews on the Move* indicate that so much residential dispersion further weakens Jewish community and organizational life.[9] However, the loosening of localized ties and the loss of a sense of place is often offset by the reinvented forms of portable ethnicity. Although only in the short-term, Yiddish retreats and workshops allow an immediate sense of community that can help to fulfill such longings. Commercial expressions of ethnic Jewishness, whether furnishings, books, foods, or decorative objects, replace institutional and neighborhood affiliations. Mail-order businesses such as the Jewish Catalog thrive especially among such highly mobile populations.

The perpetuation of Yiddish in cyberspace also thrives among these populations. With the founding in 1993 of the on-line Yiddish Network, followers of Yiddishkeit worldwide are becoming electronically connected without ever having to leave the comfort of home and with minimal logistical demands or personal sacrifice. This is a user-friendly Yiddishkeit that is escalating rapidly. At the first TYN—The Yiddish Network—(face-to-face) conference held at the University of Maryland, there were 128 delegates. Four years later, in 1996, the number had jumped to 347, and the organization boasted of contacts in all fifty states and in twenty-five countries. At the *Mame-Loshn* '96 retreat, one could sign up for Internet workshops for an introduction to "Mendele On Line" or the "Virtual Shtetl" Web pages. Cyberspace ethnicity means that people can visit symbolic ancestral homelands without having to spend the time and money for an actual journey. Indeed, even taking the short trip to the mall is becoming unnecessary with the growing availability of on-line ethnic shopping. Just click on to the "http://www.jewishmall.com" Web site to find everything from UFO dreidels to ceramic-baseball menorahs for sale.

Certainly, a major requirement of convenience ethnicity is a sense of feeling secure enough in this culture to be able to accentuate differences and to distinguish oneself from mass society. As Ruth Wisse, Professor of Yiddish Literature at Harvard, succinctly stated it:

> The more comfortable Jews feel in America, the more open they are to reclaiming a culture of exile. This is the paradox of the American diaspora: the wish to feel different *and* at home. Yiddish, with all its complex, contradictory associations, is the language of that desire.[10]

A Vogue for the Brogue: Irish America on Display

In reference to the Irish-American fear of standing out, Andrew Greeley has written:

> If brilliance and flair are counterproductive, the slightest risk-taking beyond the limits of approved career and personal behavior is unthinkable. Art, music, literature, poetry, theater, to some extent even academia, politics of any variety other than the traditional, are all too risky to be considered. The two most devastating things that can be said to the young . . . Irishman who attempts to move beyond these rigid norms are "Who do you think you are?" and "What will people say?"[11]

During the last two decades, there has been a shift from the usual pattern of concealment that has been so intrinsic to Irish-American identity to a much more outspoken display of Irish pride. Whereas Irish political clubs and genealogy societies have been in existence for many decades furthering ethnic identification in cities throughout the United States, attention to the fostering of interest in Irish cultural forms is more recent. Again, the 1970s were the turning point. In the metropolis of New York alone, at a time when the Irish population seemed to be slipping into assimilated obscurity, a flurry of initiatives put Irish-Americans right back on the city map. In the space of a few years, the Irish Arts Center and the Irish Repertory

Theater were founded; Columbia University inaugurated a seminar in Irish Studies and New York University opened the Glucksman Ireland House. Project Irish Outreach, the Emerald Isle Immigration Center, the New York Irish History Roundtable, the American Irish Teachers Association, and a second weekly newspaper, the *Irish Voice*, were all organized. Part of the impetus came from the infusion of new Irish immigrants into the city, but the long-standing Irish-American residents were also ripe to reemerge and become involved in the renaissance.

In the Boston area, the organization of the Irish Cultural Centre, founded in 1990 by a small group of Irish-Americans and naturalized Irish, most clearly exemplifies the new trend. Their statement of purpose specifically declared that they are a nonpolitical and non-partisan collectivity. Membership skyrocketed in the last few years as plans to establish a major site for Irish-American cultural activity in the Boston area took hold. The Centre, located on forty-seven acres in Canton, Massachusetts, is a multimillion-dollar facility that will house a performing arts center, a museum (including Irish Thatched Cottage), a library, a gift shop, a banquet hall, function space, and extensive playing fields for Gaelic sports. The last use is the primary reason that, after much debate, the Centre decided not to locate itself in the traditional south Boston Irish neighborhood and to move to the wide-open suburbs instead. To mark Phase I of the ICC's new campus, a grand-opening celebration was held on the weekend of October 16, 1999, to dedicate the activities building and the playing fields. To the accompaniment of a lone piper from the Boston Police Gaelic Column, both the American and Irish flags were raised. Afterward, the Boston Gaelic Athletic Association (GAA) sponsored exhibition games of hurling and football, the national sports of Ireland, against rivals from New York and Phila-delphia, as well as teams that had flown in from Ireland for the fes-tivities. The local GAA has been in existence for more than a hundred years, but the establishment of the ICC fields signifies the first time that the organization has had a permanent home.

Much of the funding for the new structure was raised through

Irish Cultural Centre activities building and playing field

the Centre's annual Irish Cultural Festival, a three-day event held in June on the campus of Stonehill College in Easton, Massachusetts. The festival is another clear example of corporate, small-business, artistic, and cultural collaboration. Indeed, in the weeks leading up to it, a huge ad for the event, listing all the corporate sponsors, can be seen on a billboard towering over Boston's central artery, a traffic-clogged highway where the volume of exposure must rank close to the top of city locations. The array of activities on the program has increased significantly each year, drawing thousands and thousands of visitors.

A related annual event is the Gaelic Roots Music and Dance Summer School and Festival at Boston College. The gathering includes week-long classes and lecture performances in Irish dance and music, recitals featuring master musicians, seisiúns in Boston's leading pubs, and a sunset Céilí Cruise in Boston Harbor. The music director, master fiddler Séamus Connolly, released a CD in 1997 called *Gaelic Roots: The Album*, produced by Connolly for the Boston College Irish Studies Program, which sponsors the event. In conjunction with Irish Studies programs at leading educational institutions and with local artists, community crafts initiatives, and Gaelic sports teams, promotion of all things Irish is a burgeoning phenomenon.

With this move toward a forthright embrace of Irish ethnicity has come an expansion of economic interests tied to an open and vocal celebration of the culture. For example, the Irish America Calendar, a complimentary insert in each January issue of the magazine *Irish America*, added a new feature for 1995. Besides the usual stunning photographs of Ireland and calendar designations of important events in Irish history, a sidebar each month describes an Irish or Irish-American corporate venture. One advertisement—opposite a shot of scenic County Wicklow with a handsome woman in the foreground—is for "The Look Is Ireland" trade show. Sponsored by The Irish Trade Board and supported by the International Fund for Ireland, the announcement promises that the spectacular event "will bring to America the greatest ever selection of Irish goods, from north and south, from crafts to crystal, fashion to home furnishings, textiles to tabletop, glass, giftware and knitwear, Ireland's finest will be marketed to retailers, wholesalers and mail-order buyers all over North America." And what is the number to call for more information? Why, of course, 1-800-BUY-IRELAND.

Indeed, one *can* actually purchase a piece of Ireland. Tiny plots of Irish dairy land are offered for sale. The consumer does not actually own the tract, but the money goes toward subsidizing it. In return, buyers receive a memento identifying their particular plot. Whether carrying an "Irish Heritage" Visa Card—in 1991, one U.S. issuer offered a free gift of a research report on your family name and a print of its coat of arms once you were approved—or "Feeling the Warmth of Ireland" with the purchase of 100 percent natural turf peat bricks from a Connecticut company, the promise is there not only to "Buy Ireland" but to buy yourself an Irish identity. More-over, consumers can bolster their Irishness not just by acquiring specialty products; marketers of mainstream merchandise are also quite willing to court Irish sensibilities as AT&T has done.

Indeed, the Irish vogue is so extensive that management at Kitty O'Shea's, the planned Irish theme bar at Boston's Logan Airport, might consider a complete historical reversal of the nineteenth-century bias against hiring Irish immigrants and put a sign in the window reading ONLY IRISH NEED APPLY. In 1999 three wait-resses, local Yankees, with a combined one hundred and three years of service at the airport Ramada Inn, filed a discrimination suit when they learned that the new ownership (the Hilton Corporation) was intending to import students from an Irish hospitality school and give them first preference over the veteran waitresses, in an attempt to create an authentic pub atmosphere replete with Irish brogues.

Irish pride is now exhibited year-round, not just on St. Patrick's Day, and celebrated coast to coast, not only in the big cities of the Northeast. Indeed, in Savannah, Georgia, in addition to a huge parade, the public schools close every March 17. This all means that the marketing of Irish merchandise is no longer restricted to the festivities surrounding St. Patrick's Day itself. The Waterstone Booksellers chain advertised an October sale last year in Boston to celebrate Irish culture, entreating shoppers with the argument that "There are so many great Irish titles right now we just couldn't wait until March." They then further enticed potential customers by offering a 10 percent discount on anything Irish they purchased.

The thirst for Irish goods has been the "key" to success for Robert Emmet Reilly, who in the mid-1980s began making shamrock key rings in the basement of his home in New Bedford, Massachusetts. Ten years later, in 1996, what had begun as a tiny cottage enterprise was bringing in $500,000 a year and had national distribution. Reilly had expanded the business to produce more than two hundred and fifty different gift items, including Christmas orna-

ments depicting pubs and crystal steins affixed with the map of Ireland. All of these items can be found in more than three hundred Irish gift shops coast to coast.[12]

Part of the constellation of sentiments that structure the ethnic revival includes longings for a mythical homeland. Such feelings

have bolstered the tourist industry, particularly in Ireland, which has become the most frequently chosen destination by visitors from the United States. Travel to the Emerald Isle grew by as much as 75 percent in the 1990s and is averaging seven times higher annually than visits to other countries in Europe. In 1996 the Irish Tourist Board (Bord Failte) launched a major marketing campaign to capitalize on this tremendous swell of interest. The moment of inspiration came when the Irish tourism minister was marching with a contingent of Irish-Americans from his native County Mayo in New York's lavish St. Patrick's Day Parade. Many Irish-Americans plan their excursions to the "homeland" in the month of March to coincide with the celebration of St. Patrick's Day. In Ireland this has customarily been a very minor holiday, a blip on the ritual calendar, though in America it has grown in importance since the late nineteenth century. Thus, when the roots-seeking American tourists arrived expectantly in Ireland, they ended up feeling sorely disappointed. Now the Irish Tourist Board has responded by committing a good chunk of money to the fabrication of entirely new celebrations, parades, and festivals to mark St. Patrick's Day on Irish soil in a process that anthropologist Dean MacCannell terms "staged authenticity," to appeal to the mid-March pilgrimage of Irish-Americans.[13]

The pattern of hyphenated Americans becoming more ethnic than their homeland peers is quite common, whether spurred by the marketplace or not. When the actor John Barry, a Dublin native, was in the Boston area shooting a film set in Charlestown, a heavily Irish neighborhood, he was surprised to find that

Everyone here is ridiculously proud to be Irish and it's great. I've seen so many people walking around with T-shirts saying "I'm Irish" and everyone has caps saying "I'm Irish" and when we were in Charlestown I've never seen so many tricolors in my life. I mean we just don't have that when you go home. People are genuinely happy to be Irish and they're genuinely proud, and it's a real thing. I just find that some of them [in Boston] find that Ireland is a different place, because they've never been there and maybe they might be third generation, or even second generation, so they have a romantic view of what it's like.[14]

In Mary Corcoran's *Irish Illegals*, a study of the "new Irish," the largely undocumented recent immigrants, she found that the new-comers had a similar view of their Irish-American counterparts but are more frustrated than Barry by what they perceive to be an oversimplified and misinformed sentimentality. Typically, Irish-Americans steeped in nostalgia would express outdated and ideal-ized notions of life in Ireland that clash with the pressing realities that drove the new Irish out of Ireland. One recent arrival com-plained, "They have a fairy tale, idyllic image of Ireland. The lakes of Killarney, the Blarney Stone kind of thing. 'Top of the morning to you'—is a phrase I never heard until I came here. They don't stop to think why people are emigrating today, and why they and their forefathers before them emigrated."[15]

Although this chapter has zeroed in on the Hispanic connection, the Yiddish revival, and the Irish-American neo-ethnicity, evidence of the complex relationship between commerce and culture could easily have been presented for any American ethnic population. Most of the examples given above illustrate strong emotional links to one particular culture. However, increasingly, Americans are self-identifying with more than one ethnic group, adding an extra hyphen to their cultural identities. Moreover, once again, as these multiply identified individuals become more visible, the market-place is finding ways to reflect their variegated allegiances.

Seven

Recipe for Multiethnicity: The Mestizo Makeover

In 1965 when the Hart–Celler Act was passed liberalizing U.S. immigration policy and setting the stage for a monumental shift in the racial and ethnic makeup of American society, it was still illegal in some states for blacks and whites to marry. Not until 1967 in *Loving v. Virginia* did the Supreme Court rule that laws forbidding interracial marriage were unconstitutional. Since that time the number of marriages that cross ethnoracial boundaries—not just black and white but Asian, Latino, Native American, and others—has steadily and, in some instances, sharply increased. For example, 60 percent of Japanese people who marry in America wed someone of another race, and Native Americans show similar levels of out-group marriages. According to census figures between 1960 and 1995, the number of interracial married couples overall increased from 150,000 to more than 1.4 million. This naturally resulted in the beginning of a biracial baby boom during the late 1960s and 1970s, and the numbers of interracial children jumped from 460,000 in 1970 to more than 1.9 million by 1990. A further twist in the multiracial mix is the increase in unions between two minority groups. African Americans, Asians, Latinos, and Native Americans are marrying one another to form new combinations of mixed-race families. Indeed, Asian-African Americans have been some of the most vocal advocates of adding a mixed-race census category. Because there are not adequate categories yet in place to keep track of these patterns officially, some demographers are referring to a silent explosion of mixed-race people in the United States.

Tendencies that at first would appear to be contradictory are increasingly characterizing contemporary American society. Through rising rates of intermarriage and mixed-race reproduction as well as the influx of newcomers with multiracial backgrounds, blended, hybrid identities are proliferating. But this trend coincides with the equally compelling social dynamic of celebrating and maintaining cultural differences. How does one simultaneously blend and remain distinctively apart? Even the scholarship reflects this dilemma. Most literature concerning ethnicity is about groups while writings about mixed or multiethnic peoples are typically focused on the individual. What is the extent of cultural hybridity? Can there be mixed groups?

One option that a mild relaxation of racial boundaries in recent years has made possible is greater acceptance of the choice to claim more than one racial ancestry. People are beginning to feel less boxed in by the color line, since even on official documentation, it is no longer necessary to select only one racial designation. In 1997 the U.S. Office of Management and Budget, which designs categories for the Census Bureau, revised its directions so that individuals can check off as many ancestries as they feel are applicable rather than having to fill in only one box under race. At high schools and universities, biracial student organizations are forming to give voice to this ever-increasing population. In the popular culture, autobiographical writings about the experience of being multiracial are pouring off the press, while mixed-race characters appear with more and more regularity in film and on television. Ramona Douglass, president of the Association of MultiEthnic Americans, a San Francisco-based advocacy group, put it succinctly when she declared: "I don't want to be invisible anymore."[1]

Just after golf phenomenon Tiger Woods signed on with American Express, after already having made monster deals with Nike and Titleist, he characterized himself as "an ethnically global person," who was a perfect spokesman for a company that specialized in selling its credit card services worldwide. From a contemporary marketing viewpoint, Woods, who when growing up invented a new ethnic identity to account for his mixed Caucasian, black, Indian, and Asian heritages, calling himself Cablinasian, is indeed the ideal representative of the global marketplace. Seth Matlins, senior vice president of Pro/Serv, a sports marketing agency, agrees that "Sociologically, he is quite the embodiment of the American melting pot. We've never seen a combination of all of his qualities in an athlete ever. . . . He transcends the boundaries of his game." Matlins is referring here both to the barriers the young athlete had already surmounted in his record-breaking play and to the transcendent possibilities that his very presence brings to the process of breaking down the legacy of American ethnoracial categories.[2]

During an interview I had with a representative from the Sebastian line of hair-care products, she pulled out a photo of the high-fashion model the company was using in its latest advertising campaign, a face that connoted a melange of indeterminate ethnic features, and proceeded to explain that "She's a mix of Yugoslavian and, I think, Asian. I just got back from a ten-day sales workshop in California, where Sebastian is based, and part of our training covered this stuff. You know, it isn't a black and white world anymore—and Sebastian wants to be more responsive to the multiethnic range of its customers."

As she boasted of Sebastian's cutting-edge approach and its environment-friendly formulas, she brought out another ad highlighting their most innovative ingredient, a green tea from Japan, "a country," she further clarified, "where they have the highest smoking but lowest cancer rates due to the restorative effect of this tea." What was noteworthy about her account was not that she championed the purported multiethnic consciousness of the hair-styling brand she represented but that she herself, a woman born and raised in a provincial New England town with no more than a high school education, was able to express ideas about global beauty and health standards, about environmental issues, and about the shifting demographics of a multiethnic world because of her employer's training program.[3]

Awareness of the demographic changes and the dynamics of multiracial communities has led some manufacturers to include pitches for racial harmony as part of their advertising strategies. Clothing companies such as Cherokee, Benetton, and Esprit started the trend. The Cherokee casual clothing label took a subtle approach by depicting two women with contrasting looks and delighted expressions on their faces, arms around each other and the lead line: "I think there's a pretty simple reason Jackie and I are so comfortable with each other. We see the world as more than just black and white." Underneath the photo is the Cherokee logo with its picture of an American Indian woman in the "O" of its name and the phrase "Make yourself comfortable."

Cross Colours, based in the south central district of Los Angeles and claiming that its merchandise is made "by true brothers from the hood," has gone further to structure its entire brand around these issues. Its logo reads: Cross Colours: Clothing Without Prejudice. Each item is tagged with a statement of the company's philosophy. Its representatives explain that its enterprise is a "microcosm of designers and artists adding to the collection their individual ethnic flair," and that its people "stand in unity as an internationally successful and ethnically diverse company, and more importantly to send our message throughout the world via our clothes." Cross Colours also lets its customers know that it donates a portion of its profits to fighting gang violence and to helping victims of domestic violence.

But it is not just clothing manufacturers who use this strategy anymore. Images of harmonious racial dynamics appear in a range of products from the acne medication Clearasil, produced by Procter & Gamble, to Mercedes-Benz and MasterCard. In 1996, when the home goods retailer Ikea ran an ad showing an interracial couple shopping in their store for some new furniture, it garnered an enthusiastic response from consumers and received a four-star rating from

Advertising Age's reviewer. A series of commercials for television, developed by Saturn features Hispanic and African-American salespeople; the underlying message emphasizes the company's inclusive, nondiscriminatory worldview. Flashbacks of his boyhood in a middle-class family, shopping with his father for a car, and the shock of being unwelcome as consumers make up the story line that the African-American salesman recounts. His past is contrasted with the contemporary scene in a Saturn dealership, bustling with customers from diverse backgrounds. The ad implies that no matter what one's racial or ethnic ancestry, prospective Saturn shoppers will receive equal, courteous treatment.

Even more direct was the 1993 Timberland campaign, a series of print ads depicting a signature Timberland boot with headlines such as GIVE RACISM THE BOOT and THIS BOOT PERFORMS BEST WHEN MARCHING AGAINST HATRED. Company executive Jeffrey Swartz maintained that "This is not about selling boots. It's about making a strong statement," but such claims are moot since strong antiracist statements and strong sales go hand in hand among Timberland's customer base, especially its younger segment. Research conducted in 1993 by the New York firm of BKG Youth, Inc., for Eastman Kodak Co. showed that only 15 percent of the teenagers surveyed said they would never want to date a person of another race. Moreover, a third of the respondents in the study had themselves been the victims of racial discrimination. Marian Salzman, the president of BKG, concluded that "The only environmental issues that sell will be urban environmental issues."[4]

Some of the rhetoric, however, borders on the grandiose, as when Sylvie Chantecaille, senior executive of creative marketing for Prescriptives cosmetics, melded contemporary interest in global beauty standards with notions of unity through multicultural marketing. In promoting their All Skins line, Chantecaille declared: "America is the first country to have a real chance to be multiracial and embrace it. In a world of ethnic wars, this approach to beauty is one way to celebrate our myriad differences." Similarly, in 1992 *Allure* magazine ran an article titled "Interracial Beauty," reporting on a study of racial attitudes. The article began with the line: "Despite increasing racial tensions in recent years, Florida investigators have found that blacks and whites agree on what constitutes good looks." In their survey of one hundred young people, half of whom were African American and half Caucasian, they asked the respondents to look at photographs of people of both races and rank them on their attractiveness. When the results showed no differences based on race, one of the researchers, a psychologist, concluded: "that with the increasing presence of minority role models in the media, popular culture now maintains a broader standard of beauty."

The appeal here is to a global consciousness, the belief that multicultural style—wearing kurtas with T-shirts or hennaed hands with combat boots—can lead to world harmony. Cross Colours states on their labels that "Ultimately, we are all human, and there is a place for everyone in our world. For those of you who seek a peaceful, healthy earth, we hope that as you wear our clothing, you will remember our message." Fashion designer Corinne Cobson takes a slightly different approach, equating multicultural chic with personal liberation. She enthusiastically proclaims: "You can mix Jamaican dreadlocks with Yugoslavian shawls or show Zulu jewelry complementing a Bolivian jacket. . . . Today, women have so many cultural references, so much freedom."[5]

Advertising is not the only aspect of commercialism to attempt to address issues of multiracial harmony. Erlich Transcultural Consultants (ETC), an ethnic marketing and consumer research firm, has a Cultural Competency and Organization Development division that works with the staffs of businesses and retail outlets to enhance their abilities to relate to a diverse range of customers. One of its clients was a large mall complex in southern California, where ETC conducted focus groups among African Americans, Latinos, Vietnamese, Filipinos, teens, mall employees, and community leaders. Its intervention resulted in the redesign of the mall space, on-going "cultural competency" training for employees, and a corresponding decrease in the incidence of negative intercultural episodes. Thus, the marketplace of the mall becomes the public site that fosters greater cross-cultural understanding and shopping, the vehicle for increased tolerance.

Sometimes, as in the case of the Sebastian brand, companies will combine environmental awareness with recognition of ethnic diversity in their marketing pitches. The Body Shop, a British-based enterprise, has put itself at the forefront of efforts to save the environment and native cultures by trading with indigenous peoples for ingredients that are then added into their cosmetic formulas. In 1992 the company unveiled a "Trade Not Aid" venture with the Santa Ana Pueblo Indians in New Mexico, purchasing blue corn for use in seven new skin-care products. It then launched the Blue Corn Range collection in its stores in the United States to coincide with Thanksgiving, promoting the line as a celebration of the country's ancestral cultures. Yet another cosmetics brand that features natural ingredients carries the slogan "one touch of nature makes the whole world kin."[6]

After the 1990 Census reports were published, beauty industry experts began to realize the potential for strengthening their faltering overall sales by targeting people of color. The findings showed, for example, that African-American women were better educated and more affluent, and their average age was younger, than ever before. Furthermore, this sector was growing at twice the rate of its white counterpart. Cosmetics companies had their eyes on the buying power of the Asian-American population as well. According to one editor at *Face*, a magazine for Asian women, "Purchases by Asians account for up to 50 percent of the sales of premium cosmetics lines in California."[7]

By 1991 new hair and skin care product lines were being launched, extended, and reformulated by mainstream cosmetics firms to accommodate every possible skin tone, with names like Maybelline's Shades of You, Prescriptives All Skins, Revlon's Fleshtones and ColorStyle, and Clinique's Stay True. Other companies have simply added new colors, from Golden Caramel to Ranch Mink, to broaden the spectrum of existing merchandise. The trend has moved beyond foundation makeup to include lipstick and eye color. Revlon's Color-

Style was designed to carry place names as well, such as West Indies Wine lipstick and Brazil Nut liquid makeup, to emphasize the varied cultural roots of the nonwhite diaspora. In 1992 Pavion Cosmetics, Ltd., the manufacturers of the Wet 'n' Wild and Black Radiance beauty lines, introduced Solo Para Ti (Only for You) for Hispanic women. Zhen Cosmetics, a smaller independent enterprise specializing in makeup for Asian skin tones, has invented a wholly different tapestry of shade names: moonbeam, bamboo, butter cream, candlelight, acorn, and almond beige. In an amusing twist, the search for just the right descriptive word to perfectly evoke an intended hue led Revlon to christen one of its newest colors Schmutz, the Yiddish word for dirt!

Multitoned marketing is so elaborate that Estée Lauder's Prescriptives All Skins brand offers no fewer than 115 different foundation shades. Launched in 1991 in a barrage of media fanfare, its initial advertising campaign drew some four thousand new customers of color a month. But this was not the first time that Estée Lauder tried to target darker-skinned customers. In the 1970s it developed a line called Tawny Bronze, but sales were so disappointing that the company discontinued it within two years. The timing was just not right, but twenty years later, not only has its All Skins collection been bringing in growing numbers of new black customers but its overall foundation makeup sales were up by 50 percent after less than a year on the market.

Not to be outdone, Cover Girl cosmetics began running ads boasting its 147 custom-made foundations. Then Maybelline took it a step further by introducing a cosmetics line, Shades of You, that instead of just adding more and more hues to the foundation mix, used a new formula altogether, one that the company claimed would wear much better on darker-skinned women because it contained less of the titanium dioxide chemical used in regular foundation makeup, a component that supposedly makes darker skin tones look ashy. This "scientific" approach caught on with other companies that for every new color remedy seemed to manufacture a skin problem to match it. In *Self* magazine's regular column on "Global

Beauty" the new color formulations were said to work "by reducing talc, which produces chalkiness on olive or velvety black skin (and frostiness on paler women), and by coating the pigments with amino acids, allowing color to blend better." Now, not only did black women have to worry about ashiness, but no matter what one's skin shade, there was chalkiness and frostiness lurking about.[8] Marketing analysts in the lucrative cosmetics industry take literally the phrase that the complexion of America is changing.

At the same time as they were developing new colors and products to reach a broader, multicultural audience, the major cosmetics corporations for the first time began to hire black models as their spokeswomen. In 1992 Revlon brought Veronica Webb in to join supermodels Cindy Crawford and Claudia Schiffer, and that same year Cover Girl, who for years had used blond-haired and blue-eyed Christie Brinkley, signed Lana Ogilvie to an exclusive contract; both companies now claim that they were the very first to hire a high-visibility African-American fashion model. As one fashion industry expert pronounced in 1994, "Issues and ethnics aside, using models of color in print is now just good business. In the changing times of America and the world, ethnicity in all its incarnations is now the norm. Advertisements using black models are at an all-time high, especially for cosmetics and beauty products."[9]

But despite the addition of African-American bodies in the business of beauty and high-fashion marketing, nothing is actually black and white anymore. Neither the classic blue-eyed blonde nor the African queen are gracing the covers of fashion magazines. Instead, the idealized beauty standard is somewhere in between, a melange of off-white features and khaki tones in a two-way process in which the black-female ideal lightened up from the 1970s Afrocentric period at the same time that the archetypical white woman was darkening, if only slightly, to a more mestizo presentation. Once black supermodels were on board, fashion magazines and cosmetic companies quickly began featuring Latina, Eurasian, and other mixed-race faces.

In 1992 the Ford agency's Supermodel of the Year was Torrey

Terrell, described as a mixture of black, white, and Native American. Daisy Fuentes, a former MTV host of Cuban ancestry, and Halle Berry, a biracial actress, soon joined Veronica Webb, Claudia Schiffer, and Cindy Crawford as Revlon spokeswomen, while Prescriptives' All Skins hired Puerto Rican model Julia Ortiz, who then appeared in advertisements for Oil of Olay. In 1997 after thirty-five years of holding a "Fresh Face" competition for girls from the United States and Canada between the ages of thirteen and eighteen, Cover Girl cosmetics in conjunction with *YM* (Young and Modern) magazine opened up the contestant pool to young women from Puerto Rico. The first year they competed, out of eleven thousand candidates, the overall "Fresh Face" winner was, indeed, a teenager from Puerto Rico, Anna Marie Kortright Martinez. She then became the first Puerto Rican model to appear in magazine advertisements for the Cover Girl line. Similarly, Avon held a Latina Model contest in which the winner appeared on four of the company's sales brochures. Yet in an ethnic marketing twist, the company's strategy for commercials for television was to feature Whoopi Goldberg's well-known voice but not her face. The visible role went to a lighter-skinned, mixed-race figure, in effect both embracing and e-racing Goldberg's blackness.[10]

Thus, the real trend is toward such a degree of ethnic and racial homogenization that racial distinctiveness actually disappears. The cover of *Time* magazine's 1993 special issue on "The New Face of America" marked a turning point when it displayed an imaginary computer-generated young woman (morphed from fourteen different racial-ethnic models) as a way to call attention vividly to the dramatic effect that increasing rates of marriage and reproduction across ethnoracial lines were having on the look of Americans. The complex formula used to create this cybergenetic figure, referred to as "the new Eve," was a combination of 15 percent Anglo-Saxon, 17.5 percent Middle Eastern, 17.5 percent African, 7.5 percent Asian, 35 percent southern European, and 7.5 percent Hispanic, and the result was a visage of modulated features, cropped hair, and muted colors that connoted no particular race, culture, or ethnicity.[11] Similarly, by 1996 General Mills had debuted a multiracial, multiethnic Betty Crocker with an equally nondescript countenance that so resembled the *Time* model, she could easily have passed for her older sister. The updated homemaker was advertised as a blend of seventy-five different women, to signify the seventy-fifth anniversary of the Betty Crocker label, and its anniversary slogan read: "There's a little bit of Betty in all of us." This type of marketing campaign clearly seeks to reach the widest possible audience, and in contemporary society, that means a rainbow coalition of consumers.

When Wrigley's Doublemint Gum doubles your pleasure in the 1990s, the twins frolicking across your TV screen are black, Asian, and mestizo Latino sets. To emphasize its new outlook, the commercial starts off in black and white showing the classic Doublemint white girls of yore before switching to its updated full-color version. The author of a coffee table book on home furnishings titled *Ethnic Style: From Mexico to the Mediterranean* defines ethnic style as "a way of life that celebrates the moment, making much of nothing. . . . Ethnic is a look based on the simplest of objects and materials."[12] In the end, ironically, the message is that ethnic is actually a universal phenomenon, one without borders.

When *People Magazine* put out its "50 Most Beautiful People" issue in 1998, ideals of multiracial beauty figured prominently in its selections and the accompanying copy. Of Ann Curry, NBC morning news anchor, it was written, "Daughter of a U.S. Navy officer and Japanese Mom, Curry, 41, says she rarely felt pretty: 'If you're of mixed race in this country, it's hard to embrace the idea of being beautiful.' Now she sees things differently. 'What I love about how I look today,' she says, 'is that so many people from all different races think I'm part of their group.' " Interestingly, given that her racial ancestry is the whole point of the narrative, Curry's father's racial background is never specified; he is simply a U.S. Navy officer. Thus, ambiguity about her origins still remains, although it is likely that her father is white since, typically, race is used only as a designator for those who are nonwhite; when left unqualified, an assumed whiteness is implied.

SPECIAL ISSUE

TIME

Take a good look at this woman. She was created by a computer from a mix of several races. What you see is a remarkable preview of . . .

THE NEW FACE OF AMERICA

How Immigrants Are Shaping the World's
First Multicultural Society

Betty Crocker 75th Anniversary Portrait

The notion of mixed-race as exotic still has its hold, as can be seen in the rationale for choosing Malia Jones, "Surfer and Model," as one of the beautiful people. Beneath a photograph that places Jones in, perhaps, the most seductive of the issue's fifty poses, it is said: "That body, along with her sultry lips and golden brown eyes brought modeling agents paddling at her Oahu door in 1996—despite the fact that she's only 5'5" Jones owes her exotic looks to her mother, Vi, a marathoner with a Hawaiian-Filipino-Spanish background, and her father, John, a dentist of German-English descent. "I'm a lot lighter than my mom but darker than my dad," Jones says.[13]

Evidence of how recent is the turn to an idealized mestizo standard of beauty can be seen in the history of the Mattel Corporation's development of black Barbie-like dolls. Although Barbie comes in a rainbow palette of ethnic varieties today and the doll is more popular than ever with young consumers, before the introduction of black dolls named Barbie in 1980, the company had tried out black renditions as early as 1967. In that year, they came up with a clone named Colored Francie, who was supposed to be Barbie's younger cousin and who was modeled after another imagined relative, the white Francie Fairchild, who had been a big commercial success when introduced the year before. Colored Francie, however, bombed completely. The name, of course, a throwback to an earlier era, demonstrates that the rhetoric of the black pride movement had not yet reached the corporate sector.

But it was not just her appellation that doomed her. What sealed her demise was the implication, since she was Barbie's cousin, that miscegenation must have taken place in the family. This offended both blacks and whites. In the climate of the late 1960s, white consumers, still reeling from the possibilities of racial integration that the Civil Rights movement had raised, saw Colored Francie as a threat, and by this time many blacks had adopted a Black Power consciousness and were unhappy, not only with Francie's antiquated name and its racist overtones but with her too-straight hair and whitewashed looks.[14] There are several Barbie variations on the market today that look as if they have had a Mestizo Makeover, with racially ambiguous features and a range of tannish skin tones, attributes that are much more acceptable to present audiences, both black and white. But, as of this writing, and even with a burgeoning mixed-race population in this country, there are no consciously designed biracial Barbies to be found on the toy store shelves.

The vision of one amalgamated race, a race of interchangeable consumer parts, bland and nonthreatening, with no protruding features, big hair, or deep skintones to distinguish it works very well with an increasingly globalized economy. More insidious is the implication that not only are racial or ethnic identities simply commodities to be bought and sold but that they can be painted on during the morning toilette and rinsed away at will, that in choosing an ethnicity, one can actually find the right fashion formula to cover one's face or the living room floor to metamorphose into some imagined notion of what that ethnicity is supposed to look like. In commenting on the versatility of a new cosmetics line, a columnist for *Self* magazine spoke of how "women of every ethnic *persuasion*" could wear it [italics mine].[15] In this sense, ethnicity is an inclination, a set of beliefs about oneself that presumably could change at any time, perhaps by simply applying a new shade of makeup. Furthermore, the idea that race and ethnicity are simply matters of style and motif obscures the very real economic and social inequalities based on racial identity that still persist in American society.

The extent of cultural hybridity, of ethnic crossovers, and cultural borrowings is increasingly reflected in the popular media. An insert in a 1998 *Newsweek* article on the American-born Muslim community was called "Serving All by Selling Islam"; it showed an I Love Allah coffee mug (with a heart to signify love), toothpaste made with halal ingredients, a compass that tells you in what direction to pray (toward Mecca), interactive high-tech teachings of the Koran, and a "Praise Allah" bumper sticker. What was remarkable, however, was that this list was introduced with the sentence: "As the United States' Muslim community grows, so does the availability of halal products and pro-Islam *tchotchkes*." That the Yiddish term *tchotchkes* (or knickknacks) has made it untranslated into mainstream American English copy is surprising enough, but to use the expression to describe pro-Islamic merchandise simply begs for an "only in America" shrug.[16]

Another striking example of multicultural mutation can be found in the Gilbert and Sullivan Yiddish Light Opera Company of Long Island. The group is composed of devotees of both Gilbert and Sullivan and Yiddish and has been performing for twenty years. In one of their recent shows, the comic operetta "Der Yiddisher Mikado," the dialogue was in English, the lyrics in Yiddish, the humor was British, and the costumes, Japanese.[17] Yiddish seems particularly conducive to ethnic blending, even in its literal sense, as in a print ad for Jewish audiences created by Tetley USA Inc. with the slogan "Think Yiddish. Drink British." to promote their British Blend Tea bags.

The multiethnic mix works in surprising and unpredictable ways. Although salsa has, indeed, displaced ketchup as America's favorite condiment, at the H. J. Heinz Co., the downturn of its most famous product has not been critical. The company grew spectacularly in the 1990s under an Irish-born CEO, Anthony J. F. O'Reilly, who credits his success at Heinz to his Irish heritage. "When you come from a little country like Ireland, you have something to prove," he told the *Boston Irish Reporter* in 1996.[18] Of course, consumption of Mexican culture within the United States is not limited solely to the Mexican-American population or to the purchase of Mexican food products. Mainstream appropriation of Mexican motifs in fashion, entertainment, architecture, southwestern decor, and linguistic colloquialisms are all widespread.

The increasingly multiethnic makeup of the American population has not escaped the attention of the small business sector either. Increasing rates of intermarriage have sparked a whole new cottage industry in the design and distribution of consumer items, including children's books, greeting cards, innovative holiday gifts, and special multiethnic travel packages. For example, the 1996 holiday season saw a record number of interfaith greeting cards being

purchased. Stores that do carry these specialty items report very brisk sales; however, their popularity has sparked a backlash among some religious leaders. Conservative Rabbi Jerome Epstein protests, "These things make me furious . . . [the] attempt to bridge over differences and blend where there is no authenticity in blending. . . . People distort both relations when they try to blend them."[19]

Despite such faultfinding, more and more instances of what can be called "blended ethnicity," the amalgamation of two or more ethnic backgrounds, are showing up in the marketplace. There's Ginsberg's Pub located on a busy corner near San Francisco's Fisherman's Wharf, whose large green-painted storefront sign advertises its sixty varieties of imported beers on tap and prominently features its Irish-Yiddish coffee for sale or its Manischewitz kosher for Passover pizza, flagged by both a seder plate and a Chef Boyardee-like figure on the eye-catching box design. Following the trend of blended ethnic products, a California Chinese/Jewish couple introduced their new kosher salad dressing with the phrase "Soy Vey!" on the label.

Apparently there is a sizable enough community of Irish-Mexicans in San Diego for a chain of restaurants known as Carlos Murphy to thrive. The Hormel Foods Corporation, producers of the Chi-Chi's brand of Mexican food, also seems to have picked up on this particular interethnic mix, running ads during March for its green salsa variety, which carry the slogan "Mucho Irish." The Irish are combined again, this time with Asians, in an *Elle* magazine spread pitching cosmetics for a multiracial market. It leads off with: "Beyond Basic Black: Now there is a makeup designed for the needs not only of African Americans, but Asians, Latinas . . . even Irish-Asians." In Manhattan, diners can choose from an array of Cuban Chinese restaurants, and in Brookline, Massachusetts, there is Shalom Hunan, which serves kosher Chinese fare. With inventions on the market, such as El Rancho's Jalapeño Rugelach (The Ultimate Jewish-Mexican Dessert), there can be no doubt that multiethnicity sells.

In a section of Palisades Park, New Jersey, where there are many Korean-American residents, passersby will notice a new trend in the

shop windows—Spanish signs alongside the Korean ones. Korean merchants have recognized that there is a burgeoning Hispanic population moving into the area, and they are making efforts to capture its business. They send out bilingual advertising circulars and carry Spanish produce alongside their large selections of Korean and Asian foods. As one wholesaler commented,

> Even if they don't write the Spanish correctly, it's there. Not in English but Korean translated into Spanish. The Koreans are aware of their Spanish consumer base but the Americans are not. . . . We carry a Spanish tea that is popular in Korea and one of our accounts is a Korean firm in the Bronx that has been distributing this Spanish tea to Korean stores.

In another case of Korean-Hispanic crossover, a study of consumer product use, conducted for a Korean-based cosmetics manufacturer, resulted in plans for the company to market their products to the U.S. Latino market.

A striking example of blended ethnicity is illustrated by one of the workshop offerings at a recent *Mame-Loshn* Yiddish culture retreat in Connecticut, sponsored by the Workman's Circle. Titled "Tsi Kenstu Shiatsu?" it promised "A hands-on workshop, with instruction in Yiddish by our certified masseur . . . in the tactile arts of Swedish massage, shiatsu, trigger point, and reflexology," with instructions to "bring your own oils (towels too)." Although many of the other conference workshops were offered in both English and Yiddish, this Judeo-Japanese-Swedish experience was available in Yiddish only.

Offspring of parents with different ethnic backgrounds are particularly receptive to the possibilities of this more occasional ethnicity, focusing on the wealth and multiplicity of cultural resources on which they can draw. When asked to describe the influences on her writing, the novelist Katherine Vaz, daughter of an Azorean-immigrant father and an Irish-American mother, credited both heritages. "The joke is that I get great material from my father's side of the family and the love of being a storyteller from my mother's. The stories that fascinated me the most were the ones that came to me from my Azorean relatives. They seemed to have a consciousness that is very beautiful."[20]

Then there is the Loyal League of Yiddish Sons of Erin, the world's only Jewish-Irish fraternal organization. It was founded in 1962 by Michael Mann of Long Island, a Jew who had emigrated from his native Ireland to Chicago in the 1930s. Since the numbers of Irish-born Jews are so small in Ireland itself, the total in this American association is nominal, less than one hundred nationwide. Yet it is significant that they organized themselves not in Ireland but in the United States, where the climate so warms to multicultural possibilities. When the members, many of whom had neighborhood and congregational ties back in Ireland, gather together they spend much of their time reminiscing. At their annual picnic, both the *hora* and the Irish jig are danced, and when one of the children of a League member married, the men in attendance wore green yarmulkes (skullcaps) and the room was decorated with an Irish flag that had a Jewish star designed on it. Although it was organized primarily as a social group, the analogy between Ireland and Israel is consciously drawn by these Yiddish Sons of Erin. Mann explains that, "The situation of the Irish people is somewhat similar to that of the Jewish people in that both have experienced subjugation by foreign powers, and both have a desire to be totally free." Although the group was at first composed of members of Jewish families who were raised in Ireland and their descendants, with the increase in Irish-Jewish intermarriage in the United States, the Yiddish Sons of Erin could see considerable growth in the future.[21]

Because of the dramatic alterations in the racial–ethnic makeup of the United States in the last decade, and the proliferation of multicultural marketing firms attempting to tap into the commercial trends that such demographic shifts present, industry experts are awaiting the 2000 Census with much anticipation. Though the findings will be much more complicated to analyze than earlier reports, those who track the country's mixed-race populations will be especially eager to sort through them. Not only will this be the first decennial census to offer the option of selecting more than one race to identify oneself, the form also expands the choices to fifteen different categories including white, African American, American Indian or Alaskan Native, Asian Indian, Chinese, Filipino, Japanese, Korean, Vietnamese, other Asians, Native Hawaiian, Guamanian or Chamorro, Samoan, other Pacific Islander, and other race. The potential for such a myriad of racial combinations is dizzying to ponder and will certainly challenge tabulators, but ultimately the statistics should reflect a far more accurate picture of the actual contours of multicultural America at the start of the new millennium.

Conclusion

In an image Andy Warhol might have appreciated, Korean immigrant Mary Paik Lee recalls her first exposure to American consumer culture as a schoolgirl in California in 1916, a vivid moment in her recollections of Americanization:

> There was a wood stove in the middle of the schoolroom. The teacher built a fire at noon and heated something in a small pot which smelled so good I asked her what it was. She said it was a can of Campbell's soup that she had bought at the store. That was my first introduction to Campbell's soups. I told Mother about the soup, and she bought one can at the store. She said it was good but that we couldn't afford to buy enough for the whole family.[1]

More than seventy-five years later, in 1994, Campbell's introduced its latest line of soups, all ethnic-based varieties, including a spicy blend of rice, beans, corn, and vegetables called Fiesta, the first Hispanic-style soup to get national distribution from the all-American Campbell's. While the company has yet to develop a Korean-flavored selection, it is likely that a direct reversal of Mary Paik's experience of identity, consumption, ethnicity, and Campbell's soup will not be long in coming.

An attempt to conjoin the study of modern consumerism with that of ethnic identity involves charting new territory. While the writing on ethnicity is vast, serious work related to the nature of consumption is still in its early stages and usually found on the periphery of sociocultural inquiry. This is not to say that research linking economic self-interest with cultural dynamics does not exist. On the contrary, the field of ethnic enterprise boasts a well-developed literature and represents, perhaps, the most explicit approach to this interrelationship by exploring how entrepreneurship, particularly the history of immigrant business ventures, is situated within the ethnic economy. Still, with a few outstanding exceptions, the role of immigrant as consumer has been overlooked.[2] But there has been a budding interest in exploring the dimensions of ethnic-based businesses that are attempting to expand beyond the immigrant enclave to sell to a wider market; an example is Levy's rye bread, whose broader advertising appeal is evident in their slogan: "You don't have to be Jewish to love Levy's." My idea in this book has been to look at the appropriation of ethnicity by businesses, whether ethnic-based or not, as a strategy to sell to wider markets in the United States. Throughout, I have been as interested in the role of ethnic marketing in more localized enterprises as at the corporate level and in the nonprofit as well as for-profit sectors of the economy.

Even the term "identity" is of relatively recent usage in the social sciences, as Philip Gleason reminded us in a 1983 *Journal of American History* essay, especially given how essential it has become to scholarship dealing with ethnicity or, for that matter, the subject of immigration. Only in the 1950s did we begin to see the concept coming into significant use in such pivotal works as Will Herberg's *Protestant, Catholic and Jew* (1955) or C. Vann Woodward's 1958 essay "The Search for Southern Identity." Of course, it was social psychologist Erik Erikson who really put "identity" on the map in the early 1960s, and America's love affair with questions of identity has been going strong ever since. Thus, the evolution of the concept of identity so intrinsic to much of the thinking in this field turns out to be an even more recent component of analysis than the category of "ethnicity." The term "ethnicity" itself was not used until the early 1940s beginning with W. Lloyd Warner and Paul Lunt's community studies of Newburyport, Massachusetts, in their Yankee City series. Trying to grapple with the relationship among all three of these relatively recent interpretive categories—identity, ethnicity, and consumption—is at once a perplexing and exhilarating project. Confounding because the traditions are not long, the models not readily apparent, and the historiography thin but exciting for precisely the same reasons, since such exploratory cross-disciplinary studies invite a sense of freedom and inventiveness.[3]

While it may no longer be fashionable for historians to engage in efforts to define the national character, as was the goal of much American Studies scholarship in the years following World War II, the notion of formulating an American identity has persisted from the early 1950s to the present, when the concept of American identity is being dissected, deconstructed, and finely splintered or redefined, reinvented, and ultimately stretched to the furthest edges of inclusivity.

Although the focus of this volume has been on commercialized expressions of ethnic identity, the way the dynamics of commerce and culture play themselves out can actually tell us quite a bit about the construction of modern identities more generally. If modernization is seen as an enormous movement from destiny to choice, the change from "being" to "becoming" ethnic perfectly exemplifies this shift. It signifies a monumental reorientation in how identity is constructed and expressed. In traditional societies, ethnicity had an ascriptive status in which cultural affinities were an imperative, but with the evolution of modernity, what characterizes ethnicity is its optionality and malleability. Individuals can decide for themselves not only the degree to which they identify with their cultural group but whether they want to identify at all. Most do. They pick and choose the when and how of ethnic expression, creating highly individualized and multidimensional variations of cultural formations. We also live in a time and a cultural milieu that magnifies ethnicity and ancestry as markers of identity. Thus, any identity is better than none. This type of ethnicity is so flexible and sporadic that it is possible to switch from one cultural form to another and then back again with ease. Not only does this mean ethnicity by choice but it also means that people's ethnic identities are often only one part of a configuration of several identity choices available to them.

Just as the marketplace develops highly customized promotions to win ethnic consumers, so do individuals invent tailor-made identities in modern societies. Nothing epitomized the extent to which modern identities are constructed like so many Lego pieces as what happened at my very first interview in conjunction with the Yiddish revival component of my research. I had arranged to meet with the head of the New York Workmen's Circle, the long-standing Jewish organization whose mission has been to foster Yiddish culture and education. One of its most successful recent programs is the annual *Mame-Loshn* retreat to celebrate Yiddish identity. I was excited that I would be starting off on this part of my study at what felt like the source, interviewing a leader of the Jewish community in the heart of New York City, the historical home to the largest influx of Yiddish-speaking Ashkenazic Jews in America. Yet the first words out of my respondent's mouth, before I had posed a single question or even begun the usual segue into interview mode, took me completely by surprise and beautifully illustrated the extent to which ethnic affiliation has become not only a matter of choice but even one of serendipity. He looked right at me and announced, "I am not Jewish." In an interview sprinkled with Yiddish phrases and expressions, he explained that he was of Irish descent, fourth generation, that he just loved the Yiddish language, thought it should continue, liked the people he met through it (his girl friend was from eastern Europe and grew up speaking Yiddish), and was deeply committed to keeping it alive.

Of course, this is an extreme case of choosing ethnicity, but most critics assume that if there is any choice involved at all, the identification is automatically less authentic, and if you then factor in any kind of commercial component, it becomes even more tainted. Consumerism thus becomes defined as a threat to cultural formation and as antithetical to the values of the ethnic revival. Yet in interview after interview, no matter if my subjects were Irish, Jewish, or Mexican, or even Irish-Jewish-Mexican, the meaning that participation in their respective movements for ethnic renewal had brought to their lives was palpable and simply could not be ignored. Their ethnicity had become a focal point and a central organizing structure in their daily lives. Moreover, the factor of choice becomes crucial because, in many ways, that is precisely what defined them. This is ethnicity by acquisition, and it is the deliberate or conscious choice involved in participation, affiliation, and consumption that remains so full of meaning-making for contemporary ethnics.

Such an identification cannot be too broadly construed, however. Richard Alba has argued that the distinctions among various European-based cultures have so waned and intermarriage among white ethnics is so widespread that a new pan-ethnic identity, what he terms "European American," has been taking shape among third- and fourth-generation descendants of the immigrants who arrived at the beginning of the twentieth century. Yet the European American self-identification has not taken hold among white ethnics. Modern ethnic identity may be convenience ethnicity, but it still needs to provide some sort of significant primordial reference for the expressive self. Europe is too nebulous a construct to serve as a mythical homeland. It lacks a symbolic matrix and the cultural particularity needed to satisfy the yearnings for a sense of belonging and a more distinctive ethnic identity.[4]

One must point out that the notion of voluntary or optional ethnicity has been relevant primarily to hyphenated Euro-American groups. Whites simply have had more options to identify with one group or another, whether as Polish, Swedish, or Greek, or to choose to ignore their ethnic heritage altogether, and the literature reflects this cleavage in analysis based on race. Voluntary ethnicity is discussed only in terms of those of European descent. Historically, nonwhites, including African Americans, Asians, Hispanics, and Native Americans, have been much more bound to their particular ethnoracial group, while the social and political liabilities of such identities have been much greater. Racial difference, even when ambiguous, is still more readily identifiable and less easily a matter of choice in contemporary America. Also, historically, the marketplace has exacerbated racial divisions, but there is evidence that these distinctions are beginning to wane in importance. It becomes more and more plausible to speak of a shift to an increasingly optional ethnicity among, for example, Chinese- or Mexican-Americans in the same way that Italian- and Irish-Americans can be selective. In actual practice, the theoretical underpinnings that explain the role of ethnicity in the lives of whites as distinct from those of nonwhites turn out to be faulty. As the nation evolves into an increasingly mestizo sociocultural entity, the separate European and non-European trajectories of identity construction edge toward collapse. In one huge arena of practice, the marketplace, such differences ultimately become irrelevant. The market is the great leveler. From kente cloth to claddagh rings, the same appeals to invented and voluntary ethnic identities are being made; the same emotional purse strings are being tugged.

Whereas participation in the emergent mass consumer culture of the early part of the century most often functioned as an effective mode of adaptation to mainstream America for new-immigrant arrivals, descendants of those same immigrants today often seek out consumer goods for the opposite purpose of accentuating their cultural distinctiveness. Conversely, more recent newcomers, like the earlier wave, discover that their ability to partake of the abundance of America and to exercise consumer choice can be the most accessible routes to rapid Americanization. Unlike their predecessors, however, they are much more likely to have already been exposed to American consumer products in their native countries, either directly or via the global media, since the marketing of American merchandise has become increasingly internationalized.

After reading a report in the *New York Times* cleverly titled "The Shmeering of America," about the "spread" of the bagel's popularity, the commentator Leonard Fein suddenly realized that the chronic fear among American Jewish leaders that Jewishness is rapidly disappearing under the weight of assimilation was completely ill-founded:

> At long last, I have figured it out. No, there is no need for us to be troubled by assimilation, that traditional terror of American Jewish life. Not, mind you, that there isn't assimilation. Very much of it. But it works in exactly the opposite direction from what we've been led to believe. It is not the Jews who are assimilating into America; it is America that is assimilating into the Jews.[5]

Indeed, today, even Dunkin' Donuts uses Yiddishisms to urge customers to try out its new bagels, with billboards that say "It's Worth the Schlep." But it is not just Jewish culture that is becoming mainstream. Whether it is the Americanization of bagels or salsa, notions of dominant versus ethnic subcultures are blurring and cultural hybridity prevails. Meanwhile, previously ethnic-identified products and services have such crossover appeal that it becomes more and more difficult to separate the hyphenated parts.

At the same time, consumer patterns have come full circle. Many now shop, as a way not of integrating but rather of distinguishing themselves from the masses. Ethnic marketing highlights the specific nature of the goods and services being offered as a way to express a distinctive identity, to become more individualized and less lost in the bland mainstream of the generic middle-class customer. Meanwhile, the children, grandchildren, and great-grandchildren of the immigrant generation have realized that in order to move forward into the future, they cannot completely let go of the past. Shopping has become a tangible instrument of hyphenated Americanization that some may continue to dismiss as "designer" ethnicity. Nonetheless, and whether we like it or not, we are all deeply immersed in a commodity-driven, consumer culture that daily shapes who we are and how we define ourselves.

Appendix:
A Note on Terminology

By and large, social scientists have had difficulty agreeing on a precise definition of ethnicity. Indeed, it has been so thorny an issue that a 1974 survey of its usage found that the majority of those who wrote on the subject avoided defining it altogether.[1] In general, though, the sense in which the term "ethnicity" has been understood within the context of the ethnic revival incorporates the features of a perceived shared culture and real or putative common ancestry. "Ethnic" originally was employed as a substitute for the much older category of race, and it further gained popularity as an identity apart from that of social class. Since the beginning of its widespread use in public discourse and scholarly writing, the word "ethnic" has usually been meant to signify the descendants of European immigrants only. Those of non-European background fell under racial designations or were subsumed under the broader category of "minorities."

Outside of academia in the world of late-twentieth-century diversified marketing, the concept of ethnicity has had a different genesis. By and large, ethnicity and race have been conflated to represent the broadest spectrum of cultural groupings. The term "ethnicity," with its more benign connotations and associations, is used to refer to all nationalities, no matter what their racial composition. The customary umbrella term for targeting blacks, Hispanics, and now Asians is "minority marketing," but such a strategy is also known as "ethnic marketing." The minority market and the ethnic market have become interchangeable segments within the field, even though they often represent very different constituencies. For example, when Information Resources, Inc., a syndicated information and consulting company that has compiled massive amounts of data on the purchasing preferences of Hispanics and African Americans, presented its comparative findings, the reports referred to the differences between "Ethnic" with a capital "E" and "Anglo" consumers. In this case, the "Ethnic" label was used to give it a parallel structure to the Anglo category, and what it actually represented were all the non-Anglo shoppers, populations that are usually designated as *racial* minorities.

It should also be noted here that the term "Hispanic," meaning the Spanish-language peoples of the Americas, and including Mexicans, Cubans, Puerto Ricans, Dominicans, and other South and Central Americans, first came into widespread use in 1970 as an official catch-all term for the purposes of U.S. Census tallies. It was a category foisted upon those with Spanish-speaking backgrounds, not a self-identifying label, but over the last thirty years, more and more Spanish-speaking Americans have identified themselves as Hispanics, a label used interchangeably with "Latinos," though the latter term also includes those from Portuguese-speaking Brazil.

More and more, the meaning of "ethnicity" has its most broad-based referent in the world of the marketplace, replacing "race" or "minority" to include nonwhite groups. For instance, when marketing specialists at the Hallmark corporation distributed material to their sales force on the demographic transition, they reported that *"Ethnic populations* in the United States have grown dramatically [italics mine]. According to the 1990 Census, 12 percent of Americans are black, 9 percent Hispanic, 3 percent Asian, 1 percent Native American, and 4 percent other. These populations are expected to grow, further diversifying the tastes, preferences, and product selection in the United States." This is a clear example of how the "ethnic" category has shifted meaning from European-origin to non-European-origin groups. The conflation of all ethnic and racial minorities serves especially to make the African-American population normative, construed as simply another ethnic group. Although one can find rare incidences of African Americans being referred to as "ethnics" as early as the 1960s, the directors of ethnic marketing departments today almost always use this approach. Thus, typically "ethnic" marketing actually means targeting the three traditional "racial" minority groups—African Americans, Hispanics, and Asians, not white Euro-Americans at all. Nonetheless, plenty of contemporary marketing campaigns are still geared to white ethnics. It's just that they do not fall into the "ethnic" category as appropriated and defined by today's marketing experts.

In another twist of the ethnic marketing rhetoric, a leading consulting firm titles some of its conferences and research publications, "Marketing to a New America." In using the phrase "New America" they mean to refer to the increasingly variegated cultural diversity and whirlwind pace of demographic change that have especially characterized the United States in the 1990s, even though their primary target populations—African Americans, Hispanics, and Asians—are hardly uniformly "new" Americans. Not only do African Americans constitute a long-standing community in this country, but many sectors of the Hispanic population and even some Asian groups have been well established for generations and do not represent new consumer segments at all. Rather, what distinguishes these so-called new ethnic categories, long invisible to corporate America, is that they are being *newly discovered* by big business executives, particularly since the results of the 1990 U.S. Census tallies were splashed across media headlines.

Another way that companies signify the contemporary demographic metamorphosis and those groups that would be synonymous with the "New America" is to refer to African Americans, Hispanics, and Asians as the "new majority." This is another euphemistic term that typically replaces the phrases "nonwhite populations" or "minority groups." In the preface of one of the latest textbooks on the subject, titled *Advertising and Marketing to the New Majority*, the author includes the following proviso: "For the purpose of this text, markets are defined in terms of ethnic groups. Subgroups of the majority population such as Italians, Poles, Jews, Greeks, and others are not dealt with."[2] Indeed, by and large, the phenomenon of multicultural marketing in the corporate context, whether it is called marketing to a "New America" or to a "new majority," means targeting the big three nonwhite categories— African Americans, Hispanics, and Asians, although, of course, some Hispanics would not self-identify as nonwhite.

Finally, in some instances, the concepts of "inner city" and "ethnic" marketing are used interchangeably. For example, Crossover Creative Group, a segmented marketing agency based in San Francisco, advertises its services with the slogan "Get in Touch with Your Urban Multicultural Side." Although there are examples of this type of geographic and ethnic convergence in various neighborhoods across the urban landscape, for the most part, such enclaves are rarely so neatly aggregated or, with the increasingly multiethnic suburban sprawl, so centered at the core of the city. Often, the term "inner city" is used euphemistically to refer to the urban poor or to minorities and thus becomes easily, if inappropriately, linked to the "ethnic" label as well. Today, the terms "ethnic," "ethnics," or "ethnicity" within the marketplace have been diluted to carry the most inclusive meaning possible. Where the use of sociocultural categories are necessary to the discourse, they are invoked as a way of differentiating and individualizing human identity without connoting interethnic divisiveness or social inequities.

Notes

One: Longings and Belongings

1. David Hollinger, *Postethnic America: Beyond Multiculturalism* (New York: Basic Books, 1995): 3.

2. Interview with Yuri Radzievsky, July 9, 1996.

3. Gail Baker Woods, *Advertising and Marketing to the New Majority* (Belmont, Cal.: Wadsworth Publishing Co., 1995): ix.

4. Raj Mehta and Russell W. Belk, "Artifacts, Identity, and Transition: Favorite Possessions of Indians and Indian Immigrants to the United States," *Journal of Consumer Research* 17 (March 1991): 408.

5. Daniel Boorstin, *The Image: A Guide to Pseudo-Events in America* (New York: Atheneum, 1987): 4.

6. Leigh Eric Schmidt, *Consumer Rites: The Buying & Selling of American Holidays* (Princeton, N.J.: Princeton University Press, 1995): 58; on "the cult of the new" see especially William Leach's study of the development of the department store, *Land of Desire: Merchants, Power, and the Rise of a New American Culture* (New York: Pantheon Books, 1993): 4–5. in *Inside Prime Time* (New York: Pantheon Books, 1985), cultural critic Todd Gitlin coined the phrase "recombinant style" to describe this phenomenon, "which collects the old in new packages and hopes for a magical synthesis": 77–78.

7. Margaret Mead, "Ethnicity and Anthropology in America," in *Ethnic Identity: Cultural Continuities and Change*, eds. George DeVos and Lola Romanucci-Ross (Palo Alto, Cal.: Mayfield Publishing Co., 1975): 189.

8. Robert Wood, "Tourist Ethnicity: A Brief Itinerary," *Ethnic and Racial Studies* 21, no. 2 (1998): 230.

9. Sociologist Richard Alba has gone so far as to view ethnicity as a form of cultural capital arguing that ethnic symbols and references can be of use in the complex signaling by which individuals establish relationships to one another, especially in the business world. *Ethnic Identity: Transformation of White America* (New Haven, Conn.: Yale University Press, 1990): 133 & 161.

10. Alba, *Ethnic Identity*, 1990; Mary Waters, *Ethnic Options: Choosing Identities in America* (Berkeley and Los Angeles: University of California Press, 1990).

11. Alba, *Ethnic Identity*, 1990; Stanley Lieberson, "Unhyphenated Whites in the United States." *Ethnic and Racial Studies* 8, no. 1 (1985): 159–180; Tom W. Smith, "Ethnic Measurement and Identification," *Ethnicity* 7 (1980): 78–95.

12. Herbert Gans, "Symbolic Ethnicity: The Future of Ethnic Groups and Cultures in America," *Ethnic and Racial Studies* 2, no. 1 (1979): 1–20.

13. Clara Rodríguez, *Puerto Ricans in the United States* (Boulder, Colo.: Westview Press, 1991): 17; Anny Bakalian. *Armenian-Americans: From Being to Feeling Armenian* (New Brunswick, N.J.: Transaction Publishers, 1993): 7–8.

14. Donald Tricarico, "In a New Light: Italian-American Ethnicity in the Mainstream," in *The Ethnic Enigma: The Salience of Ethnicity for European-Origin Groups*, ed. Peter Kivisto (Philadelphia: The Balch Institute Press, 1989): 29.

15. Lawrence Fuchs, "What We Should Count and Why," *Social Science and Modern Society* 34, no. 6 (Sept./Oct. 1997): 26.

16. Warren Belasco, "Ethnic Fast Foods: The Corporate Melting Pot," *Food and Foodways* (1987): 9.

17. Historian Andrew Heinze refers to this phenomenon as the "stigma of consumption" in his study of Jewish identity and consumer culture at the turn of the century, *Adapting to Abundance: Jewish Immigrants, Mass Consumption and the Search for American Identity* (New York: Columbia University Press, 1990): 8

18. Marjorie Esman, "Tourism as Ethnic Preservation: The Cajuns of Louisiana," *Annals of Tourism Research*, 11 (1984): 451–467.

19. Sociologist Viviana Zelizer argues that a false contradiction exists within the U.S. economy pitting connectedness and differentiation against one another in "Multiple Markets: Multiple Cultures," in *Common Values, Social Diversity and Cultural Conflict*, eds. Neil Smelser and Jeffrey Alexander (Princeton, N.J.: Princeton University Press, 1999).

20. Jocelyn Linnekin, "Consuming Cultures: Tourism and the Commoditization of Cultural Identity in the Island Pacific," in *Tourism, Ethnicity and the State in Asian and Pacific Societies*, eds. Michel Picard and Robert E. Wood (Honolulu: University of Hawaii Press, 1997): 215–250.

21. Mary Corcoran, *Irish Illegals: Transients Between Two Societies* (Westport, Conn.: Greenwood Press, 1993): 127; *Boston Irish Reporter*, February 1997: 9 & 23.

22. Grace Goldin, "Christmas-Chanukah: December Is the Cruelest Month," *Commentary*, November 1950: 417; Diego Ribadeneira, "Hanukkah's Rising Cost," *Boston Globe*, 13 December 1998: B1 & B10.

23. Schmidt, *Consumer Rights*, 1995: 300–301.

24. Elizabeth Buck, *Paradise Remade: The Politics of Culture and History in Hawai'i* (Philadelphia: Temple University Press, 1993): 187–191.

25. Jennifer Gates, "Strangers in New York: Ethnic Tourism as Commodity, Spectacle, and Urban Leisure in Three Manhattan Neighborhoods." Doctoral Dissertation, Department of Anthropology, New York University, 1997.

26. Ryan Mathews, "Marketing to a New World of Taste," *Progressive Grocer* (July 1995): 73–74; Timothy Taylor, *Global Pop: World Music, World Markets* (New York: Routledge, 1997): 27.

27. Umberto Eco, *Travels in Hyperreality* (New York: Harcourt, Brace and Jovanovich, 1986): 8.

28. Robert Bellah *et al.*, *Habits of the Heart: Individualism and Commitment in American Life* (Berkeley: University of California Press, 1985): 152.

29. Arlene Dávila, *Sponsored Identities: Cultural Politics in Puerto Rico* (Philadelphia: Temple University Press, 1997): 220–229.

30. Dávila, *Sponsored Identities*, 1997: 232–247

31. Interview with Richard Joel, December 18, 1995.

Two: From Community to Commodity

1. New York *Forverts*, "New Season, New Hats," 7 September 1905.

2. Christopher Sullivan, "Firms Court a Once-Ignored Market: Minority Consumers," *Philadelphia Inquirer*, 2 August 1992: D9; Peter Alan Harper, "Wealthy Blacks Are Targeted as Investors," *Standard Times*, 21 September 1998: A4.

3. For an explanation of the terms used to label these populations, see the Appendix: "Note on Terminology."

4. James B. Kirk, "The Negro in Advertising" *Printer's Ink*, 8 November 1895: 22; classified advertisement, *Printer's Ink*, 25 January 1917: 111.

5. Robert E. Weems, *Desegregating the Dollar: African American Consumerism in the Twentieth Century* (New York: New York University Press, 1998): 16–17.

6. George Sanchez, *Becoming Mexican American: Ethnicity, Culture and Identity in Chicano Los Angeles*, 1900–1945 (New York: Oxford University Press, 1993): 172–175.

7. Ingrid Oter-Smart, Marketing to a New America Conference, May 22, 1996.

8. Susan Strasser, *Satisfaction Guaranteed: The Making of the American Mass Market* (New York: Pantheon, 1989): 10–15.

9. Heinze, *Adapting to Abundance*, 1990: 174 & 177.

10. Heinze, *Adapting to Abundance*, 1990: 158–160; Shuli Berger, "Special to the *Forverts*: Advertising Campaigns, 1910–1930," slide-lecture, Mame-Loshn '97, May 25, Fairfield, Conn.; Diane Hotten-Somers, "From a Moral Character to a Consumer Personality: The Evolution of the Relationship Between American Mistresses and Irish Maids from 1850–1920," unpublished paper, 1998: 32–33.

11. Lizabeth Cohen, *Making a New Deal: Industrial Workers in Chicago, 1919–1939* (Cambridge: Cambridge University Press, 1990): 105–106, 113, and footnote 51, 407–408.

12. Victor Greene, *A Passion for Polka: Old-Time Ethnic Music in America* (Berkeley and Los Angeles: University of California Press, 1992): 247–248; Lisa Gitelman, "Unexpected Pleasures: Phonographs and Cultural Identities in America, 1895–1915," in *Appropriating Tech-*

nology, eds. Ron Eglash *et al.* (Minneapolis: University of Minnesota Press, forthcoming). Gitelman makes the insightful point that unlike the ethnic press, whose readership was necessarily limited to co-ethnic speakers because of the language barriers, anyone could play ethnic music whether the listener shared the ancestry of the music being represented or not, so that exposure to foreign cultures through phonograph records was a much more widespread form of mass media than were foreign language newspapers.

13. Erica Bsumek, "Commerce, Tradition, Ethnicity," paper presented at the American Historical Association Annual Meeting, Washington, D.C., January 9, 1998.

14. Helen Lee Schifer, "Rich Rewards," *Self*, November 1992: 141–143.

15. Weems, *Desegregating the Dollar*, 1998: 49–53; Kathy M. Newman, "The Forgotten Fifteen Million: Black Radio, the 'Negro Market' and the Civil Rights Movement," *Radical History Review* 76 (Winter 2000): 115–135.

16. Dan Sewell, "Purchasing clout of blacks is rising," *Standard Times*, 30 July 1998: A6.

17. Ann Ducille, "Dyes and Dolls: Multicultural Barbie and the Merchandising of Difference," *differences: A Journal of Feminist Cultural Studies* 6, no. 1 (1994): 49–50.

18. Harper, "Wealthy Blacks Are Targeted," 1998: A4.

19. Interview with Amy Hilliard-Jones, June 18, 1996.

Three: The New Ethnic Marketing Experts

1. As of this writing, the only ways to obtain copies of the newsletter are by subscription or by contacting the editor, Lisa Skriloff, directly at Multicultural Marketing Resources, 286 Spring Street, Suite 201, New York, NY 10013, Tel: 212-242-3351, e-mail: *infobrokr1@aol.com*; "Niche-market Focus Takes Multicultural Ad Spotlight," *Advertising Age*, 16 November 1998: S16.

2. Wei-Na Lee and Koog-Hyang Ro Um, "Ethnicity and Consumer Product Evaluation: A Cross-Cultural Comparison of Korean Immigrants and Americans," *Advances in Consumer Research* 19 (1992): 429–436.

3. Marketing to a New America Conference, New York City, May 22, 1996.

4. John Ellis, "TV Breaks Through Language Barrier," *Advertising Age*, 16 Nov. 1998: s20; Interview with Yuri Radzievsky, July 9, 1996.

5. Gary Levin, "Marketers Learning New Languages for Ads," *Advertising Age*, 10 May 1993: Section 1.

6. Lisa Penaloza, "*Atravesando Fronteras*/Border Crossings: A Critical Ethnographic Exploration of the Consumer Acculturation of Mexican Immigrants," *Journal of Consumer Research* 21 (June 1994): 32–54; Wayne D. Hoyer and Rohit Deshpande, "Cross-Cultural Influences on Buyer Behavior: The Impact of Hispanic Ethnicity," in *Proceedings of the AMA Educators' Conference*, eds. Bruce J. Walker *et al.* (Chicago: American Marketing Association, 1982): 89–92; Frederick Sturdivant, "Business and the Mexican-American Community," *California Management Review* 26 (fall 1969): 120–134.

7. Interview with Yuri Radzievsky, July 9, 1996.

8. Sathi Dasgupta, *On the Trail of an Uncertain Dream: Indian Immigrant Experience in America* (New York: AMS, 1989).

9. Interview with Yuri Radzievsky, July 9, 1996.

10. Steve Hess reported in *Hallmark Noon News*, August 9, 1994: 1.

11. Patricia Nelson Limerick, "Insiders and Outsiders: The Borders of the USA and the Limits of the ASA," *American Quarterly* 49, no. 3 (September 1997): 449–469.

12. Steve Hess, *Hallmark Noon News*, March 30, 1994.

13. Interview with Yuri Radzievsky, July 9, 1996.

14. Janet L. Willen, "Marketers to the World," *Nation's Business*, February 1994.

15. Conversation with Julia Huang, president, InterTrend, December 1, 1999.

16. Strasser, *Satisfaction Guaranteed*, 1989: 143.

17. "How to Make It in the World Market," January 1996.

18. Interview with Amy Hilliard-Jones, June 18, 1996.

19. *Forward*, 6 December 1996: 11.

20. Mitchell Zuckoff, "Reaching Out to Minority Consumers," *Boston Globe*, 28 June 1992: 77.

Four: The Romance of Ethnicity

1. Eva Hoffman, *Lost in Translation: A Life in a New Language* (New York: Penguin, 1989): 262–263.

2. Gans, "Symbolic Ethnicity," 1979.

3. Josh Kun, "New Jews," *Boston Phoenix*, 9 October 1998: 14; Bakalian, *Armenian-Americans*, 1993: 7; John Bukowczyk, *And My Children Did Not Know Me: A History of the Polish-Americans* (Bloomington: Indiana University Press, 1987): 117.

4. Aaron Lansky, June 15, 1997.

5. Interview with Yuri Radzievsky, July 9, 1996.

6. Natalie Wexler, "How Do You Say Cross-Dressing in Yiddish? On One Family's Return to the Mother Tongue," *Forward*, 9 August 1996: 12.

7. Wexler, "How Do You Say Cross-Dressing," 1996.

8. MSR&C Ethnic Market Report: 330.

9. Raffi Ishkanian, "Roots Paper," in *Becoming American, Becoming Ethnic: College Students Explore Their Roots*, ed. Thomas Dublin (Philadelphia: Temple University Press, 1996): 75.

10. Peter Ephross, "Harley's Angels: 'Yidden on Wheels,' " *Forward*, 18 October 1996: 14.

11. *Forward*, 15 November 1996: 14.

12. Renée Graham, "Quinn-essential," *Boston Globe*, 9 May 1999: N9 & N11.

13. Donna Gabaccia, *We Are What We Eat: Ethnic Foods and the Making of Americans* (Cambridge: Harvard University Press, 1998): 182–187.

14. Interview with James Berry, January 11, 1994.

15. Interview with Eileen Leahy, September 8, 1994.

16. Interview with James Berry, January 11, 1994.

17. *Boston Irish Reporter*, November 1996: 31.

18. Marcella Bombardieri, "Food is the star of Armenian festival," *Boston Globe*, 20 July 1998.

19. Ishkanian, "Roots Paper," 1996: 75–76.

20. Interview with Charles Sahasian, October 18, 1994.

21. Interview with Karen Kazanjian, September 28, 1994.

22. Suzanne Sinke, "Tulips Are Blooming in Holland, Michigan: Analysis of a Dutch-American Festival," in *Immigration and Ethnicity: American Society—"Melting Pot" or "Salad Bowl"?*, eds. Michael D'Innocenzo and Josef P. Sirefman (Westport, Conn.: Greenwood Press, 1992): 3–14; Gerard J. Brault, *The French-Canadian Heritage in New En-*

gland (Hanover, N.H.: The University Press of New England, 1986): 177; Gabaccia, *We Are What We Eat*, 1998: 189; Greene, *A Passion for Polka*, 1992: 245.

23. Matthew Goodman, "One Yiddish Festival That's 'Not About Nostalgia,' " *Forward*, 22 August 1997: 11–12.

24. *Boston Irish Reporter*, May 1997: 18.

25. William Kates, "First Americans Festival Aims to Educate in an Entertaining Way," *Standard Times*, 3 August 1997: E10.

26. Gates, "Strangers in New York," 1997: 386–387.

27. Micaela Di Leonardo, *The Varieties of Ethnic Experience: Kinship, Class and Gender Among California Italian Americans* (Ithaca: Cornell University Press, 1984): 18.

28. Interview with Karen Zehnder on, "The World," Radio Broadcast, co-produced by WGBH Boston, the BBC and Public Radio International, November 11, 1999.

29. Wendy Belzberg, "On-Line Jewish Communities," *Forward*, 31 October 1997: 23. URLs: http://www.ideasign.com/olamkatan; http://www.mishpacha.com

30. The California Portuguese Immigrant Community in the Year 2000," presentation given for the Conference on the Portuguese-American Experience, University of Massachusetts, Dartmouth, Mass., October 12, 1996.

31. Dávila, *Sponsored Identities*, 1997: 169.

Five: Ethnic by Design: Marketing to a "New America"

1. Interview with John and Melissa Gregorian, June 11, 1996.

2. Francine Farnes, "Metro's handbags are functional—and hip," *Standard Times*, 16 September 1998: C1.

3. Thomas Morgan, "The Latinization of America," *Esquire*, May 1983: 54;

4. Gabaccia, *We Are What We Eat*, 1998: 198; Waters, *Ethnic Options*, 1990: 188–121; Alba, *Ethnic Identity*, 1990: 85–91 & 122.

5. Mathews, "Marketing to a New World of Taste," 1995: 74.

6. Frank Hammel, "An Ear for the Exotic," *Supermarket Business* 50, No. 12 (December 1995): 74.

7. Frank McCoy, "Goya: A Lot More than Black Beans and Sofrito," *Business Week*, 7 December 1987: 137–138.

8. Chris Reidy, "New Star Market to Be an Epcot of Cuisine," *Boston Globe*, 3 June 1997: C14; Andrew McCoy, "Star Jumps into Ethnic Markets," *Boston Business Journal*, 2 June 1997; Marvin Howe, "Bodegas Find Prosperity," *New York Times*, 19 November 1986.

9. "Kosher Supermarket Makes Waves on the Web," (staff) *Forward*, 20 November 1998: 2; URL: http://www.koshersupermarket.com

10. *Forward*, 16 February 1996: 12; 9 January 1998: 8; 18 July 1997: 16.

11. Robert Eisenberg, *Boychiks in the Hood: Travels in the Hasidic Underground* (New York: Harper San Francisco, 1995): 179.

12. "A Brew for the Jew Taps into a New Market," *Forward*, 7 November 1997: 8.

13. Evan Spingarn, "Beaujolais Goes Kosher," *Forward*, 27 November 1998: 28.

14. Benjamin Smith, "At the Food Show: Rugelach, Strudel and Bible Bread," *Forward*, 3 July 1998: 15.

15. *New York Times*, 14 Jan. 1996: 39; Hugh Mulligan, "Ethnic Weddings Are Back in Style," *Standard Times*, 9 September 1997, B2.

16. *Forward*, 29 May 1998: 18.

17. Kevin McDonough, "Tune in Tonight," *Standard Times*, 16 October 1998: B7; Maureen Dezell, "Beyond the High-Stepping," *Boston Globe*, 1 November 1998: M1 & M6.

18. *Boston Globe*, 22 March 1998; *Standard Times*, 15 March 1998.

19. Author's note: No you don't see Mickey Mouse in "Long Journey Home"—not to worry, because you can find him in any number of Disney Chanukah menorah designs; Patti Hartigan, "PBS Traces Irish-American Experience," *Boston Globe*, 25 January 1998: N1 &. N8.

20. Taylor, *Global Pop*, 1997: 6; Robin Estrin, "Irish Culture Catching on in the Mainstream," *Standard Times*, 17 April 1999: B1.

21. Scott Alarik, "A Great Time to Hear Irish Music," *Boston Globe*, 28 February 1999: N7.

22. Scott Alarik, "Gael Force: Irish Music Sweeps into Boston College this Weekend for the Gaelic Roots Festival," *Boston Globe*, 29 September 1995: 58; David Gates, "The Marketing o' the Green," *Newsweek* 121 (5 April 1993): 60.

23. *Boston Globe*, 8 August 1997: D13; *Forward*, 19 June 1998: 11.

24. Interview with Holly Poirier and Anita Daly, August 4, 1998.

25. Glenn Collins, "To Build Attendance at 'the Glory of Byzantium,' " *New York Times*, 10 April 1997: D6.

26. Amy Wallace, "Hollywood Courts Latino Audiences," *Boston Globe*, 4 August 1998: E6.

27. Paul Southrada, "Banc One Corporation Goes Hollywood," *Standard Times*, 6 April 1997: F2

28. *Marketplace*, April 24, 1998 (public radio).

29. Guy Garcia, "Caliente! Latin Pop is Hot, Hot, Hot—Again," *Standard Times*, 29 June 1999: B1 & B2.

30. David Brauder, "TV Company Tried to Reach Homesick Ethnic Market," *Standard Times*, 9 December 1998: C1 & C4; John Ellis, "TV Breaks through Language Barrier," *Advertising Age*, 16 November 1998: s20; Paul Singman, "Reaching an Increasingly Diverse and Affluent Ethnic Population through Television," *The Source Book of Multicultural Experts*, 1999–2000: 35–36.

Six: A Rainbow Coalition of Consumers

1. Judith Ortiz Cofer, "Silent Dancing," in *Visions of America: Personal Narratives from the Promised Land*, eds. Wesley Brown and Amy Ling (New York: Persea Books, 1993): 182–183.

2. Daniel McQuillen, "Cities of Gold," *Incentive* 170 (February 1996): 38–40.

3. Frances Ryan, "If Opportunity Knocks—Let It In! Franchise Business Is a Natural for Puerto Rican Entrepreneurs," *Caribbean Business*, 31 March 1994: 1.

4. Interview with Eric Vieland, July 2, 1996.

5. Interview with Aaron Lansky, July 4, 1996.

6. Rick Lyman, "A Culture Preserved," *New York Times* 16 June 1997: B4.

7. Correspondence with Aaron Lansky, December 16, 1996.

8. Trudy Tynan, "Saving Yiddish: From Dumpster to Cyberspace," *Standard Times*, 30 November 1998: B3.

9. Sidney Goldstein and Alice Goldstein, *Jews on the Move: Implications for Jewish Identity* (Albany: State University of New York Press, 1996).

10. Jonathan Rosen, "A Dead Language, Yiddish Lives—And So

Does the Fight over Why," *New York Times Magazine*, 7 July 1996: 26–27.

11. Andrew M. Greeley, *That Most Distressful Nation: The Taming of the American Irish* (Chicago: Quadrangle Books, 1972).

12. Patricia O'Connor, "Irish Past—Bright Business Future," *Sunday Standard Times*, 10 November 1996: F1–2.

13. *Boston Irish Reporter*, December, 1996: 29; Dean MacCannell, *The Tourist: A New History of the Leisure Class* (New York: Schocken Books, 1976).

14. Bill Forry, "Denis Leary's Irish Roots on Display in Charlestown Film," *Boston Irish Reporter*, June, 1997: 36

15. Corcoran, *Irish Illegals*, 1993: 127.

Seven: Recipe for Multiethnicity

1. Paul Shepard, "Mixed Race Stirs Census Debate," *Standard Times*, 3 April 1997: 1.

2. Paul Farhi, "AmEx Gets into the Game of Selling Tiger Woods," *International Herald Tribune*, 21 May 1997: 20.

3. Interview with Kristina Nowak, October 15, 1996.

4. Bruce Horovitz, "Harmonic Convergence: Racial Tolerance Is Suddenly a Hot Topic in Advertising," *Los Angeles Times*, 19 January 1993: D1 & D6.

5. Laurel Gaeber, "Beyond Basic Black," *Elle*, August 1993: 118; "Interracial Beauty," *Allure*, December, 1992; "Vogue's View," *Vogue*, September 1992: 276.

6. *Self*, November 1992: 34.

7. Gaeber "Beyond Basic Black," 1993: 123.

8. *Self*, October 1992: 48.

9. Jill Hudson, "Does Racism Lurk Beyond Fashion Runways?" *Washington Post*, 22 April 1994: C4

10. Caroline Clarke, "Redefining Beautiful," *Black Enterprise*, June 1993: 243–252; *San Juan Star*, 5 February 1999: 36.

11. Though a letter to the editor in the New Bedford, Massachusetts, daily newspaper, the *Standard Times*, about the cover written by a Cape Verdean-American—Cape Verdeans are of mixed Portuguese and African heritage—insisted that the model had to be a compatriot.

12. Miranda Innes, *Ethnic Style: From Mexico to the Mediterranean* (New York: Cross River Books, 1992).

13. *People,* 11 May 1998: 143 & 154.

14. Ducille, "Dyes and Dolls," 1994: 51.

15. *Self,* November 1992: 40.

16. *Newsweek,* "The New Islam," 16 March 1998: 34–37.

17. *Forward,* 30 January 1998: 10.

18. *Boston Irish Reporter,* November 1996: 16

19. *Forward,* 6 December 1996: 11

20. Ric Oliveira, "Portuguese Speakers on Tap at Umass Dartmouth," *Standard Times,* 12 October 1996: A5.

21. "Kosher Irish," *Irish America,* September 1987: 20–21.

Conclusion

1. Mary Paik Lee, *A Quiet Odyssey: A Pioneer Korean Woman in America,* ed. Sucheng Chan (Seattle: University of Washington Press, 1990): 37–38.

2. Examples of book-length treatments that do include substantial discussions of immigrants and ethnics as consumers are: Andrew Heinze, *Adapting to Abundance: Jewish Immigrants, Mass Consumption and the Search for American Identity* (New York: Columbia University Press, 1990); Victor Greene, *A Passion for Polka: Old-Time Ethnic Music in America* (Berkeley: University of California Press, 1992); Donna Gabaccia, *We Are What We Eat: Ethnic Foods and the Making of Americans* (Cambridge, Mass.: Harvard University Press, 1998); Jenna Weissman Joselit, *The Wonders of America: Reinventing Jewish Culture, 1880–1950* (New York: Hill and Wang, 1994); George Sanchez, *Becoming Mexican American: Ethnicity, Culture and Identity in Chicano Los Angeles, 1900–1945* (New York: Oxford University Press, 1993); Lizabeth Cohen, *Making a New Deal: Industrial Workers in Chicago, 1919–1939* (Cambridge: Cambridge University Press, 1990.)

3. Philip Gleason, *Journal of American History* 69 (March 1983): 910–931, reprinted as Chapter 5, "Identifying Identity: A Semantic History," in Gleason's *Speaking of Diversity: Language and Ethnicity in Twentieth-Century America* (Baltimore: The Johns Hopkins University Press, 1991): 123–149.

4. Alba, *Ethnic Identity,* 1990.

5. Leonard Fein, "Goldi-Lox and the Three Bagels," *Forward*, 3 January 1997: 7.

Appendix

1. Wsevold Isajiw, "Definitions of Ethnicity," *Ethnicity* 1 (1974): 111.

2. Gail Baker Woods, *Advertising and Marketing to the New Majority* (Belmont, Cal.: Wadsworth Publishing Co, 1995): ix.

Bibliography

Alarik, Scott. 1995. "Gael Force: Irish music sweeps into Boston College this weekend for the Gaelic Roots Festival." *Boston Globe*, 29 September: 58.

————. 1999. "A Great Time to Hear Irish Music." *Boston Globe*, 28 February: N7.

Alba, Richard. 1990. *Ethnic Identity: Transformation of White America*. New Haven, Conn.: Yale University Press.

Bakalian, Anny. 1993. *Armenian-Americans: From Being to Feeling Armenian*. New Brunswick, N.J.: Transaction Publishers.

Bamberger, Joan. 1986–1987. "Family and Kinship in an Armenian-American Community." *Journal of Armenian Studies* III, no. 1-2: 77–86.

Barth, Fredrik. 1969. *Ethnic Groups and Boundaries: The Social Organization of Culture Difference*. London: Allen & Unwin.

Bauer, Raymond A., and Stephen A. Greyser. 1968. *Advertising in America: The Consumer View*. Cambridge, Mass.: Harvard University Press.

Belasco, Warren. 1987. "Ethnic Fast Foods: The Corporate Melting Pot." *Food and Foodways:* 1–30.

Bellah, Robert, *et al.* 1985. *Habits of the Heart: Individualism and Commitment in American Life*. Berkeley: University of California Press.

Belzberg, Wendy. 1997. "On-Line Jewish Communities." *Forward*, 31 October: 23.

Berman, Sara. 1997. "Venturing into Some Novel Niches." *Forward*, 31 October: 8.

Bombardieri, Marcella. 1998. "Food is the Star of Armenian Festival." *Boston Globe*, 20 July.

Boorstin, Daniel. 1987. *The Image: A Guide to Pseudo-Events in America*. New York: Atheneum.

Brauder, David. 1998. "TV Company Tried to Reach Homesick Ethnic Market." *Standard Times*, 9 December: C1 & C4.

Brault, Gerard J. 1986. *The French-Canadian Heritage in New England*. Hanover, N.H.: The University Press of New England.

Bsumek, Erica. 1998. "Commerce, Tradition, Ethnicity," paper presented at the American Historical Association Annual Meeting, Washington, D.C., January 9.

Buck, Elizabeth. 1993. *Paradise Remade: The Politics of Culture and History in Hawai'i*. Philadelphia: Temple University Press.

Bukowczyk, John. 1987. *And My Children Did Not Know Me: A History of the Polish-Americans*. Bloomington and Indianapolis: Indiana University Press.

Clarke, Caroline. 1993. "Redefining Beautiful." *Black Enterprise* 23 (June): 243–252.

Cofer, Judith Ortiz. 1993. "Silent Dancing." In *Visions of America: Personal Narratives from the Promised Land*, eds. Wesley Brown and Amy Ling. New York: Persea Books: 179–186.

Cohen, Abner, ed., 1974. *Urban Ethnicity*. London: Tavistock.

Cohen, Lizabeth. 1990. *Making a New Deal: Industrial Workers in Chicago, 1919–1939*. Cambridge: Cambridge University Press.

Cohen, Ronald. 1978. "Ethnicity: Problem and Focus in Anthropology" *Annual Review of Anthropology* 7:379–403.

Collins, Glenn. 1997. "The Americanization of Salsa." *New York Times*, 9 January: D17.

———. 1997. "To Build Attendance at 'the Glory of Byzantium.'" *New York Times*, 10 April: D6.

Corcoran, Mary. 1993. *Irish Illegals: Transients Between Two Societies*. Westport, Conn., and London: Greenwood Press.

Costa, Janeen Arnold and Gary Bamossy, eds. 1995. *Marketing in a Multicultural World: Ethnicity, Nationalism, and Cultural Identity*. Thousand Oaks, Cal.: Sage Publications.

Crispino, James. 1980. *The Assimilation of Ethnic Groups: The Italian Case*. Staten Island, N.Y.: Center for Migration Studies.

Dasgupta, Sathi. 1989. *On the Trail of an Uncertain Dream: Indian Immigrant Experience in America.* New York: AMS.

Dávila. Arlene. 1997. *Sponsored Identities: Cultural Politics in Puerto Rico.* Philadelphia: Temple University Press.

Dezell, Maureen. 1998. "Beyond the High-Stepping." *Boston Globe*, 1 November: M1 & M6.

Di Leonardo, Micaela. 1984. *The Varieties of Ethnic Experience: Kinship, Class and Gender Among California Italian Americans.* Ithaca, N.Y.: Cornell University Press.

Dinnerstein, Leonard, Roger Nichols, and David Reimers. 1996. *Natives and Strangers: A Multicultural History of Americans.* New York: Oxford University Press.

Dublin, Thomas, ed., 1996. *Becoming American, Becoming Ethnic: College Students Explore Their Roots.* Philadelphia: Temple University Press.

Ducille, Ann. 1994. "Dyes and Dolls: Multicultural Barbie and the Merchandising of Difference." *differences: A Journal of Feminist Cultural Studies* 6, no. 1: 46–68.

Earl, Peter. 1986. *Lifestyle Economics: Consumer Behavior in a Turbulent World.* New York: St. Martin's Press.

Eco, Umberto. 1986. *Travels in Hyperreality.* New York: Harcourt, Brace and Jovanovich.

Eisenberg, Robert. 1995. *Boychiks in the Hood: Travels in the Hasidic Underground.* New York: Harper San Francisco.

Ephross, Peter. 1996. "Harley's Angels: 'Yidden on Wheels.' " *Forward*, 18 October: 14.

Esman, Marjorie. 1984. "Tourism as Ethnic Preservation: The Cajuns of Louisiana." *Annals of Tourism Research* 11: 451–467.

Esterik, Penny Van. 1982. "Celebrating Ethnicity: Ethnic Flavor in an Urban Festival." *Ethnic Groups* 4: 207–228.

Estrin, Robin. 1991. "Irish Culture Catching on in the Mainstream." *Standard Times*, 17 April: B1.

Farhi, Paul. 1997. "AmEx Gets into the Game of Selling Tiger Woods." *International Herald Tribune*, 21 May: 20.

Farnes, Frances. 1998. "Metro's Handbags Are Functional—and Hip." *Standard Times*, 16 September: C1.

Fein, Leonard. 1997. "Goldi-Lox and the Three Bagels." *Forward*, 3 January: 7.

Bibliography   219

Forry, Bill. 1997. "Denis Leary's Irish Roots on Display in Charlestown Film." *Boston Irish Reporter* (June): 36.

Fuchs, Lawrence H. 1990. *The American Kaleidoscope: Race, Ethnicity and Civic Culture.* Hanover, N.H.: Wesleyan University Press/The University of New England.

———. 1997, "What We Should Count and Why." *Social Science and Modern Society* 34, no. 6 (September/October): 24–27.

Gabaccia, Donna. 1998. *We Are What We Eat: Ethnic Foods and the Making of Americans.* Cambridge, Mass.: Harvard University Press.

Gaeber, Laurel. "Beyond Basic Black." *Elle,* August 1993: 118.

Gans, Herbert. 1979. "Symbolic Ethnicity: The Future of Ethnic Groups and Cultures in America." *Ethnic and Racial Studies* 2, no. 1:1–20.

———. 1992. "Second-Generation Decline: Scenarios for the Economic and Ethnic Futures of the Post-1965 American Immigrants." *Ethnic and Racial Studies* 15, no. 2:173–192.

———. 1993. "Symbolic Ethnicity and Symbolic Religiosity: Towards a Comparison of Ethnic and Religious Acculturation." *Ethnic and Racial Studies* 17, no. 4: 577–92.

Gates, David. 1993. "The Marketing o' the Green." *Newsweek* 121 (5 April): 60.

Gates, Jennifer A. 1997. "Strangers in New York: Ethnic Tourism as Commodity, Spectacle, and Urban Leisure in Three Manhattan Neighborhoods." Doctoral Dissertation. Department of Anthropology, New York University.

Gitelman, Lisa. Forthcoming. "Unexpected Pleasures: Phonographs and Cultural Identities in America, 1895–1915," in eds. Ron Eglash *et al., Appropriating Technology.* Minneapolis: University of Minnesota Press.

Gitlin, Todd. 1985. *Inside Prime Time.* New York: Pantheon.

Gleason, Philip. 1991. *Speaking of Diversity: Language and Ethnicity in Twentieth-Century America.* Baltimore: The Johns Hopkins University Press.

Goldin, Grace. 1950. "Christmas-Chanukah: December Is the Cruelest Month." *Commentary,* November: 417.

Goldstein, Sidney, and Alice Goldstein. 1996. *Jews on the Move: Implications for Jewish Identity.* Albany: State University of New York Press.

Goodman, Matthew. 1997. "One Yiddish Festival That's 'Not About Nostalgia.' " *Forward*, 22 August: 11–12.

Gordon, Mary. 1991. *Good Boys and Dead Girls and Other Essays*. New York: Viking Penguin.

Graham, Renée. 1999. "Quinn-essential." *Boston Globe*, 9 May: N9 & N11.

Greeley, Andrew M. 1972. *That Most Distressful Nation: The Taming of the American Irish*. Chicago: Quadrangle Books.

Greene, Victor. 1992. *A Passion for Polka: Old-Time Ethnic Music in America*. Berkeley and Los Angeles: University of California Press.

Hammel, Frank. 1995. "An Ear for the Exotic." *Supermarket Business* 50, No. 12 (December): 74.

Harper, Peter Alan. 1998. "Wealthy Blacks are Targeted as Investors." *Standard Times*, 21 September 1998: A4.

Hartigan, Patti, 1998. "PBS Traces Irish-American Experience." *Boston Globe*, 25 January: N1 & N8.

Heinze, Andrew. 1990. *Adapting to Abundance: Jewish Immigrants, Mass Consumption and the Search for American Identity*. New York: Columbia University Press.

Herberg, Will. 1955. *Protestant, Catholic, Jew*. Garden City, N.Y.: Doubleday.

Hirschman, Elizabeth C. 1981. "American Jewish Ethnicity: Its Relationship to Some Selected Aspects of Consumer Behavior." *Journal of Marketing* 45 (summer): 102–110.

Hoffman, Eva. 1989. *Lost in Translation: A Life in a New Language*. New York: Penguin.

Hollinger, David. 1995. *Postethnic America: Beyond Multiculturalism*. New York: Basic Books.

Hout, Michael, and Joshua R. Goldstein. 1994. "How 4.5 Million Irish Immigrants Became 40 Million Irish Americans: Demographic and Subjective Aspects of the Ethnic Composition of White Americans." *American Sociological Review* 59 (February): 64–82.

Howe, Marvin. 1996. "Bodegas Find Prosperity." *New York Times*, 19 November

Hoyer, Wayne D. and Rohit Deshpande. 1982. "Cross-Cultural Influences on Buyer Behavior: The Impact of Hispanic Ethnicity," in

Proceedings of the AMA Educators' Conference, eds. Bruce J. Walker *et al.* Chicago: American Marketing Association, 89–92.

Hudson, Jill. 1994. "Does Racism Lurk Beyond Fashion Runways?" *Washington Post*, 22 April 1: C4

Ibson, John Duffy. 1990. *Will the World Break Your Heart? Dimensions and Consequences of Irish-American Assimilation*. New York: Garland Publishing.

Innes, Miranda. 1992. *Ethnic Style: From Mexico to the Mediterranean*. New York: Cross River Books.

Isajiw, Wsevold. 1974. "Definitions of Ethnicity." *Ethnicity* 1:111–124.

Ishkanian, Raffi. 1996. "Roots Paper," in *Becoming American, Becoming Ethnic: College Students Explore Their Roots*, ed. Thomas Dublin. Philadelphia: Temple University Press, 75–81.

Joselit, Jenna Weissman. 1994. *The Wonders of America: Reinventing Jewish Culture, 1880–1950*. New York: Hill and Wang.

Kates, William. 1997. "First Americans Festival Aims to Educate in an Entertaining Way." *Standard Times*, 3 August: E10.

Kazal, Russell A. 1995. "Revisiting Assimilation: The Rise, Fall and Reappraisal of a Concept in American Ethnic History." *American Historical Review* 100, no. 2: 437–471.

Kirk, James B. 1895. "The Negro in Advertising," *Printer's Ink*, 8 November: 22.

Kleeblatt, Norman, ed. 1996. *Too Jewish?: Challenging Traditional Identities*. New York: The Jewish Museum and New Brunswick, N.J.: Rutgers University Press.

Kun, Josh. 1998. "New Jews." *Boston Phoenix*, 9 October: 14.

Leach, William. 1993. *Land of Desire: Merchants, Power, and the Rise of a New American Culture*. New York: Pantheon Books.

Lee, Mary Paik. 1990. *A Quiet Odyssey: A Pioneer Korean Woman in America*, ed. Sucheng Chan. Seattle: University of Washington Press.

Lee, Wei-Na, and Koog-Hyang Ro Um. 1992. "Ethnicity and Consumer Product Evaluation: A Cross-Cultural Comparison of Korean Immigrants and Americans," *Advances in Consumer Research* 19: 429–436.

Levin, Gary. 1993. "Marketers Learning New Languages for Ads," *Advertising Age*, 10 May: Section 1.

Lieberson, Stanley. 1985. "Unhyphenated Whites in the United States." *Ethnic and Racial Studies* 8, no. 1: 159–80.

Limerick, Patricia Nelson. 1997. "Insiders and Outsiders: The Borders of the USA and the Limits of the ASA." *American Quarterly* 49, no. 3 (September): 449–469.

Linnekin, Jocelyn. 1997. "Consuming Cultures: Tourism and the Commoditization of Cultural Identity in the Island Pacific," in *Tourism, Ethnicity and the State in Asian and Pacific Societies*, eds. Michel Picard and Robert E. Wood. Honolulu: University of Hawaii Press, 215–250.

Lyman, Rick. 1997. "A Culture Preserved." *The New York Times*, 16 June: B4.

MacCannell, Dean. 1976. *The Tourist: A New History of the Leisure Class*. New York: Schocken Books.

Marchand, Roland. 1985. *Advertising the American Dream: Making Way for Modernity, 1920–1940*. Berkeley and Los Angeles: University of California Press.

Market Segment Research & Consulting, Inc. 1966. *Ethnic Market Report: A Portrait of the New America*. Coral Gables, Fla.

Mathews, Ryan. 1995. "Marketing to a New World of Taste." *Progressive Grocer*, July: 73–74.

McCoy, Andrew. 1997. "Star Jumps into Ethnic Markets." *Boston Business Journal*, 2 June.

McCoy, Frank. 1987. "Goya: A Lot More than Black Beans and Sofrito," *Business Week*, 7 December: 137–138.

McCracken, Ellen. 1993. *Decoding Women's Magazines: From Mademoiselle to Ms.* New York: St. Martin's Press.

McCracken, Grant. 1988. *Culture and Consumption*. Bloomington: University of Indiana Press.

McDonough, Kevin. 1998. "Tune in Tonight." *Standard Times*, 16 October: B7.

McQuillen, Daniel. 1996. "Cities of Gold," *Incentive* 170 (February): 38–40. Available: Lexis-Nexis.

Mead, Margaret. 1975. "Ethnicity and Anthropology in America," in *Ethnic Identity: Cultural Continuities and Change*, eds. George DeVos and Lola Romanucci-Ross. Palo Alto, Cal.: Mayfield Publishing Co., 173–97.

Medding, Peter Y. 1987. "Segmented Ethnicity and the New Jewish Politics." *Studies in Contemporary Jewry* 3: 26–48.

Mehta, Raj, and Russell W. Belk. 1991. "Artifacts, Identity, and Transition: Favorite Possessions of Indians and Indian Immigrants to the United States." *Journal of Consumer Research* 17 (March): 398–411.

Morgan, Thomas. 1983. "The Latinization of America," *Esquire*, May: 54

Mulligan, Hugh. 1997. "Ethnic Weddings Are Back in Style." *Standard Times*, 9 September: B1–2.

Nathan, Joan. 1994. *Jewish Cooking In America*. New York: Alfred A. Knopf.

Newman, Kathy M. 2000. "The Forgotten Fifteen Million: Black Radio, the 'Negro Market' and the Civil Rights Movement," *Radical History Review* 76: (Winter): 115–135.

O'Connor, Patricia. 1996. "Irish past—bright business future." *Sunday Standard Times*, 10 November: F1–2.

Oliveira, Ric, 1996. "Portuguese Speakers on Tap at Umass Dartmouth." *Standard Times*, 12 October: A5.

Penaloza. Lisa. 1994. "*Atravesando Fronteras*/Border Crossings: A Critical Ethnographic Exploration of the Consumer Acculturation of Mexican Immigrants." *Journal of Consumer Research* 21 (June): 32–54.

Phillips, Jenny K. (1978) Symbol, Myth and Rhetoric: The Politics of Culture in an Armenian-American Population, Boston University Ph.D. thesis in Anthropology (#23 in AMS Press Series 32).

Reidy, Chris. 1997. "New Star Market to Be an Epcot of Cuisine." *Boston Globe*, 3 June: C14.

Ribadeneira, Diego. 1998. "Hanukkah's Rising Cost." *Boston Globe*, 13 December: B1 & B10.

Rodríguez. Clara. 1991. *Puerto Ricans in the United States*. Boulder, Colo.: Westview Press.

Rosen, Jonathan. 1996. "A Dead Language, Yiddish Lives–And So Does the Fight Over Why." *New York Times Magazine*, 7 July: 26–27.

Rubin-Dorsky, Jeffrey and Shelley Fisher Fishkin, eds. 1996. *People of the Book: Thirty Scholars Reflect on Their Jewish Identity*. Madison: University of Wisconsin Press.

Ryan, Frances. 1994. "If Opportunity Knocks—Let It In! Franchise Business Is a Natural for Puerto Rican Entrepreneurs." *Caribbean Business*, 31 March: 1

Sanchez, George. 1993. *Becoming Mexican American: Ethnicity, Culture and Identity in Chicano Los Angeles, 1900–1945*. New York: Oxford University Press.

Sarna, Jonathan D. 1978. "From Immigrants to Ethnics: Toward a New Theory of Ethnicization." *Ethnicity* 5:370–378.

Scanlon, Jennifer. 1995. *Inarticulate Longings: The Ladies' Home Journal, Gender, and the Promises of Consumer Culture*. New York and London: Routledge.

Schifer, Helen Lee. 1992. "Rich Rewards." *Self*, November: 141–143.

Schmidt, Leigh Eric. 1995. *Consumer Rites: The Buying & Selling of American Holidays*. Princeton, N.J.: Princeton University Press.

Sewell, Dan. 1998. "Purchasing Clout of Blacks Is Rising." *Standard Times*, 30 July 1998: A6.

Shepard, Paul. 1997. "Mixed Race Stirs Census Debate." *Standard Times*, 3 April : 1.

Sinke, Suzanne. 1992. "Tulips Are Blooming in Holland, Michigan: Analysis of a Dutch-American Festival," in *Immigration and Ethnicity: American Society—"Melting Pot" or "Salad Bowl"?*, eds. Michael D'Innocenzo and Josef P. Sirefman. Westport, Conn.: Greenwood Press, 3–14.

Smith, Tom W. 1980. "Ethnic Measurement and Identification." *Ethnicity* 7: 78–95.

Southrada, Paul. 1997. "Banc One Corporation Goes Hollywood." *Standard Times*, 6 April: F2.

Strasser, Susan. 1989. *Satisfaction Guaranteed: The Making of the American Mass Market*. New York, Pantheon.

Sturdivant, Frederick D. 1969. "Business and the Mexican-American Community," *California Management Review* 26 (fall): 120–134.

Sullivan, Christopher. 1992. "Firms Court a Once-Ignored Market: Minority Consumers." *Philadelphia Inquirer*, 2 August: D9

Taylor, Timothy. 1997. *Global Pop: World Music, World Markets*. New York: Routledge.

Tricarico, Donald. 1989. "In a New Light: Italian-American Ethnicity in the Mainstream," in *The Ethnic Enigma: The Salience of Ethnicity for European-Origin Groups*, ed. Peter Kivisto, Philadelphia: The Balch Institute Press, 24–46.

Tynan, Trudy. 1998. "Saving Yiddish: From Dumpster to Cyberspace." *Standard Times*, 30 November: B3.

Urry, John. 1990. *The Tourist Gaze: Leisure and Travel in Contemporary Societies.* London: Sage Publications.

Wallace, Amy. 1998. "Hollywood Courts Latino Audiences." *Boston Globe*, 4 August: E6.

Waters, Mary. 1990. *Ethnic Options: Choosing Identities in America.* Berkeley and Los Angeles: University of California Press.

Weems, Robert E. 1998. *Desegregating the Dollar: African American Consumerism in the Twentieth Century.* New York: New York University Press.

Wexler, Natalie. 1996. "How Do You Say Cross-Dressing in Yiddish? On One Family's Return to the Mother Tongue." *Forward*, 9 August: 12.

Wisse, Ruth. 1996. "Shul Daze." *The New Republic.* 27 May: 16–19

Wood, Robert E. 1998. "Tourist Ethnicity: A Brief Itinerary," *Ethnic and Racial Studies* 21, no. 2: 218–242.

Woods, Gail Baker. 1995. *Advertising and Marketing to the New Majority.* Belmont, Cal.: Wadsworth Publishing Co.

Woodward, C. Vann. 1958. "The Search for Southern Identity." *Virginia Quarterly Review* 34: 321–338.

Zelizer, Viviana. 1999. "Multiple Markets: Multiple Cultures," in *Common Values, Social Diversity and Cultural Conflict*, eds. Neil Smelser and Jeffrey Alexander. Princeton, N.J.: Princeton University Press.

Zuckoff, Mitchell. 1992. "Reaching Out to Minority Consumers." *Boston Globe*, 28 June: 77.

Index

Illustration Credits

Page 181. Betty Crocker 75th Anniversary Portrait: Betty Crocker®
is a registered trademark of General Mills, Inc., and is used
by permission

Page 185. Think Yiddish. Drink British: Reprinted with the permission of Tetley USA Inc.

Page 187. Ginsberg's Pub: Photo by the author

Page 188. Manischewitz Pizza Mix: Collection of the author

Page 189. El Rancho Rugelach: Collection of the author

About the Author

Marilyn Halter is Associate Professor of History and Research Associate at the Institute for the Study of Economic Culture at Boston University, where she also teaches in the American and New England Studies Program. She is the author of *Between Race and Ethnicity: Cape Verdean American Immigrants, 1860–1965* (1993) and *New Migrants in the Marketplace: Boston's Ethnic Entrepreneurs* (1995).